D1336419

The Execution Process Volume 1

IMPLEMENTATION
IN A BUREAUCRACY

Government and Administration Series
Edited by F. F. RIDLEY, *Professor of Political Theory and Institutions, University of Liverpool, England.*

Control in a Bureaucracy
The Execution Process Volume 2
ANDREW DUNSIRE

The Government of Education
KEITH FENWICK AND PETER MCBRIDE

The Organisation of Local Government
R. GREENWOOD, C. R. HININGS, S. RANSON, K. WALSH

Policy Analysis:
A Political and Organizational Perspective
W. I. JENKINS

Pressure Groups and the Policy Process:
Policy-making in a post-Parliamentary Democracy
J. J. RICHARDSON AND A. G. JORDAN

The Politics of the Firm
LEONARD TIVEY

The Execution Process Volume 1

IMPLEMENTATION
IN A BUREAUCRACY

Andrew Dunsire

MARTIN ROBERTSON

First published in 1978 by Martin Robertson & Co. Ltd., 108 Cowley Road, Oxford OX4 1JF

ISBN 0 85520 173 8

Phototypeset in V.I.P. Sabon by Western Printing Services Ltd, Bristol
Printed and bound by Richard Clay at The Chaucer Press, Bungay.

Contents

Preface

What is your understanding of the process of 'execution'? Most people seem to think first of – you know – *an* execution: the Chair or the Rope, Madame la Guillotine, a Mafia 'contract', the firing squad. Very well. Let us examine it.

Imagine that a soldier has been court-martialled and judged guilty of desertion in the face of the enemy, for which the penalty (it is wartime) is death by firing-squad. He is in a garrison cell, awaiting the appointed hour; the hour comes, the little procession of garrison commander, chaplain, guards, medical officer and prisoner makes its way to an inner courtyard, and the prisoner is offered a blindfold; prayers are said as the riflemen take their places. In a few seconds it is over.

To describe what has happened, we may say either that the prisoner has been executed, or that the sentence of death has been executed. In the first version, execution means a judicial killing. In the second, it clearly means no more than that the sentence has been 'carried out', fulfilled, brought to completion. This book (perhaps disappointingly) is about 'execution' in this second sense, not the first.

It is clear enough who has 'executed' the prisoner. Apart from nominating an abstraction like the 'Law', or 'Society', you would surely agree that the firing-squad has executed the prisoner. They have acted as the 'executioner'. Who, then, has 'executed' the sentence of death? Not *only* the riflemen pulling their triggers: all the members of the little procession are also involved, at the least. The riflemen, in a way, are but the implements the others have wielded. Firing rifles is their trade: at the enemy one day, practice range targets another day, convicted deserters the next – all in a day's work so far as pulling triggers goes. The riflemen obey the order: 'Fire!';

they are probably unaware of any command: 'Execute this sentence'.

Whoever receives *that* command does not, it would seem, execute either the prisoner or the sentence by himself. It would be better, perhaps, to say that he sets machinery in motion towards that end. A great deal of paperwork will undoubtedly be necessary: regimental headquarters to notify, next of kin, pay and allowances section, army records, barracks, and so on. A firing-squad has had to be detailed, ammunition issued, medical officer and chaplain warned, mortuary and burial arrangements commissioned. A large number of little processes are started by the pronouncement of the sentence, go through their separate routines and, as it were, converge at the appointed hour and place. Then, afterwards, a number of other processes begin: a formal report to the President of the Court Martial, with medical certificates; return of the body, or burial; return of the man's kit and equipment to stores; rearrangement of rotas and lists on which the man's name had appeared, and so on.

These activities, it will be plain enough on brief consideration, are perhaps 'set in motion' by the pronouncing of the sentence of death, but they are not 'set up' by it: there are structures already in being, there are people used to giving such instructions and people used to obeying them; there are reporting procedures and accounting procedures and means of co-ordinating them. The riflemen execute the prisoner; but a whole apparatus of perhaps hundreds of persons, organised in a form of bureaucracy and employing its characteristic practices, has some part in executing the sentence.

Everyone is more or less aware of this sort of thing – the processes that have to be gone through to turn a sentence (made up of words) into a rattle of rifle fire or the like (physical and mechanical action), that definitively changes aspects of the real world – even if they might not find it easy to spell it out. It is these implicit general principles we are setting out to make explicit. What it is necessary to do or have done, the requisite processes, can be called 'implementation' – the choosing, linking and wielding of the implements by which words become action-on-the-world. This is the theme of this volume.

A description of the processes of implementation is not, assuredly, a complete description of the execution process in a bureaucracy. There are several ways in which it falls short of that, and it may be helpful to set out some of them now. Briefly, the book: (1) does not deal with policy making; (2) 'leaves the people out'; (3) makes use of a very loose definition of 'bureaucracy'; (4) uses an old-fashioned 'ideal type' framework, rather than a behavioural or contingency approach; and (5) concerns itself with purely internal processes and not with what happens in the outside world at all. I shall try to justify these idiosyncrasies.

(1) This book is predicated on what may seem an obsolete, mistaken, and dangerous premise: that execution can be separated from decision, or implementation from policy making, and the like. Now, so great were the falsities of the 'policy/administration dichotomy' in American writing in the early decades of the century, that many political scientists still look askance at anything other than a 'seamless web model', in which what a policy is and how it will be activated are indistinguishable. To my mind, however, the dichotomy is not false, it is semantically inescapable; and the layman in these matters (to whom *not* making this simple distinction would seem absurd) is using words quite properly when he says 'policy is one thing, implementation is another' (or the like) – provided he recognises that this analytical separation of processes is no ground for the normative separation of persons, or of roles. The fact that it is permissible to distinguish in principle between the making of a policy and the carrying out of a policy in no way implies (as some would have it imply) that civil servants should not make policy. There are five or six suppressed premises in any such asserted conclusion, each of which can be impugned.

However, although we will not spend much time on policy making as such, there will be a good deal of discussion of the relations between decision and implementation, at all levels in a bureaucracy.

(2) This book is also predicated on what may appear an equally obsolete, mistaken and dangerous premise: that it is feasible to discuss the analytical structure of administrative processes while 'leaving the people out' – that is, while ignoring the 'human factor' – motivation, interpersonal conflict, group dynamics and so on. Rather than adopt any uncompromisingly 'structuralist' stance over the entire universe of discourse, I shall plead first the 'analyst's defence' (which is that analysis requires the stressing of some parts of the subject at the expense of others, in order to reveal the existence of patterns that might otherwise be missed), and say that, whereas in any real-life situation an official will, of course, take account of the personalities and individual characteristics of those with whom he must work, as investigators we shall never appreciate the weight of the organisational processes as such, unless we deliberately try to

hold constant the psychological and social-psychological variables.

More positively, I have endeavoured to include in the analysis behaviour ascribable to *official role* (e.g. the superior–subordinate relation, the autonomy of the specialist), and have concentrated on cognitive factors in explanation of behaviour, while setting aside the affect component. The 'people' are in, all right; but I have been concerned to demonstrate the difficulties that are inherent in the logic of the structure and of the process by reason of limitations on the capabilities and capacities of people – apart from their emotions, beliefs and preferences. There are at least these two components to the 'human factor' (cognition and affect), and they should be distinguished.

(3) The third apparently perverse premise of this book (given the title) is that no precise definition of 'bureaucracy' is necessary. It will soon be evident that the term is not being used in the sense of 'red tape' or excessive use of forms and rigid procedures, nor in the sense of a usurpation by officials of powers that rightly belong only to elected representatives; and that it is not even being used to describe certain common features of all large-scale organisations, but to refer to only one type of organisation – the government department and similar public bodies. The term is used here quite colloquially: 'bureaucrats' means civil servants in Whitehall, and their near kin in one particular public corporation.

I am not at all concerned with approving or disapproving of bureaucracies, nor am I concerned to show how Weber misunderstood something about them, or to test some proposition derived from post-Weberian scholarship. If a stipulative definition is required, 'bureaucracy' here refers to an organisation which employs hierarchy of authority and division of jurisdiction internally, with an output consisting mainly of marks on pieces of paper, and externally accountable for its internal processes as well as its output performance and impact. My argument will be that bureaucracies, by their very nature and not from any concession to the liberal *Zeitgeist*, do not and cannot operate by commands from the top, or in simple expression of the 'will of the Minister'; and that it is not the 'department' which collectively enjoys the degree of independence and autonomy that is often observed, while the individual bureaucratic official is subject to authoritarian rule; *it is the other way around*.

(4) The fourth foolish assumption (as it may be thought) which informs this book is that it is legitimate to describe the internal

processes of 'a' bureaucracy (in the abstract), to speak of 'the' implementation process (in general) and so on. Correct contemporary outlook might be that it is silly to pretend that any one description will do equally well for all the (quite various) bodies included within the term 'bureaucracy', especially in the loose formulation employed here. One should rather look for the conditions under which one's variables would take up this or that set of particular values, and attempt a typology of execution processes within different bureaucracies. With that kind of criticism I am in deep sympathy (in principle).

My reply must only be, 'Yes, but not yet.' Beginnings have been made, in implementation and in other aspects of execution, in the construction of typologies, developing theories of contingent influences on execution processes. In this book, however, we shall remain in the realm of definition; and of constitutive rather than operational definition at that, in Kerlinger's terms (1964; quoted in Hinings *et al.*, 1967,62). We are to be concerned with exploring the necessary relations between concepts, the logical entailments of certain assumptions, the building of a model of what it must be that people mean by the words they use in describing implementation in a bureaucracy. Explanations of observed phenomena, of the configuration of empirical variables in concrete situations, will no doubt come later if a pay-off seems promised.

(5) In the literature of this subject, 'implementation' has been used in two broad senses. In the first, implementation of a policy means the producing of a desired effect upon the world. Scholars interested in the public policy process have set out to measure impact or effect of a new policy or a change in policy, and to explain gaps that might then be seen between what the policy makers intended or thought they would achieve, and what they actually did achieve. But it is not always noticed that the explanation must take two elements into account: there is not only the relationship between policy input and impact outcome, but also that between policy input and bureaucratic output. That is to say, the intentions of the policy makers have first to be transformed into the actions of officials, before they can have any effect upon the world whatever. 'Impact studies' have tended to concentrate on environmental reactions to *policy* change, while leaving opaque the relationship of policy and output: yet it is clear enough that the processes of implementing policy within the bureaucracy are part of what is reacted to. A general model of those may

therefore assist in the evaluation of the impacts of particular policy changes.

(6) A sixth aspect of the lack of completeness of the treatment of execution in this book must be mentioned. Implementing a decision or new policy, 'setting machinery in motion' as it was put above, is one thing: 'running' a bureaucracy, providing and maintaining the machinery, ensuring a generalised capability for implementing policies, is surely another. This (which can be designated 'control') is in many ways the complement of 'implementation' in the execution process in bureaucracies, as may become evident by the end of the book: it is the subject of a separate volume, entitled *Control in a Bureaucracy*.

These books had their genesis as long as twenty-five years ago, when I began teaching Public Administration and wished to find a book that would provide as close and as theory-based an account of what went on in government departments *below* the level of Permanent Secretary as was available for the relationship between top civil servants and Ministers, or for the recruitment and training of top civil servants, and some other topics of that kind. At the time, there were very few even purely descriptive accounts of British central administrative practice, whether of the teaching textbook or special case-history sort. During a stay in the United States I had been introduced to Simon-Smithburg-Thompson (1950), and tried to adapt this material for British classes. But my main intellectual debt in this field (as will be obvious by the end of the book) came to be to March and Simon (1958). It has been superseded in some respects, and I do not share the psychological assumptions at its base; but the book is still, twenty years on, a mine of new concepts and insights. Time and again for the present book I have (as I thought) laboriously worked something out for myself, and then come across the basic idea in March and Simon, perhaps in a single throw-away sentence.

Drafts of some of these chapters have been in existence for ten years. Several years ago Professor W. J. M. Mackenzie was kind enough to read some of them and make detailed and valuable comments. Above all he encouraged me to persevere, even with such an odd, esoteric, abstract and theoretical kind of Public Administration writing as this – which had led another mentor of mine, Professor W. A. Robson, to ask whether I was still 'whoring after strange gods'. To them both I wish a long and happy retirement.

I am grateful also to former colleagues in the Ministry of Transport and Civil Aviation and friends in British Rail, in London and in Regional Headquarters at York (including the officers of the Area Transport Users' Consultative Committee) for generous help with the case-study which forms Chapter 3. They may consider it a mouse of a result from our mountainous labours at the time: the book as then envisaged was a somewhat different one, and the material has been boiled down more than once. They did their best to correct errors of fact in the account of a branch line closure, but I am responsible for any that remain, and for all matters of interpretation. (It should perhaps be made clear that the procedures described in Chapter 3 were those in force at the time of the closure in question; many changes, in both legislation and Ministry and railway practice, have taken place since.)

Some parts of the book were written while I was the holder of a personal research award from the Social Science Research Council, and I gladly acknowledge my indebtedness to them for this opportunity. To my family, who have had this work around their necks for many a summer, my debt is incalculable, and I dedicate the book to them.

York
April 1978

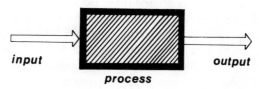

input **output**

process

Fig. 1 The 'black box'

CHAPTER 1

The 'P/Q Relation'

The separation of powers

At least since the time of Marsilius of Padua in the fourteenth century
(Vile, 1967, 27)* men have distinguished clearly between the making
of law, the legislative function, and the execution or putting into
effect of the law, the executive function. Until the seventeenth century they tended to include in 'execution of the law' all that we would
call 'judicial' as well; and Bentham's formulation was that the
'Administrative' and the 'Judiciary' together formed the 'Executive'
(Bentham, 1843, IX, 154), but that need not detain us here. By the
end of the eighteenth century, writers on government and learned
people generally were quite accustomed to order their thoughts
around the three-fold division of the 'powers of the state' into
legislative, executive, and judicial. It is worth emphasising that there
never was anything particularly right or inevitable about this way of
classifying, but it has proved useful ever since – too useful, perhaps,
for it has stopped most people thinking about alternative ways.

Montesquieu in the eighteenth century held that the liberties of
Englishmen were safeguarded because these three powers were exercised by separate organs of government, so that no one organ might
use to the full the coercive sanctions of the state without the concur-
rence of the other two:

When the legislative and executive powers are united in the

---

* References throughout the book will be given as here. 'Vile, 1967, 27' means that
the quotation or point referred to will be found on page 27 of the book by Vile that
was published in 1967, full details being given under 'Vile' in the booklist at the end of
this volume. 'Montesquieu, (1748) 1949, 151' indicates page 151 of a book by
Montesquieu that was first published in 1748, although the edition actually being
used is that of 1949, details again appearing in the booklist under 'Montesquieu'.

same person, or in the same body of magistrates, there can be no liberty ... Again, there is no liberty, if the judiciary power be not separated from the legislative and executive. (*Montesquieu, (1748) 1949, 151–2*)

The impact of this idea upon the emerging constitutionalists of America was liberating and permanent; the 'separation of powers' became the equivalent of an Eleventh Commandment. Nor is Montesquieu's account of the British Constitution wholly wrong: the overlap between our Legislative and Executive from the dual membership of Ministers of the Crown, and between the Legislative and the Judiciary from the dual membership of the 'Law Lords', should not blind us to the fact that no Member of the House of Commons can be a civil servant at the same time, no civil servant can be a judge, and so on (Plamenatz, 1963, I: 289). And it is a solid English tradition (owing, perhaps, as much to Mammon as to Montesquieu) that makes judges of the Common Law wary of the encroachment of the Executive upon their functions, whether it be by the Court of the Star Chamber in the seventeenth century or 'administrative tribunals' in the twentieth.

So what began as a simple logical classification scheme, an aid to understanding the nature of government, became a rule about how things ought to be and a set of prescriptive rights. The same process was repeated at the end of the nineteenth century, on a somewhat smaller stage: beginning in a paper of 1887 by Woodrow Wilson exploring the transferability of foreign administrative techniques, and separating such 'administrative questions' from the 'political questions' of monarchy or republicanism and so on (Wilson, 1887, 211), this distinction became caught up in the struggle for reform of the 'spoils system' of appointment, as indeed Wilson may have intended. If administration is a technical matter, it needs trained people with job security to do it well. From a different starting point, Frank. J. Goodnow looked analytically at activities in a single state:

Political functions group themselves naturally under two heads, which are equally applicable to the mental operations and the actions of self-conscious personalities. That is, the action of the state as a political entity consists either in operations necessary to the expression of its will, or in operations necessary to the execution of that will. (*Goodnow, 1900, 9*)

And there are

> in all governmental systems two primary or ultimate functions
> of government, viz. the expression of the will of the state and the
> execution of that will. . . . These functions are, respectively,
> Politics and Administration. (*Goodnow, 1900, 22*)

NB.

But Goodnow holds quite clearly that the functions cannot be separated except analytically; that although, in the nature of complex
modern governments, some organs will specialise in one rather than
the other, it is not feasible for any one or even any group to do so
exclusively. There must be harmony between the law and its execution, and

> in order that this harmony between the expression and the
> execution of the state will may be obtained, the independence
> either of the body which expresses the state will or of the body
> which executes it must be sacrificed . . . practical political
> necessity makes impossible the consideration of the function of
> politics apart from that of administration. Politics must have a
> certain control over administration. . . . (*Goodnow, 1900,
> 23–4; Waldo, 1948, 108*)

However, administration is not homogeneous: there is purely
executive administration, quasi-judicial administration and statistical and semi-scientific administration, and only the first kind is 'of
necessity subordinated to the function of politics'. The rest 'should
be relieved very largely, if not altogether, from the control of political
bodies' (Goodnow, 1900, 86).

Types of admin

Here I think we see the conventional nomenclature of the American governmental system influencing the analysis, as it did with
W. F. Willoughby's similar treatment of the relationship between
'administration' and 'execution' (Willoughby, 1919, 231ff.; Waldo,
1948, 112) and other writers of the period (see extracts in Lepawsky,
1949, Part I). For Willoughby, however, it is the 'executive' function
that is all-embracing; it

> is distinctly political in character. It involves the making of
> far-reaching decisions in respect to governmental policies. In
> respect to the actual conduct of governmental affairs it has to do
> with seeing that policies that are adopted, or lines of action that
> are decided upon, are properly carried into effect rather than in
> undertaking the work proper of putting these policies and pro-
> grammes into execution. . . . The latter function, the administra-

tive, on the other hand, strictly speaking, involves the making of no decisions of a political character. (*Willoughby, 1919, 385*)

So the 'executive function' stops short of 'execution', which is the job of the 'administrative function'. These words, like Humpty Dumpty's, clearly mean what they are told to mean by whoever pays them most.

Both Goodnow and Willoughby were looking for a theoretical justification for letting the politicians on Capitol Hill into the White House and the Cabinet, as it were, and letting the party men into the top direction of the Departments, but not beyond a certain line: the 'executive function' is acceptably political, but not the 'quasi-judicial', or 'statistical and semi-scientific', or 'quasi-business or commercial' activity (Goodnow, 1900, 86); 'executive', yes, but not 'the putting of policies and programmes into execution' (Willoughby, 1919, 385). These aims, with their confusion of terminology and their lack of philosophical success in drawing the desired boundary, continued to distort political science for half a century. The distinctions of the more careful pioneers were lost, rather than clarified: 'policy' was made interchangeable with 'politics', 'execution' with 'administration'. 'Almost without exception', said the historian of this movement, Dwight Waldo, later writers

accept it as plain fact that there are but two parts of functions in the governmental process: decision and execution, politics and administration; that administration is a realm of expertise from which politics can be and should be largely excluded. (*Waldo, 1984, 114*)

Thus, the writer of the first textbook on public administration, Leonard D. White: 'Public Administration consists of all those operations having for their purpose the fulfilment or enforcement of public policy' (White, 1926, 3).
Or another:

Politics is . . . an inevitable and necessary part of the process of government. It must, however, be controlled and confined to its proper sphere which is the determination, crystallisation, and declaration of the will of the community. Administration, on the other hand, is the carrying into effect of this will once it has been made clear by political processes. From these premises, therefore, is derived the keystone of the new public administration – the conclusion that politics should stick to its policy-determining sphere and leave administration to apply its own technical processes free from the blight of political meddling. (*Pfiffner*, 1935, 9)

Wallace S. Sayre summarised thus the first of the premises on which the pioneer texts were founded:

> The politics—administration dichotomy was assumed both as a self-evident truth and as a desirable goal; administration was perceived as a self-contained world of its own, with its own separate values, rules, and methods. (*Sayre*, 1958, 102)

By 1935 the pendulum was already beginning its swing the other way again, but as late as 1966, in England, an official committee was obliged to deal with the same attempt to employ an invalid theory to draw the same dividing line. Time after time witnesses expressed the need to distinguish between policy and administration: 'If only policy could be separated from administration, the former to be exercised by members and the latter by officers, this would be a solution. . . .' (Maud, 1967, para. 109). The Committee on Management in Local Government rejected the view that the function of elected members is to decide 'policy' and that of officers is to 'execute' or 'administer' it, because, they argued, 'policy' could not be defined (Maud, 1967, para. 143). (They did not argue that 'execution' or 'administration' could not be defined.)

> We argue that 'policy' cannot be defined and indeed that it should not be defined. Some issues are, to reasonable men, so important that they can safely be termed 'policy issues'. But what may seem to be a routine matter may be charged with political significance to the extent that it becomes a matter of policy. Other routine matters may lead by practice and experience to the creation of a principle or a policy. . . . (*Maud, 1967, para. 143*)

The Committee's report goes on to use the arguments against 'the policy/administration dichotomy' that had by then become standard among political scientists: Luther Gulick's note in 1933 that 'where there is *discretion*, there is the making of policy' – yet discretion is inseparable from decision, at any level (Waldo, 1948, 123); E. Pendleton Herring showing how policy is everywhere made on the indispensable advice of administrators (Herring, 1936); Carl Friedrich in 1937 devising the 'rule of anticipated reactions' to explain how official-level policy makers could yet be under the control of representative politicians (Friedrich, 1937, 16); Chester Barnard noting that 'a considerable part of administrative work consists in the interpretation and reinterpretation of orders in their application to concrete circumstances that were not or could not be taken into account initially' (Barnard, 1938, 165); above all, perhaps, Paul Appleby making the whole distinction *relative*: 'In the perspective of each successive level everything decided at that level and above is 'policy', and everything that may be left to a lower level is 'admini-stration' (Appleby, 1949, 21).

Thus did American scholars redress the balance disturbed by the enthusiasms of the reformers: the contemporary position is that, if there is an analytical distinction to be drawn between 'policy' and 'administration' (and if there is not, why use two words?), or be-tween the making of policy and the carrying out of policy, or the like, such a distinction will not serve (as the Maud Committee put it) to distinguish between the responsibilities of politically appointed per-sons and those of 'civil service' personnel. If there is a political need, or any other need, for a boundary between territories, or group rights, elected politicians on one side and career officials on the other, then a threshold of some kind must be devised: but the discrimination between what is 'policy' and what is 'administration' or 'execution' simply will not bear that weight – to shift the metaphor. On the whole, European political science has never been driven to the attempt, for the governmental systems have not pre-sented the problem so acutely. The Reorganisation Committee of 1920 called the duties proposed for the new Administrative Class of the British civil service 'those concerned with the formation of policy' – and no hairs were turned. (For a dicussion of the evo-lution of this position, see Fry, 1969; Dunsire, 1973, 18–37, 153–65.)

Willing and acting

But if the whole policy/execution dichotomy debate was a wrong turning leading to a dead end, insofar as the theory was designed to support a political platform and failed to do so, there is nevertheless a dichotomy of some kind implicit in the mere idea of 'execution'. If the word has the ordinary or dictionary meaning of 'carrying into effect', 'implementation', 'effectuation', etc., that presupposes the existence of something to be carried into effect:

> There must be something out there prior to implementation; otherwise there would be nothing to move toward in the process of implementation. A verb like 'implement' must have an object like 'policy'. (*Pressman and Wildavsky, 1973, xiii*)

– or 'plan, command, law, judicial sentence, will, etc.' as the dictionary has it, and we could add 'intention, decision, order' and a number of other such concepts, each perhaps distinct from the others, but sharing one meaning at least. They all stand for what comes before, in the relationship in which 'execute', 'implement', 'carry out', and so on, all stand for what comes after. The rationale of such a dichotomy is a separate matter from the appropriateness of any particular labels one might choose for the two aspects (although names must be given or there is no way of talking about it); and that in turn is a separate matter from the success or failure of the instrumental use that someone may have tried to make of it. Though the policy/administration dichotomy may not satisfactorily discriminate between the work of politicians and the work of officials, that does not necessarily mean that there is no policy/administration dichotomy; and even if we found that, indeed, a policy/administration dichotomy is a false one, that would not mean that a command/execution dichotomy was also false.

So as to be able to discuss it without avoidable connotations, let us name the basic before/after idea, the 'P/Q relation', and explore what the writers we have quoted thought about it.

Goodnow's conceptual apparatus was explicit. First, political functions could be grouped under two heads and, second, the same two heads applied to the 'mental operations and the actions of self-conscious personalities'. There is an analogy between the 'self-conscious personality', or individual human being, and the state as a political entity; and there is a psychology which dichotomises between mental operations and actions. There was ancient and contemporary support for both positions. Parallelism between 'head' and 'members', or bodily organs and the 'head and members of the body politic', has scriptural authority; and the emerging discipline of 'sociology' talked of the birth, growth and death of societies and the like in considerable (and well considered) detail. An 'idealist' school of political philosophers tended to present evidence that the State *is* a 'self-conscious personality':

> After pointing out the analogy between the organised structure of minds and the organised structure of society, we now go on to show that minds and society are really the same fabric regarded from different points of view. (*Bosanquet (1899) 1951, 158*)

– building on the new and fashionable psychology which distinguished a mere *association* of ideas from organic control through a dominant idea, and so could be held identical with Tönnies's (1887) distinction between *Gesellschaft* and *Gemeinschaft*. It could also support Rousseau's distinction between the 'will of all' and the 'general will', a construction essential for the idealist theory of the state (Bosanquet, (1899) 1951, 145–66). But after the use made of it by the dictators Mussolini and Hitler, the full Hegelian identification of the state with a transcendental mind and purpose fell decidedly out of favour, and among political scientists even the analogy between parts of the individual and parts of the society is avoided.

The second aspect of Goodnow's theoretical assumptions is also gravely suspect. More than a century earlier, Rousseau himself had made the dichotomy the basis of his 'separation of powers' in the state:

> Every free action has two causes which concur to produce it, one moral – the will which determines the act, the other physical – the strength which executes it. When I walk towards an object, it is necessary first that I should resolve to go that way, and secondly that my feet should carry me. (*Rousseau, (1762) 1968, 101*)

There is a similar distinction in the organs of the government. It was this understanding of how things actually work in the human being that (as Vile says) dominated the minds of constitution builders for many years, as they sought a basis for dividing the functions of government. The 'mind/body dualism' (as such distinctions between will and strength, thought and action, mental operations and physical operations and the like appear to the philosoper today) also has classical Greek and early Christian warrant: relatively crudely in the notion of a 'spirit' or 'soul' inhabiting the 'body' or material human manifestation and leaving it at death; less crudely in the emerging notions of 'awareness of reason' or 'self-consciousness' as we now call it. The problem with the cruder formulations is understanding how the two substances interact: if, as Descartes, for instance, postulated, they are two different kinds of existence, it becomes difficult to explain what happens at the 'interface' – how a motion in one causes an effect in the other. The problem with later formulations is testability; no one can be conscious of more than one 'self'. Koestler, on the other hand, pin-points the problems of trying to abandon the dualism: he reports an experiment in which a scientist, by means of electrodes implanted in a patient's brain, caused the patient's hand to be raised. On being asked, 'Why did you lift your hand?', the patient replied, very reasonably, 'I didn't do it. You made me do it.' An experimenter using hypnotism can also 'make' a patient act in such a way, and when similarly asked why he did it, the patient will commonly manufacture a 'reason' why he acted in the conditioned way. 'One is tempted to say', Koestler concludes, 'that the hypnotist imposes his will on the subject's mind – the surgeon merely on his brain' (Koestler, 1967, 204).

There have been many attempts to deal with these problems, ranging from solipsism (the 'It's *all* in the mind' of Bishop Berkeley) to the unworried materialism of the modern psychologist, by way of occasionalism, epiphenomenalism and other attempts at accommodation. Rousseau spoke of 'concurrent' causes; G. F. Stout, the psychologist on whom Bosanquet relied, used a theory which neither denied nor asserted dualism, but insisted that every event in human life had two aspects, one physical, the other mental, each complementing the other in an unresolved way (Stout, 1896). The logical positivists' approach is to assert 'category confusion': the notions of 'mind', 'idea' and so on are on one plane of discourse, and anyone who finds it useful to talk in this way is welcome to do so; the notions of 'brain', 'motion' and so on are on another plane of discourse, and only on this plane can experimental science proceed (Ryle, 1949; Sluckin (1954) 1960, Chap. 10). 'Mind' statements are useful as summations of behaviour or predispositions to behave in some identifiable way, but they do not relate to anything 'real', and have to be translated on to the other plane before they can do so. 'Mind' interacting with 'body' is not a problem; it is meaningless.

The ancient versions of the state/organism analogy kept clear of mind/body dualism just because they were so crude: parallels of 'head' and 'members' do not raise the difficulty. Some of this older imagery survives. 'Thought' *vis-à-vis* 'action' retains a 'head/body' image. Koestler's juxtaposition of 'mind' and 'brain', both seen as 'head', sharpens the puzzle: the plane shift, if that is what it is, is clearly indicated. But different versions of operations all going on in the head do not produce an image useful to the protagonist of 'separation of powers'. The state organism analogy and thought/action dualism is still implied in Pfiffner's use of the phrase 'will of the community' in 1935; but as positivism spread among the learned, the rationale of a discrimination between politicians and officials, where one was required, began to alter; the politics/administration dichotomy became, in Appleby's hands, a *relative* thing, a 'P/Q relation' that occurred at all levels in a bureaucracy, and there was no need to employ an analogy between the organism and the organisation for that purpose.

Yet, if we are to conduct a discussion about the execution process in organisations, about the relationship between 'plan' and 'implementation' or whatever we name it, it seems that we must take up a position in these matters: do organisations decide, or is it only organisms (men and women) that decide? Can organisations act, or is it only organisms that can act? What is the nature of the 'P/Q relation', whether we speak of it in relation to the individual human being or in relation to the organisation? It would be useful if some fresh approach to all the puzzles just presented could bring into a single perspective the organism/organisation analogy and the thought/action dualism so that we could see whether there is indeed a single 'P/Q relation'.

There is another matter. Rousseau spoke of 'every *free* action' being the effect of two causes. When are actions 'free'? Is the consciousness of sometimes being able to choose one course of action rather than another mere illusion? Are all our decisions the resultants of the influences that bear upon us – our heredity, our history, our environment? If we knew more about a man's setting, could we predict more of his behaviour? And so on: the 'free will' puzzle has occasioned as much disputation as mind/body dualism or any other of the classic philosophical problems and is at the centre of the modern questions about a 'social science'. It is also, in an inverse way, at the centre of the questions about the 'authority' and 'compliance' relationship in an organisation: does the rational man merely pursue his own interests via the organisation? Can there be autonomy in a bureaucracy?

Finding a single perspective on all these questions would seem to require the reduction of three scientific disciplines – physiology, individual psychology and social psychology – to a single discipline. But that is not the case: the need is for something less daunting, a common language and set of concepts with which to discuss these several bodies of knowledge, as indeed mathematics, in a limited way, already provides. It will be enough if we can find an interpretation of 'self-consciousness', 'identity', the 'I' of the patient in Koestler's story, that is not inconsistent with the corresponding interpretation of concepts like 'brain', 'motor nervous system' and so on, and not inconsistent either with the interpretation into the same language of concepts concerned with interaction between persons, social groupings, 'organisational behaviour' and the like. That is still a tall order, but perhaps we can make a beginning.

The TOTE cycle

Let us begin by putting the self-conscious actor in focus. Now, however conscious of self he may be, there are many events taking place in his own body of which he is *not* conscious (and this is true whether by 'he' we mean 'mind' or 'brain' or whatever). He can, for instance, sense his heart beating and his stomach rumbling, but he cannot sense the operation of his kidneys and he can bring about a change in that operation only by rather indirect methods, by 'making arrangements' rather than by willing it, doing it, taking thought or acting in any direct manner. And if we went into the matter deeply enough (we shall, later), we would find that the self-conscious actor actually cannot so much as lift his hand except by a similar process of 'arranging for it to happen' through several levels of nerve centre. 'Self-consciousness' does not extend very far down into the physiological hierarchy and, so far as we can tell, there is no 'self-consciousness' at any other level.

If we begin again from the self-conscious actor and move outwards instead of inwards, we make a similar finding. Again, he can arrange for things to happen in regions of his environment beyond those he can actually sense, but he can 'participate in' events only when he can use his senses directly. If in the first image the self-consciousness of the actor is seen as at the top of a physiological hierarchy descending through levels of the nervous system, in the second image the self-consciousness of the actor is seen as at the bottom of a social hierarchy ascending through levels of larger and larger social groupings (which we can name differently according to our interest, but obvious ones are: individual, family, neighbour-hood, community, society, etc.). At no other level is there 'self-consciousness' – at least, that would be my belief; as already noted, some philosophers have postulated sentience at group or nation level. It is one thing to slip into shorthand signs such as 'The Labour Party intends...' or 'Britain has always felt...': it is another thing to believe it.

However many inconvenient corners it knocks off physiological knowledge and knowledge of individual and social psychology in order to make that knowledge fit the image, this concept of a single hierarchy extending outwards and inwards from the self-consciousness of the actor is undoubtedly a concept that brings the three bodies of knowledge into a single perspective. 'Consciousness' is seen as a unique property of only one 'level' in that hierarchy (if we who write and read happened to be kidneys or societies – kidneys and societies that could write and read – we might have a different conception of where that level is located). This idea in no way solves any puzzles about consciousness, but it lets us go around them.

If no sentience at other levels, then no 'identity' either, unless with care in metaphor. The question of whether there can be 'intention', or 'choice', or 'decision' at other levels can either be answered logically and dogmatically ('all such usages are mistaken'), or else it can be left a little more open for the time being – it may be obviously fanciful to think of a kidney having a plan or making a decision, but reference to a party's intentions is, after all, so very frequent that people must find some meaning in the phrase.

What of 'action'? In view of what was said about a man 'arrang-ing' to lift his own hand, the question might appear to be whether 'action' is appropriately predicated of the self-conscious actor, let alone of any other level in the hierarchy inwards or outwards. But that nonsense comes from confusing 'a man' and 'some (or even all) of the parts of a man': a brain can arrange for a man's hand to lift; the man lifts his hand. Nevertheless, on such an understanding of what is happening, a man's 'action' is either a description of his movements as someone else sees them, or it is a description of what is 'arranged to happen' internally – that is, a sort of programme for the motor nervous system and various sets of muscles. The 'will/action' dichotomy was simple: any analysable components of the process were either one or the other. The newer physiological approach cannot make such an either/or distinction: it is impossible to say when a process stops being 'will' and begins being 'action'. Nor, in this approach, are action processes individually identifiable in that manner. We learn how to make muscle movements by trying out motor nervous system discharges: we learn sequences of such nerve—muscle activities; we learn to stand erect, to walk, to climb, by combining such learned sequences; we learn how to assemble whole volleys of such movements into complex activities like riding a bicycle. The 'action' that a self-conscious actor decides upon, then, is almost inevitably some programme of such relatively complex behaviours from his repertoire, or possibly a combination of that and 'arrangements' for other people's behaviour that in some way he can expect or command.

But selecting such a programme is not the once-for-all event that the concept 'decides upon' implies. Rather does learning continue to have a role: it is less (this approach says) like setting a train going on a railway track than like driving a car through traffic; monitoring what is actually happening, avoiding accidents and coping with the unforeseen, moving always towards the completion of the action intended but altering the selection of behaviour sequences as changing circumstances dictate – sometimes, of course, all in the twinkling of an eye, as when a man wielding a hammer alters its direction and force in mid-stroke as the nail wobbles. How quickly it is done; yet how many sheets of paper would be required to describe, in terms of signals in the nervous system and alterations in the muscles, what happened?

All human activity, at the subconscious as well as the conscious level (according to one particular version of this approach put forward by Miller, Galanter and Pribram in their book *Plans and the*

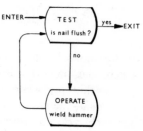

Fig. 2 A TOTE unit for hammering nails (*Annett, 1969, 21: after Miller, Galanter and Pribram, 1960*)

Structure of Behavior), is governed by a cycle of neural processes they call TOTE – for Test Operate Test Exit. This embodies, first, a *test* for incongruities in the immediate environment – things that should not be there, strangers, departures from expectations, changes in settled values, etc.; second, the *operation* of a standard response, whatever the programme in question is; third, *test* to see whether the incongruity has disappeared; if it has, fourth, *exit* to next cycle; if not, shunt down (or 'in') a level and do a TOTE at that level, or several, until the incongruities disappear, which should have made them disappear at the higher level. Any TOTE can in this way trigger an internal search and test, a TOTE-within-a-TOTE, and *that* TOTE can trigger an internal TOTE, and so on. There is no limit to the number of times one can go another level inwards (at least, it is a high number) (Miller, Galanter and Pribram, 1960; Annett, 1969).

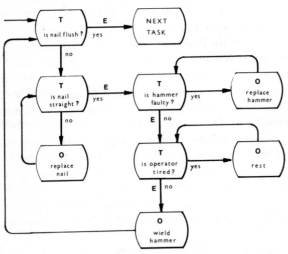

Fig. 3 Expanded TOTEs-within-a-TOTE for hammering nails (*Annett, 1969,* 22)

Much of this activity does not take place in the brain but in lower centres; and of that which does, most of it is at subconscious level. But the process of 'conscious thinking' is considered to be the same in principle: search (environment, memory, etc.), test, operate, test, exit. The 'operate' in any such cycle may refer to what we think of as 'physical action' or it may be a surrogate for that, an *imagined* action, depending upon more or less conscious calculations of probabilities which in turn we base on memory and association. In such a construction, 'planning', 'predicting', 'forecasting' and so on embody this notion of 'operate-without-action', a simulation of the future without commitment, a species of game, like the army's Tactical Exercises Without Troops. 'Think Ahead', thus, is an instruction to 'Act Ahead – in your Head'. But a surprising corollary is that there is, in the structure of the cycle as such, no difference between 'acting first and seeing what happens' and 'giving careful thought to all the alternatives before deciding', or between 'incremental' decision making and 'synoptic planning', to use some trade terms we will explore later. The first of each pair uses real feedback from the environment, the second uses conjectural feedback from the subject's own resources – and each is best in some circumstances. There is also a complete range of intermediate positions.

Again, this idea does not explain 'will' or even 'thought', but it does give some account of what 'mental operations' may be involved, and it does provide a non-dichotomous, non-dualistic working theory of the relationships between the accepted categories 'thought' and 'action' in the individual human being. Whether or not the same theory is applicable at group and organisational decision levels had better be left open for the moment. We certainly have a hypothesis to start from, and if we were as sure as Rousseau, Bosanquet, Goodnow and others that what is the case for the individual is also the case for the social grouping, we would replace the 'P/Q relation' with a hierarchy of TOTE cycles. Let us not, however, attempt to argue from any analogy (or even a homology). Let us, instead, look at a case-study which will provide some examples of the phenomenon we are studying, and see what concepts and processes seem helpful in understanding it.

But before going on to that, we should look at some more modern accounts of the implementation process, the literature of the subject.

CHAPTER 2

The Literature

Books and articles about the implementation process are remarkably few, as Pressman and Wildavsky found when preparing their own book, which is entitled:

Implementation: How Great Expectations in Washington are Dashed in Oakland; Or, Why It's Amazing That Federal Programs Work At All, This Being a Saga of the Economic Development Administration as told by Two Sympathetic Observers Who Seek to Build Morals on a Foundation of Ruined Hopes (1973)

They write:

> There is (or there must be) a large literature about implementation in the social sciences – or so we have been told by numerous people. None of them can come up with specific citations to this literature, but they are certain it must exist. Surely, they will say, the vast scholarly attention paid to poverty programs and efforts to secure compliance in the field of civil rights has generated work on problems of implementation. It must be there; it should be there; but in fact it is not. There is a kind of semantic illusion at work here because virtually everything ever done in public policy or public administration must, in the nature of things, have some bearing on implementation. Analytical study (as opposed to mere mention) of implementation seems so eminently reasonable that few can imagine it does not exist. (*Pressman and Wildavsky, 1973, 166*)

The authors admit (as must the present writer) that there may have been something they overlooked; but with the assistance of their research team they had searched a number of indexes to periodicals for articles with 'implementation' or 'execution' in the titles, bibliographies on poverty and civil rights and a number of texts in Public

16

Administration; and nowhere found more than a sentence or two, never a list of citations to the literature on the subject.

Having done much the same for my own purposes, perhaps over a somewhat wider area, I can agree – with reservations. Books and articles with this subject as their central theme, treated analytically, are indeed rare, though no longer non-existent; this literature is now conveniently summarised in an article by Van Meter and Van Horn (1975). But there are two other 'literatures' to be explored. Books and articles in which one can find accounts of the implementation of particular laws, judgements and decisions, treated as history or biography, or as evidence to support some point or other, are not at all rare. In the business administration world, and to a lesser extent in Public and Social Administration, whole training programmes have been built around the study of case histories, among which are many narratives of the introduction of new products and other innovations, which do in practice deal with 'implementation problems'. What is missing is the specific focusing on the classification of these problems rather than on the development of generalised competence in innovation on the part of managers for whom the programmes are designed. The literature brought together by Van Meter and Van Horn is in this genre, comprising empirical case-studies but differing from the earlier literature in that attempts at generalisation about the problems of implementation as such are begun.

The second literature that Pressman and Wildavsky might have explored more thoroughly is in a different tradition, that of the abstract account or ideal type of the process. Most textbooks and manuals on administration and management in general contain some treatment of the implementation process, though a titles search would not reveal it. There is also writing in the field of organisation theory (in which for this purpose we can include bureaucracy theory and the work of the American economists Tullock and Downs) which deals with what is here being thought of as the execution process.

The present book is in the second of these two traditions rather than the first. There is, however, another kind of distinction between the two literatures, which begins from the difference between what Van Meter and Van Horn call 'policy implementation studies' and 'policy impact studies' (1975, 448). Policy impact studies attempt to evaluate policies by measuring the amount of change brought about by them, comparing it with the amount intended and accounting for any difference. A policy decision, put into practice, might solve the problem presented, or actually make it worse, or create fresh problems. Impact studies are concerned with the substantive results or outcomes of (usually) government action, and their aim is the improvement of policy preparation and decision.

Policy implementation studies are less concerned with outcome than with output and attempt to identify the conditions under which an intended output may be achieved. Government (or other policy makers) may devise a policy to solve a problem, meaning that they envisage an output from governmental agencies which, if produced, would in their estimation solve it: but it is common experience that the output actually produced is not that which was envisaged. Either no output is produced at all (the policy intentions never reach the point of being transformed into action upon the environment), or else an output different in quantity, quality or direction from that intended is produced. Implementation studies attempt to evaluate not policies but agency capacity to 'deliver', or carry through to output stage whatever policies are agreed and promulgated, by measuring output intended, comparing it with output achieved and accounting for any difference.

It will be apparent that an 'implementation gap' of this latter kind may well be a factor in an 'impact gap' of the former kind. Evaluators of policies will go astray if they assume that the effects they measure are a function of the policies decided rather than of the policies-as-implemented. Governments will be ill advised to change their policies as a consequence of complaints from dissatisfied clients, without first assuring themselves that the service or action complained of was one inherent in the policy rather than the result of its faulty implementation. Governments, indeed, may be well advised to build their policies wherever feasible out of known and reliable outputs ('off-the-peg solutions'), which if less tailor-made in impact terms are likely to be more predictable in implementation terms.

The school of writers summarised by Van Meter and Van Horn, while being primarily concerned with 'policy implementation' rather than 'policy impact', is more ambitious in its scope than the school of writers to which Tullock, Downs and the present writer can be said to belong. The former attempts to account for the whole of any difference between intended output and actual output ('programme performance'), or the degree to which 'anticipated services are actually delivered' (Van Meter and Van Horn, 1975, 449). The latter school is, by and large, interested in only one aspect of any such difference: the factors implicit in the nature of a bureaucracy.

Thus Dolbeare and Hammond, in their study *The School Prayer Decisions* (1971), identify four categories of factors at work in the response of other agencies to rulings of the US Supreme Court: (1) those associated with the differing response to the substance of the decisions; (2) those depending upon differences in institutional structures and procedures; (3) those arising from the specific political and cultural context; and (4) those turning on the interests, priorities, preferences and behaviours of the actors involved. In their own model, Van Meter and Van Horn postulate seven variables:

1. The nature of the policy to be carried out, according to
   1.1 the amount of change involved
   1.2 the degree of consensus upon its goals present among the actors
2. The standards by which performance is to be measured
3. The resources and incentives made available
4. The quality of inter-organisational communication and control (or enforcement)
5. The characteristics of the implementing agencies, according to
   5.1 size and competence of staff
   5.2 degree of hierarchical control
   5.3 amount of political support available
   5.4 the 'vitality' of the organisation
   5.5 'openness' of internal communications
   5.6 kind of linkages with policy-making body
6. The economic, social, and political conditions
7. The disposition of the implementors, made up of
   7.1 their cognition (comprehension, understanding) of the policy
   7.2 the direction of their response (accept, neutral, reject)
   7.3 the intensity of their response.

By contrast, Anthony Downs's book *Inside Bureaucracy* (1967), which will be examined in some detail later, can be said to advert only to items 4, 5 and 7 in this list, and so can the present book. We will not be in any way concerned with measuring performance as a whole; only with the organisational structures and processes which influence the implementation or delivery of policy, its operationalisation or transformation from ideas to actions. Moreover, unlike Downs, we shall not be concerned with the direction or intensity of the actors' response; only with their cognition and the cognitive processes involved in implementation.

We shall, then, be working far behind the frontiers being carved out of the unknown by the pioneers of policy implementation studies (e.g., Gross, 1966, 1967; Gergen, 1968; Dolbeare and Hammond, 1971; Derthick, 1972), and by the equally intrepid explorations of Hood (1976) in Britain. (A valuable but non-theoretical British study by a serving senior civil servant is Johnstone, 1975). We shall be cultivating ground already broken, many years ago, by March and Simon (1958) and others. Some of the literature cited by Van Meter and Van Horn, however, is also relevant to these narrower concerns: the study by Pressman and Wildavsky (1973), already quoted, and the work of Kaufman (1973), amongst others, will be analysed. (See, on the theory of policy implementation, Bauer and Gergen, 1968; Jones, 1970; Gross *et al.*, 1971; Dye, 1972, 1976; Backoff, 1974. For individual studies with implementation aspects, see Selznick, 1949; Johnson, 1967; Yates and Nelson, 1967; Novogrod *et al.*, 1969; Allison, 1971; Crenson, 1971; Williams, 1971; Sapolsky, 1972; Heclo, 1974; Rose, 1974. On policy evaluation, see Dolbeare, 1975; Katz *et al.*, 1975; Rose, 1976; articles in *Evaluation Quarterly*. A recent *jeu d'esprit* is Bardach, 1977.)

Prehistory of the literature

Scholars, and advisers to princes, have been aware of the seven implementation variables, if not in so many words, since the beginning of the literature of civilised man. Jethro, Moses' father-in-law, has been said to have 'invented' the artificial hierarchy of jurisdiction and the 'exception principle' of delegation during the wanderings of the Jews in the desert (*Exodus*, 18; George, 1968); and the constitution of Chow about 1100 BC shows a complete understanding of the use of rank, favour and attention, as well as appointment and emoluments, in the control of high officials, and the use of regulations, procedure and accounting in the control of government departments (George, 1968, 12). Plato was quite clear on the division of labour (*Republic*, Book II) and Cyrus on the utility of standard routines (George, 1968, 18). Closer to our own day, the early nineteenth-century writings on the functions of a manager, though using recognisable terms like planning, direction and control, do not greatly add to the understanding implicit in the writings of the ancients.

With the increase in the complexity of manufacturing processes and industrial integration around the turn of the twentieth century, sophistication of thought about organisation increased also in the relative explosion of literature associated with 'scientific management'; mainly in terms of shop-floor operations and production control, but also in terms of organisational structure and management. The first comprehensive textbooks on management in industry (rather than on political economy with passages on this) began to appear.

Meanwhile, or perhaps somewhat earlier, the study of governmental administration, with a long pedigree in 'cameralistics' on the continent of Europe, and with the work of Jeremy Bentham inaugurating an English school of pragmatic writing and doing, had achieved a higher level of sophistication than that of the industrial writers, particularly in the analysis of 'bureaucracy'. Most sophisticated of all, without doubt, were the early sociologists Comte, Spencer and Le Play, who discovered the basic principles of what we would now call theory of organisations and general systems theory (for an expanded account, see Dunsire, 1973; Fletcher, 1971, 1974).

During the second decade of this century, this work was synthesised and given a new impetus for further development in the writings of two very different men, Henri Fayol (1841–1925) and Max Weber (1864–1920). Fayol was a French mining engineer, Weber a German professor of sociology. An appreciation of their work as a whole would be quite out of place here, but to them can be traced two styles of discussing the process we are investigating: to Fayol, the 'stages of the administrative process' style; to Weber, the 'organisational dynamics' style. We shall briefly trace the developments in each style separately.

Fayol, Gulick and others

Fayol saw management activity as comprising 'planning, organising, commanding, co-ordinating, and controlling', and asserted that this was the same in all settings – industry, government, society and even in the home. He assumed a 'scalar chain', or sequence of subordination, and 'order' – expanded as 'a place for everyone and everyone in his place' – and prescribes several rules of managerial duty, such as 'Formulate clear, distinct, precise decisions' and 'Have everything under control'. Fayol's writing and lecturing had enormous impact, even in America, on the articulation and integration of the principles of 'good administration'; but there was no analysis of the process by which the good manager's intentions are transformed into production operations other than by 'command' (Fayol, 1916, 1929; Brodie, 1962, 1967; Cuthbert, 1970; etc.)

When President Harry S. Truman was about to hand over the White House to General Dwight D. Eisenhower, he is said to have commiserated with his successor in these words: 'He'll sit here, and he'll say, "Do this! Do that!" And nothing will happen. Poor Ike – it won't be a bit like the Army. He'll find it very frustrating' (Bailey, 1966; quoted in Sharkansky, 1970, 170). Truman himself evidently had an odd idea of what 'the army' was like: he saw it as the stereotype of a military command structure which *would* involve obeying orders, the stereotype from which the early theoreticians of industrial management drew their models.

Luther Gulick, in a paper called 'Notes on the Theory of Organisation' which he had prepared for the celebrated President's Committee on Administrative Management, reformulated Fayol's list into a mnemonic word POSDCORB, which summarised the work of the chief executive, the letters standing for Planning, Organizing, Staffing, Directing, Co-ordinating, Reporting and Budgeting (Gulick, 1937, 13). Gulick's analysis of the different bases of specialisation that are necessary when 'building up' from the operating level of an organisation and 'building down' from the top, is acute; but from the present point of view his significant contribution is his statement of the two primary methods of co-ordinating a complex subdivision of work:

1. By organisation, that is, by interrelating the subdivisions of work by allotting them to men who are placed in a structure of authority, so that the work may be co-ordinated by orders of superiors to subordinates, reaching from the top to the bottom of the entire enterprise.
2. By the dominance of an idea, that is, the development of intelligent singleness of purpose in the minds and wills of those who are working together as a group, so that each worker will of his own accord fit his task into the whole with skill and enthusiasm. (*Gulick, 1937, 6*)

Gulick saw the second as 'the more important and the more difficult': 'The absurdities of the hierarchical system are made sweet and reasonable through unity of purpose' (Gulick, 1937, 39). But it is the first of these two methods, with all its absurdities, which represented (and largely still represents) the most widely held and commonsense assumption about the way the purposes of those at the head of a hierarchy of authority are translated into the corresponding actions of those who serve them – 'by orders of superiors to subordinates, reaching from top to bottom'. (For a formalisation of the 'monistic' model, see Thompson, 1961, 74.)

Lyndall F. Urwick, who was Gulick's partner in publishing *Papers on the Science of Administration* in 1937, himself published in 1943 a very successful book, *The Elements of Administration*, which is notable from the present point of view in distinguishing for the first time in a systematic way the different qualities of each level in a gradation, not so much of authority as of scope:

Broadly speaking ... in almost every form of complex organisation, seven such levels may be distinguished, which involve, not gradations in the same kind of activity, but activities which differ in quality and character. These are:

(1) *Criticism and Review* and/or *Legislative*. These are the activities carried out by the Houses of Parliament in our British system of government, or by the shareholders in their corporate capacity in a limited liability company.

(2) *Governing Authority*, i.e. the activities carried out by the Cabinet or a board of directors in their corporate capacity.

(3) *Liaison between Policy and Operation*. This activity is not very clearly isolated in British practice. But it forms the most vital part of the duties of a Minister *vis-à-vis* the department ... [and of] the duty of those members of the board of directors who also occupy executive positions as employees of the company (managing directors). ...

(4) *Operating Authority*, i.e. the activity of the principal executive officer of any undertaking . . . the Permanent Under-Secretary of State or general manager. . . .

(5) *Supervision of Operation*. This activity includes all those of every grade who exercise the delegated authority of the principal executive in supervising the work of others – in government the hierarchy of officials and in business the various ranks of managers, foremen and so on.

(6) *Operation*. At the end of any chain of authority the point

is reached where what is delegated is not further authority, but responsibility for the discharge of specific functions. Such activities are operation. They may, of course, include activities of considerable importance and status, such as the work of a highly skilled research chemist or engineer. (*Urwick*, (*1943*) *1963, 63–4*)

The seventh 'level' is *Jurisdiction*, by which Urwick means the juridical function. It does not really fit into his own scheme here, and does not concern us. In the first six, however, we have for the first time a plausible structure of gradation for the execution process, beginning at 'legislation' and ending with 'operation' – even if other intermediate terms might seem more suitable for our purposes.

Recognising that the fifth level, *Supervision of Operation*, includes rather a lot (he notes that 'between the commander-in-chief of any army in the field and the private soldier there are approximately fourteen separate grades or ranks', in the British civil service equivalent, about ten grades or ranks, and in a typical manufacturing organisation, nine grades), Urwick reproduces a classification of supervisory work which he says 'has been worked out in the United States':

General Superintendence   Discussion as to policy: no intervention as to means or methods – over principal subordinates and technical chiefs.
Administrative Superintendence   Instructions as to policy and occasional discussion of means and methods – over heads of Divisions and Departments and independent workers of equal rank.
Executive Superintendence   Frequent consultation, advice and guidance – over supervisory positions and trained and independent workers.
General Supervision   Supervisor available, but does not intervene in minor phases of the work – over employees thoroughly familiar with their duties and the methods of accomplishing them.
Executive Supervision   Frequent of results secured – over employees who have learned the routine of their work, but require instruction as to any deviation from it.
Oversight   Constant watch over manner and method of work in all details – over a learner or apprentice. (*Urwick, 1943, 66*)

This might be put alongisde the proposed duties of the three general classes of the British civil service, as seen by the Reorganisation

Committee of the National Whitley Council in 1920. The duties of the highest class, the Administrative Class, were to be:

> those concerned with the formation of policy, with the co-ordination and improvement of Government machinery, and with the general administration and control of the Departments of the public service.

The upper grades of the next class, the Executive Class, would be:

> concerned with matters of internal organisation and control, with the settlement of broad questions arising out of business in hand or in contemplation, and with the responsible conduct of important operations;

and the lower grade would have as their duties:

> the critical examination of particular cases of lesser importance not clearly within the scope of approved regulations or general decisions, initial investigations into matters of higher importance, and the immediate direction of small blocks of business.

Finally, the Clerical Class would embrace staff

> dealing with particular cases in accordance with well-defined regulations, instructions, or general practice; preparing material for returns, accounts, and statistics in prescribed forms; undertaking simple drafting and précis work; and collecting material on which judgements can be formed. (*Mackenzie and Grove, 1957, 62; Bourn, 1968, 449; Fry, 1969; Dunsire, 1973, 23*)

On an assumption that the process of execution in an organisation does follow a path from top to bottom of the hierarchy of authority, one could construct, from grading classifications of this sort, the implied model of the stages of that process: from legislation, through the formation of policy under that legislation, and the drafting of regulations and instructions under such policy, to the dealing with particular cases under these regulations and instructions.

Edward H. Litchfield put forward some 'Notes on a General Theory of Administration' in 1956, which saw the administrative process as a 'cycle of action' found both in policy making and in 'the executive function': the five actions were

A	Decision making	D	Controlling
B	Programming	E	Reappraising
C	Communicating	(A	Decision making)

'Programming' was the interpretation of decisions in the form of specific programmes 'which provide the direction for detailed operation', and so become 'guides to action'; programme planning is 'an activity designed to implement decisions'. Programme planning

> rests on a wide range of specific methods and techniques. These include capital budgets, operating budgets, manning tables, organisation charts, tables of equipment, and a variety of similar means of translating a decision into specific programs for the allocation of money, manpower, authority, physical resources, and so on. . . . (*Litchfield, 1956, 17*)

But that is as far as we get down the road between decision and action.

Preston Le Breton, in his chapter 'A Model of the Administrative Process' of the book edited by himself (1968) sees it as essentially dichotomous: planning followed by implementation. There are, he says, fourteen steps in the planning process and fourteen more in the implementation process, the latter being:

1. Receipt of approved plan
2. Obtaining an understanding of the technical components of the plan
3. Interpretation of ramifications of plans
4. Determination of role of implementor
5. Organising implementation staff and assigning responsibility
6. Preparation of an implementation plan
7. Taking action and making necessary commitments
8. Notifying organisation members of the new program
9. Interpretation of operational plans to subordinates
10. Instruction of subordinates in their control assignments
11. Gathering data on progress of plan
12. Review and evaluation of plan
13. Taking corrective action when necessary
14. Report of progress to authorised personnel. (*Le Breton, 1968, 172*)

However, we are given no hints about how to do any of these things, or what 'taking action' (in 7) means.

The pioneering work of Yehezkel Dror in the field of public policy analysis is so notable that one hesitates to draw attention to his treatment of what he called the 'post-policy-making stage':

Phases that from a lower level look like policy making often from a higher level look like a carrying out of policy. That is, these two stages are enough alike in composition and content that I can merely mention the main post-policy making phase, the execution of policy, without discussing it in detail. (*Dror, 1968, 188*)

Fourteen phases have gone before: phase 15 is 'Motivating the executing of the policy', and phase 16 is 'Executing the policy'. This includes 'field operations (such as building a dam, paying a pension, etc.,) that involve relatively little decision making' (Dror, 1968, 191). Phase 17 is 'Evaluating policy making after the policy has been executed'.

There is a sizeable modern literature on 'administrative reform', many of the treatments embodying a four-, five- or six-stage process in which 'implementation' is one of the stages. For instance, Gerald Caiden's subheadings under 'The Process of Administrative Reform' are: Awareness of Need; Formulation of Goals and Objectives, Strategy and Tactics; Implementation of Reforms; Evaluation. He cites a six-stage process from Goodenough, of which stage 5 is 'Enacting a Program', in which 'concrete steps are taken systematically to alter the conditions of life, and to forge a new order' (Goodenough, 1963, 298), and another six-step sequence by Mosher, of which the last is 'Implementation'. Caiden notes the similarity of these sequences to general classifications of social change, by Lasswell (1963) – 'intelligence, promotion, prescription, invocation, application, appraisal, termination'; by Pages – 'recognition, diagnosis, and action'; and by Parsons – 'dissatisfaction, symptoms of disturbance, coping with tension, tolerance of new ideas, translation of these new ideas into practicalities, implementation of innovations, and routinisation of innovations' (Parsons and Smelser, 1956; Caiden, 1969, 129). He might have noticed their general resemblance to the model of John Dewey in *How We Think* (1933), consisting of five stages: (1) feeling a difficulty, (2) locating and defining it, (3) suggesting possible solutions, (4) developing, by reasoning, the implications of the suggestions, and (5) making further observations and experiments that lead to acceptance or rejection of each suggestion (Dewey, 1933; Dror, 1968, 79; Katz and Kahn, 1966, 274).

In his discussion of 'implementation of reforms', Caiden classifies under 'reforms imposed through political revolution' 'reforms introduced to remedy organisational rigidity', 'reforms through the legal system' and 'reforms through changes in attitude'. Very little of the discussion, therefore, is relevant to the question of the implementation of a policy decision through the workings of a single organisation, or several such; and, indeed, the discussion is concerned largely with what Pressman and Wildavsky found 'implementation' to *mean* in the Operational Research usage: getting people to accept innovation and adopt changes proposed (Pressman and Wildavsky, 1973, 197). The same is true, by and large, of the chapters in the very influential textbook by Simon, Smithburg and Thompson (1950) devoted to 'Implementing Planning Goals', 'The Tactics of Execution: Reducing the Costs of Change' and 'The Tactics of Execution: Securing Compliance' (Simon, Smithburg, Thompson, 1950, 437–87). That is a significant aspect of implementation in any setting, undoubtedly; but getting people to accept change does not exhaustively describe the process of putting plans into operation, or the like. By and large, therefore, the writing in this first style hardly goes beyond mere mention of 'implementation' or 'execution'. Let us turn to some examples within the second style, organisational dynamics.

Barnard and the early Simon

This second style is distinguished from the first mainly by having a sociological and sociopsychological outlook rather than an engineering and military one; and its obvious 'first name' would be Max Weber, as already noted – except for the awkward fact that Weber's work in this field, mainly his writings on 'bureaucracy', were not widely available in English until the late 1940s. They then had enormous influence; but it is strictly anachronistic to put him earliest in this section. We will nevertheless do so, partly because in logic he belongs there, partly because it does not much matter anyway – important though his general approach was, he had little to say about the precise process we are investigating.

Like Mooney and Reiley (1931) of the classic 'administrative management' school, but with enormously greater scholarship, Weber scoured world history in search of the principles (not the 'one best way' of the scientific management writers) of the *rational* administrative organisation. The kind of organisation that has been most successful, he concluded, was one based on a clear-cut division of labour both horizontally and vertically, each lower office under the supervision of a higher one, but the duties and responsibilities of each office fixed by law, or by rule or regulation, so that a higher office is not free to 'take over' the business of a lower one at will. The people filling these offices, he saw, were appointed for their capacities for the work, were trained for it and were remunerated by salaries so that they had no pecuniary interest in deciding one way or another in the course of the business; and the business was conducted without personal involvement of any other kind on the part of the staff, according to general rules that were more or less exhaustive, more or less stable, and which could be learned and so provide officials with their 'technical' equipment. Work processes were typically based upon written documents, carefully preserved; particular cases would be dealt with by application of the rules and not by 'commands' from higher authority. This rational form of organisation Weber called 'bureaucratic'. 'The fully developed bureaucratic mechanism compares with other organisations exactly as does the machine with the non-mechanical modes of production' (Weber, in Gerth and Mills, (1948) 1961, 196–7, 214; see Albrow, 1970; Bendix, 1960; etc.)

Another school that was very significant for the general development of organisation theory but of comparatively little importance for the present purposes grew from the research at the Hawthorne Works of the Western Electric Company in Chicago conducted under the supervision of Elton Mayo, which produced discoveries about the role, in the relationship between 'management' and 'worker', of the intervening social grouping, the face-to-face work group (see Mayo, 1933; Roethlisberger and Dickson, 1939; Landsberger, 1958; etc.). This work was absorbed, along with the more conventional orthodoxies of scientific management, by the man who is the true 'first name' in this section, Chester I. Barnard.

Barnard was a businessman (president of Bell Telephone of New Jersey) who enjoyed close relations with L. J. Henderson of the Harvard Business School (to which Mayo also belonged) and had read widely in management literature; his major work, *The Functions of the Executive* (1938) was originally delivered in lectures at the Lowell Institute. Again, a full description of this book or of its general importance in organisation theory, is hardly relevant here. Charles Perrow wrote: 'It would not be much of an exaggeration to say that the field of organisational theory is dominated by Max Weber and Chester Barnard, each presenting different models, and that the followers of Barnard hold numerical superiority' (Perrow, 1972, 75). Among theorists acknowledging their debt to Barnard Perrow placed those of three distinct schools of organisation theory: the institutional school as represented by Philip Selznick, the decision-making school as represented by Herbert Simon, and the human-relations school as represented by such as Likert, McGregor and Argyris.

The basis of Barnard's approach was to see all organisations not, as practically all existing theory assumed, as coercive arrangements dominated by power and held together by sanctions, but as *co-operative* systems which by their very nature depend mainly on their members' mutual desire for them to continue in being and on the tolerance of their 'environment' – other organisations, the community. Organisations require to be in equilibrium, as regards both what their members put in and what they take out, and with respect to the exchanges with the environment. The motivational balance of compliance and inducements leads Barnard to a 'cognitive' reciprocity of authority and its acceptance:

> A person can and will accept a communication as authoritative only when four conditions simultaneously obtain: (a) he can and does understand the communication; (b) at the time of his decision he believes that it is not inconsistent with the purpose of the organisation; (c) at the time of his decision, he believes it to be compatible with his personal interest as a whole; and (d) he is able mentally and physically to comply with it. (*Barnard, 1938, 165*)

Some of this is restatement of management lore (cf. Taylor: 'One should be sure, beyond the smallest doubt, that what is demanded of the men is entirely just and can certainly be accomplished.' Taylor, 1910; Urwick, 1937, 83), but it is restatement from the 'men's' point of view. Perrow considered that the Barnard pendulum had swung too far, that these 'conditions of acceptance' of authority grossly distort the reality, which is that most organisations even today are still coercive systems with power at the top (Perrow, 1972); but from our point of view in the present context, it is only the first condition that is interesting. Barnard goes on:

> A communication that cannot be understood *can* have no

authority. An order issued, for example, in a language not intelligible to the recipient is no order at all – no one would so regard it. Now, many orders are exceedingly difficult to understand. They are often necessarily stated in general terms, and the persons who issue them could not themselves apply them under many conditions. Until interpreted they have no meaning . . . Hence, a considerable part of administrative work consists in the interpretation and reinterpretation of orders in their application to concrete circumstances that were not or could not be taken into account initially. (*Barnard, 1938, 165*)

Barnard's account of what this 'interpretation and reinterpretation' consists of is, I believe, the earliest treatment in quasi-analytic and generalised terms of the process we are studying:

. . . the critical aspect of this function is the assignment of responsibility – the delegation of objective authority. Thus in one sense this function is that of the scheme of positions, the system of communication, already discussed. That is its potential aspect. Its other aspect is the actual decisions and conduct which make the scheme a working system. Accordingly, the general executive states that 'this is the purpose, this the objective, this the direction, in general terms, in which we wish to move, before next year'. His department heads, or the heads of his main territorial divisions, say to their departments or sub-organisations: 'This means for us these things now, then others next month, then others later, to be better defined after experience.' Their sub-department or division heads say: 'This means for us such and such operations now at these places, such others at those places, something today here, others tomorrow there.' Then district or bureau chiefs in turn become more and more specific, their sub-chiefs still more so as to place, group, time, until finally purpose is merely jobs, specific groups, definite men, definite times, accomplished results. But meanwhile, back and forth, up and down, the communications pass, reporting obstacles, difficulties, impossibilities, accomplishments; redefining, modifying purposes level after level.
Thus the organisation for the definition of purpose is [also] the organisation for the specification of work to do; and the specifications are made in their final stage when and where the work is being done. I suspect that at least nine-tenths of all organisational activity is [done] on the responsibility, the authority, and the specifications of those who make the last contributions, who apply personal energies to the final concrete objectives. There is

no meaning to personal specialisation, personal experience, personal training, personal location, personal ability, eyes and ears, arms and legs, brains and emotions, if this is not so. What must be added to the indispensable authority, responsibility, and capability of each contributor is the indispensable co-ordination. This requires a pyramiding of the formulation of purpose that becomes more and more general as the number of units of basic organisation becomes larger, and more and more remote in future time. Responsibility for abstract, generalising, prospective, long-run decision is delegated *up* the line, responsibility for definition, action, remains always at the base where the authority for effort resides. (*Barnard, 1938, 232–3*)

Then appears what from a later point of view is the cloven hoof:

In this fact lies the most important inherent difficulty in the operation of co-operative systems – the necessity for indoctrinating those at lower levels with general purposes, the major decisions, so that they remain cohesive and able to make the ultimate detailed decisions coherent; and the necessity, for those at the higher levels, of constantly understanding the concrete conditions and the specific decisions of the 'ultimate' contributors from which and from whom executives are often insulated. Without that up-and-down-the-line co-ordination of purposeful decisions, general decisions and general purposes are mere intellectual processes in an organisational vacuum, insulated from realities by layers of misunderstanding. (*Barnard, 1938, 233*)

The 'indoctrination' will bear further discussion; but for the moment let us note the emphasis on *interpretation* of orders, and on the curiously upside-down effect of piling authority and responsibility on what even in Barnard's imagery is the bottom layer of the pyramid: a pyramid that embraces wider and more general not narrower concerns at higher levels. The imagery needs sorting out. (For commentary on Barnard, see Tillett, 1970, 312–41; Perrow, 1972, 74–95. On the inversion of authority and power, cf. Mechanic, 1962, 351; Tannenbaum *et al.*, 1974; Golembiewski and Munzenrider, 1977).

Herbert Simon repeated some of this basic thought and applied it to the military situation in a 1944 article:

It is clear that the actual physical task of carrying out an organisation's objectives falls to the persons at the lowest level of the administrative hierarchy. The automobile, as a physical object, is built not by the engineer or the executive, but by the mechanic on the assembly line. The fire is extinguished, not by the fire chief or the captain, but by the team of firemen who play a hose on the blaze.

It is equally clear that the persons above this lowest or operative level in the administrative hierarchy are not mere surplus baggage, and that they too must have an essential role to play in the accomplishment of the agency's objectives. Even though, as far as physical cause and effect are concerned, it is the machine-gunner, and not the major, who fights battles, the major will likely have a greater influence upon the outcome of a battle than will any single machine-gunner. (*Simon*, 1944, 16)

Conventional organisation charts, Simon goes on, are unrealistic pictures of the authority distribution because they do not indicate the *degree* of influence exercised:

Influence is exercised in its most complete form when a decision promulgated by one person governs every aspect of the behaviour of another. On the parade ground, the marching soldier is permitted no discretion whatsoever. His every step, his bearing, the length of his pace are all governed by authority. . . . Few examples could be cited, however, from any other realm of practical affairs where influence is exercised in such complete and unlimited form.

Most often . . . a subordinate may be told what to do, but given considerable leeway as to how he will carry out the task. The 'what' is, of course, a matter of degree also and may be specified within narrower or broader limits. The commands of a captain at the scene of a fire place much narrower limits on the discretion of the firemen than those placed on a fire chief by the city charter which states in general terms the function of the fire department. (*Simon*, 1944, 18)

Simon then proceeds to a distinction between premises of decision (factual premises and value premises) into which we need not follow him now. He returns to the theme of influence:

In ancient warfare, the battlefield was not unlike the parade ground. An entire army was often commanded by a single man, and his authority extended in a very complete and direct form to the lowest man in the ranks. This was possible because the entire battlefield was within range of a man's voice and vision and because tactics were for the most part executed by the entire army in unison. (*Simon, 1944, 19*)

Leaving aside the historical validity of this assertion, it is thought-provoking. Simon is distinguishing, within the 'monocratic' or single-headed form of organisation, between an extremely short, vertical hierarchy without vertical differentiation except as to number, and a longer hierarchy with vertical differentiation in function — different levels having different jobs to do:

> The modern battlefield presents a very different picture. Authority is exercised through a complex hierarchy of command. Each level of the hierarchy leaves an extensive area of discretion to the level below, and even the private soldier, under combat conditions, exercises a considerable measure of discretion. (*Simon, 1944, 20*)

Simon then briefly recapitulates Barnard's scheme of successive interpretations of top decisions, adding, however, a new thought — the 'internal autonomy' of each sub-unit:

> Under these circumstances, how does the authority of the commander extend to the soldiers in the ranks? How does he limit and guide their behavior? He does this by specifying the general mission and objective of each unit on the next level below and by determining such elements of time and place as will assure a proper co-ordination among the units. The colonel assigns to each battalion in his regiment its task; the lieutenant-colonel to each company; the captain to each platoon. Beyond this the officer ordinarily does not go. The internal deployment of each unit is left to the officer in command of that unit. The United States Army Field Service Regulations specify that 'an order should not trespass upon the province of a subordinate. It should contain everything that the subordinate must know to carry out his mission, but nothing more'.
> So far as field orders go, then, the discretion of a subordinate officer is limited only by the specification of the objective of his unit and its general schedule. He proceeds to narrow further the discretion of his own subordinates so far as is necessary to specify what part each subunit is to play in accomplishing the task of the whole. (*Simon, 1944, 20*)

This may sound a mere elaboration of Gulick's 'orders of superiors to subordinates, reaching from the top to the bottom of the entire enterprise', but Barnard and Simon add two extremely significant elements to the theory of the process (not, let us note well, necessarily to *practice* in organisations). These are, first, the precise recognition of the *double* interpretation – the need for each level of command not only to understand what the instruction received from higher up means for that level, but also to specify for the next lower level what the instruction means for *them*. The chief executive or four-star general issues an order. The suborganisation heads or colonels listen and digest, but do not simply repeat either what they have heard or what they have understood to the department heads or lieutenant-colonels. Each breaks it up; he rephrases it, uses words generals don't use. Each department head or lieutenant-colonel listens, but he does not simply repeat what he hears to the division heads or the captains: he goes through the same process of first interpreting for his own level and then interpreting again for his subordinates. The division heads and captains also, in their turn, do the same. Neither Barnard nor Simon articulates this double interpretation in their brief analyses: but it is implicit in their logic. It is clearly a complex matter: their accounts do not spell out what the words they use imply, and I have done it for them – it becomes important later.

The second new element in Simon's description is the somewhat surprising *regulation* of the US army that requires respect by the superior for the 'province' of a subordinate. We are all well aware that throughout political history kings and other commanders have had to have a care for the susceptibilities and problems of their barons and nobles and generals. But we have thought of this as being, in the machiavellian tradition of writing, a matter of the power game. An army regulation is a different thing altogether. Simon goes on to quote Barnard on the concept of authority; it rests on the acceptance by the subordinate of the rights of the superior. There is what Barnard called a 'zone of indifference', which Simon prefers to call a 'zone of acquiescence'; and if the superior attempts to carry authority beyond this zone, Simon says, 'disobedience will follow' (Simon, 1944, 21). Now, the discussion of 'authority' is a separate one, but the point to be made here is that Simon's own analysis, and the US Army Field Service Regulations (1941), p. 31, which he quotes, show there to be more than a 'zone of acquiescence' involved. The subordinate officer appears to have rights which conflict with those of his superior; he has a command of his own which is not simply part of the command of his superior (to be exercised or delegated by that superior at will). The idea of a 'zone of acquiescence' only comes into play insofar as the subordinate decides whether or not to stand on these rights. Standing up for rights that are guaranteed by regulation cannot be construed as disobedience.

Obviously, the US army may be unique in having such a regulation. Simon does not make it clear whether he thinks there are analogies in other types of organisation. However, even in the US army, the subordinate officer's discretion within his own command is far from total:

> To be sure, the field order . . . specifies only the 'what' of his action. But the officer is also governed by the tactical doctrine and general orders of the army which specify in some detail the 'how'. When the captain receives field orders to deploy his company for an attack, he is expected to carry out the deployment in accordance with the accepted tactical principles in the army. In leading his unit, he will be held accountable for the 'how' as well as the 'what'.
>
> The same kind of analysis could be carried out for the man who actually does the army's 'work' – the private soldier; and we would see that the mass of influences that bear upon his decisions include both direct commands and tactical training and indoctrination. (*Simon, 1944, 20*)

These few lines are also rich with theory to be explored. What is the precise difference between 'what' and 'how'? Are there categories implied here, in some wider scheme of classification? What is the significance of an official 'no trespass' sign at the boundary of a subordinate's jurisdiction, if the subordinate already has been trained and indoctrinated and will be held to account for 'what' he does and 'how' he does it, perhaps by the same superior who faces the 'no trespass' sign? What exactly is the nature of the 'autonomy' of those who do 'the actual work' of an organisation? Is there a similar 'autonomy' at other levels, 'province' by 'province'? It needs much clarification.

Extracts from this 1944 article of Simon's were reprinted in *Reader in Bureaucracy*, edited by Merton *et al.* (1952, 185–94). In the same volume there is an article from the *Political Science Quarterly* by Lyman Bryson (1951; Merton *et al.*, 1952, 202–16), who without reliance on previous administrative theory literature sets out to guide those who are called upon to be consultants and expert advisers through the pitfalls of organisational politics, and incidentally deals with the 'decision—action process'. Execution, he says,

> is not a merely mechanical performance in which the intentions of the policy maker are automatically realised. Execution always involves a series of subsidiary decisions which arise in carrying out the powers that have been delegated to the executive by the policy maker. Opposition, treachery, political manipulations or useful inventiveness may make or mar the policy as it is realised. The adage 'If you want something well done, do it yourself' is an admonition to an administrator not to trust his executives. The other adage, 'A man who is his own lawyer has a fool for a client', may incidentally express the other side of the case. Or we might find it in the Chinese maxim of political administration which states that the good administrator does nothing; he does nothing, in order to give his executives the opportunity to do their best. This ambivalence in popular folklore shows that the decision as to how much he shall personally intervene in the execution of his own policies is one of an administrator's most sticky problems. (*Bryson, 1951, 322*)

H. G. Creel, writing about the beginnings of bureaucracy in China, speaks of his 'considerable surprise' on finding a cardinal dictum of Shen Pu-hai, a philosopher who died in 337 BC, quoted in almost verbatim translation in the *Political Science Quarterly* as a "Chinese maxim" '. Shen Pu-hai, Creel considers, stands comparison with

> contemporary scholars working in the field of administrative theory, such as Max Weber, Chester I. Barnard, Herbert A. Simon, Talcott Parsons, Robert K. Merton and Peter M. Blau. . . . That there are differences goes without saying, yet in general Shen Pu-hai twenty-three hundred years ago and these scholars working today are dealing with the same kind of problems and sometimes arriving at remarkably similar answers. (*Creel, 1964, 161–2*)

'Shen Pu-hai repeatedly says that the skilful ruler "does nothing", and various contexts show that the purpose is that his ministers shall not be mere "yes-men", but shall rather develop their own ideas and exert themselves' (Creel, 1964, 162n.).

Bryson's 'decision—action process' turns out to be a version of the Dewey 'thinking' model, and does not justify his promising preamble:

The decision—action process is a series of decisions whose nature and scope must be studied if we are ever to conceptualise fully, and arrange logically, the co-operation between the elements of knowledge and power that make the world go round. . . . (*Bryson, 1951, 323*)

He seems to be much more interested in the 'power' than in the 'knowledge':

The fact is observable and inescapable, whatever moral judgement one may insist on passing on it, that the decision-making process is a field of personal ambition and sharp competition in all practical situations, whether business, government or institutional. (*Bryson, 1951, 327*)

We shall encounter shortly some further examples in this long tradition of 'practical wisdom' writing, which looks rather like science but isn't.

March and Simon

The next contribution to this constructive 'literature' of the execution process was a considerable landmark in several ways. In 1958 James G. March and Herbert A. Simon published the first textbook to be written entirely from the viewpoint of the student of organisations as such. The use of the term in this sense, as equivalent to or a generalisation of the terms 'undertaking', 'enterprise', 'institution' and so on, does not much antedate the twentieth century, and 'organisation theory' begins to emerge only around 1950 – sometimes meaning 'theory of organising', sometimes 'theory about organisations' (Rapoport and Horvath, 1960, 90; Silverman, 1970; Dunsire, 1973, 111; etc.).

March and Simon (1958) is not, however, itself organised in such a way as to present a coherent and relatively simple account of the authors' view of the execution process: once more, as with nearly all other works being quoted here, it is necessary to select passages from different parts of the book so as to put together the set of assumptions they worked with. We may begin on p. 3. The authors are pointing to the *specificity* of influence processes in organisations, as contrasted with the *diffuseness* of many other influence processes in society:

A concrete example will help to point up the contrast we have in mind. Compare rumor transmission with the transmission of a customer order through a manufacturing company. Rumor transmission is truly a process of diffusion. Seldom does a rumor move outward along a single channel; indeed, in most cases it would soon die if it did not spread out broadly from its original source. The customer order, on the other hand, is transmitted along definite channels, and usually relatively few of them, to specific destinations. (*March and Simon, 1958, 3*)

The concept of the customer order moving through a factory is the one we are looking for. The communication comparison leads to an analogy we have met before:

Organisations are assemblages of interacting human beings and they are the largest assemblages in our society that have anything resembling a central co-ordination system. Let us grant that these co-ordinative systems are not developed nearly to the extent of the central nervous systems in higher biological organisms – that organisations are more earthworm than ape. Nevertheless, the high specificity of structure and co-ordination within organisations – as contrasted with the diffuse and variable relations *among* organisations and among unorganised individuals – marks off the individual organisation as a sociological unit comparable in significance to the individual organisms in biology. (*March and Simon, 1958, 4*)

March and Simon begin by examining 'classical' organisation theory of both the physiological ('time-and-motion study') and the administrative management ('departmentalisation') kinds, considering the latter as a formal 'assignment problem' solution, and finding the assumption that the 'task to be done' is given in advance of the designing of the organisation to be an unrealistic one: 'the determination of which precise activities are to be performed at which times and places' is itself one of the important processes in real organisations. They therefore propose to introduce two generalisations that may bring formal theory more into line with what is said in a commonsense way by the 'classical' writers. The first is that 'the activities of the organisation may belong to well-defined, highly routine types, but the occasion for the performance of any particular activity may depend on environmental stimuli. . . .' (March and Simon, 1958, 26) – that is, there may be, for example, only a few 'skills' available in an organisation, but which of them are brought

into play depends on what 'orders' come in. The second generalisation takes us one further stage into dynamic complexity, recognising
that 'often not even the *contingent* program of activities is given in
advance; that, in fact, one of the important activities that goes on in
organisations is the development of programs for new activities that
need to be routinised for day-to-day performance' (March and
Simon, 1958, 26) – that is, those who run the organisation are not
merely allocating work to predetermined specialised units or 'skills',
but redesigning the assembly of 'skills' according to what 'orders'
come in.

(It can sometimes help towards clarity if a point is paraphrased
using different imagery. Converting from 'organism' analogy to
'machine' analogy, then: what March and Simon are saying is that
classic theory gives rules for designing a machine to make certain
objects from certain raw materials. Their first new 'generalisation'
suggests that organisations are like machines that can select from
among their internal mechanisms so as *either* to continue producing
the same objects from different materials *or* to produce different
objects. The second 'generalisation' turns them into machines that
can not only select among internal mechanisms, but add new ones or
redesign the existing ones.)

In real organisations, March and Simon go on, the limits to the
operation of either organising capability are not formal principles
like unity of command and span of control, but such factors as ease
of communication (easier between some skill groups than others),
ease of acquiring new skills, economics of training, and so on.

We can construct March's and Simon's assumptions about the
execution process from two of their principal concepts: first, that
activity in an organisation (as in an individual; but I will omit in this
account their frequent references to the organism/organisation analogy) is broadly either 'programmed' or 'non-programmed'; second,
that programmes are linked in chains, or more complex sets where
programmes are contained in programmes, to any necessary number
of levels.

'Non-programmed' activity is exemplified by innovation and
planning, problem solving and design of new programmes, in
response to stimuli for which no appropriate ready-made response is
available. An organisational 'performance programme' is a sequence
or pattern of activities that has been developed and learned in the
past as an appropriate response to some particular class of stimulus

from outside – outside the organisation or outside the organisational unit concerned. Such routinised behaviour can be quite elaborate and can involve several people and hundreds of discrete movements or actions: the key is that it is all 'set off' by a simple stimulus and follows a single sequence or pattern. Examples given are: a customer order in a firm; a fire gong in a fire station; the appearance of an applicant at a social worker's desk; the appearance of an automobile chassis in front of the work station of a worker on an assembly line (March and Simon, 1958, 141). The more often the stimulus has been experienced in the past, the more routinised is the response likely to become:

> Situations in which a relatively simple stimulus sets off an elaborate program of activity without any apparent interval of search, problem solving, or choice are not rare. They account for a very large part of the behavior of all persons, and for almost all of the behavior of persons in relatively routine positions. Most behavior . . . in organisations is governed by performance programs. (*March and Simon, 1958, 142*)

Programmes may contain choice of a routinised form, such as the application of a formula to the stimulus to determine which of a small number of responses is appropriate; this we can call a performance *strategy* (142). Every programme contains a specification of the circumstances under which it is to be begun, and a specification of the circumstances under which it can be considered completed ('program-evoking step' and 'program-execution step'); a programme-executing step by one member of an organisation may serve as a programme-evoking step for another member (147).

A programme can specify activities (means) or it can specify product or outcome (ends). 'The further the program goes in the latter direction, the more *discretion* it allows for the person implementing the program to supply the means—end connections' (147). Discretion is also involved in any search activity, in the application of a strategy, where a programme is implanted by previous professional training or apprenticeship, or by learning from experience rather than being organisationally-derived.

'Programme', then, is being used in exactly the same sense as in the housewife's automatic washing machine, on which by setting a knob or inserting a key she can select, according to the type of fabric being washed, etc., a sequence combining a certain water temperature, length of wash, number of rinses, length of spin, and so on, and the machine will go through its performance when the switch is pushed. Or it is like a dance routine, which can be an extremely complex series of movements lasting several minutes, learned off and repeated night after night and often by a number of dancers simultaneously. Activity in an organisation (any organisation), say March and Simon, is *mostly* like that. Some of it contains a little more choice, more discretion; as if the washing machine could itself sense what type of fabric was being loaded, or as if the dancers had some opportunity to express their own interpretation of the theme.

The programmes in an organisation do not, however, exist in isolation. If all programme-evoking stimuli were from outside the organisation, programmes would compete for resources and hence pose an allocation problem; but they would not otherwise require interrelation with one another. Where the programme of one organisational unit is the stimulus for another, on the other hand, where there are discretionary elements and where outcomes are specified rather than activities – then control is needed. 'Control programmes' form another category of programme. Finally, some programmes may be 'higher-level': that is, they may contain a degree of problem-solving activity aimed at modifying existing 'lower-level' programmes:

> In organisations there generally is a considerable degree of parallelism between the hierarchical relations among members of the organisation and the hierarchical relations among program elements. That is to say, the programs of members of higher levels of the organisation have as their main output the modification or initiation of programs for individuals at lower levels. (*March and Simon, 1958, 150*)

'Higher-level', it seems, has two distinct connotations: it describes a *programme* which has as its output the modifying of other (subsidiary, related or lower-level) programmes; and it describes a *status* or rank, of persons usually associated with that type of programme. But it may be important to keep the two concepts analytically separate.

Then there follows a key passage for our present concerns:

> Any organisation possesses a repertory of programs that, collectively, can deal in a goal-oriented way with a range of situations. As new situations arise, the construction of an entirely new program from detailed elements is rarely contemplated. In most

cases, adaptation takes place through a recombination of lower-level programs that are already in existence. An important objective of standardisation is to widen as far as possible the range of situations that can be handled by combination and recombination of a relatively small number of elementary programs. (*March and Simon, 1958, 150*)

The whole concept of a more or less stable organisation coping with a variety of demands made upon it, in fact, depends upon this process:

Our treatment of rational behavior rests on the proposition that the 'real' situation is almost always far too complex to be handled in detail. As we move upwards in the supervisory and executive hierarchy, the range of interrelated matters over which an individual has purview becomes larger and larger, more and more complex. The growing complexity of the problem can only be matched against the finite powers of the individual if the problem is dealt with in grosser and more aggregative form. One way in which this is accomplished is by limiting the alternatives of action that are considered to the recombination of a repertory of programs. (*March and Simon, 1958, 150*)

Here is the 'opposite side of the medal' to the earlier Simon formulation of a progressive narrowing of discretion level by level, from higher to lower. It can be expressed as a progressive increase in discretion as higher levels are reached, which is the simple mirror image; but the emphasis in this passage is on the necessary change in the shape of the problem – it has to be seen 'in grosser and more aggregative form'.

However, the programmes that are combined and recombined in this way are not mere parts of a machine; they are the activities of persons. March and Simon go on to consider how perception of role and of subgoals can affect outputs, and how important the quality of the communication between organisational units and persons is. From this material we have to construct their assumptions about the relationship between the steps or elements of the execution process.

First, the material is concerned with relations between individual persons and between organisational units, not between subordinate and superior as such, as levels in a status hierarchy. Status or rank undoubtedly adds a dimension to communication, but it may be useful to consider the relationships as they are without that dimension.

Second, they consider it important to separate motivational aspects from cognitive aspects: ways in which relationships are affected by wishes, hopes, fears and so on, and ways in which they are affected purely by the mechanisms of the senses and of the brain in perceiving, storing and using information. We will concentrate here on what they say about the cognitive aspects and leave the affective aspects until later – recognising, of course, that it is possible to do this only analytically, and that in any real situation the two are interlinked. as March and Simon put it: 'What a person wants and likes influences what he sees; what he sees influences what he wants and likes' (March and Simon, 1958, 151).

An actor chooses, or decides, by virtue of a definition of the situation that is his own subjective appreciation: to that extent, he selects what he will regard as the stimulus to which he then responds. The 'real' situation is always too complex; he pays attention to part of it, according to what he thinks significant for him. When tasks are allotted to an organisational unit by some factorisation of the task of the organisation as a whole, other units' subtasks can be and are ignored; stimuli that would set off *their* programmes tend not to be seen, and his own unit's stimuli are seen as 'larger than life'. In-unit habits, language and frames of reference reinforce the tendency. Information is 'filtered' in entering the unit and repeatedly filtered in use (151–3).

Information leaving the unit is also selective: very often summarised, only the 'conclusions' passing to other units, as when a host of temperature, humidity and barometric pressure observations from a hundred weather stations are converted into a short weather report – and then, perhaps, into a weather *forecast* upon which other people act without in the least knowing how it has been arrived at. Classification is a form of summarisation: once an input has been classified as belonging to a particular species of case, all the attributes of the species can be predicated of it without closer inspection; only the name of the *class* need be communicated, perhaps to act as the evoking step for an appropriate programme. Enormous amounts of original information can be 'absorbed' or soaked up inside the unit, and prevented from occupying communication channels unnecessarily, by drastic 'classifying' – turning it into 'either/or' information, by establishing a threshold of 'satisfactory performance' of some appropriate kind and signalling only when this is crossed. In a modern car, for instance, the driver is seldom told what his oil pressure or water temperature actually is, only (by means of red warning lights) that it is not satisfactory. Much 'inspection' activity involves dichotomous decisions, evoking alternative programmes (163). Thus the organisation's repertory of performance programmes can be brought into action in a quite elaborate pattern of detailed action by communication of relatively few and simple internal stimuli: the organisation can operate, in a relatively stable environment, by having:

(a) a repertory of standard responses;
(b) a classification of program-evoking situations;
(c) a set of rules to determine what is the appropriate response for each class of situations. (*March and Simon, 1958, 164*)

Communication in such a highly-programmed organisation is easiest, and so most frequently found, in terms of the technical vocabulary used for these classification schemes and rules. Anything that does not fit into this vocabulary is communicated only with difficulty:

> Hence, the world tends to be perceived by the organisation members in terms of the particular concepts that are reflected in the organisation's vocabulary. The particular categories and schemes of classification it employs are reified, and become, for members of the organisation, attributes of the world rather than mere conventions (Blau, 1955). (*March and Simon, 1958, 165*)

Information enters an organisation, because of specialisation, at highly specific points. The perceptions of the environment generated at these points are the 'facts' about the environment that the organisation uses. This is another instance of summarisation, or the transmission of inferences from data rather than the data themselves. When this occurs, not only information but also *uncertainty* is absorbed. The man who transforms the data obtained from the original replies to a questionnaire, for example, into a set of averages and summary tables, knows the range of values that has been summarised into each average: in communicating the average only, he absorbs this information and with it his knowledge of the degree of uncertainty it represents. To others, his average is a 'fact'.

Direct perception of production processes is limited largely to employees in a particular operation on the production floor. Direct perception of customer attitudes is limited largely to salesmen. Direct evidence of the performance of personnel is restricted largely to immediate supervisors, colleagues, and subordinates.

In all of these cases, the person who summarises and assesses his own direct perceptions and transmits them to the rest of the organisation becomes an important source of informational premises for organisational action. The 'facts' he communicates can be disbelieved, but they can only rarely be checked. Hence, by the very nature and limits of the communication system, a great deal of discretion and influence is exercised by those persons who are in direct contact with some part of the 'reality' that is of concern to the organisation. Both the amount and the locus of uncertainty absorption affect the influence structure of the organisation. (*March and Simon, 1958, 165*)

Where different persons have access to the same raw evidence, but it is important that all parts of the organisation act on the same premises of decision, a formal uncertainty-absorbing point will be established to produce the 'stipulated facts', the 'legitimate estimates', the 'official forecasts' (166). Whether it is the formal decision point or not, however, 'to a considerable extent the effective discretion is exercised at the points of uncertainty absorption' (167).

The title of the chapter from which I have been quoting is 'Cognitive Limits on Rationality'. The idea that where discretion is exercised, power can be wielded, is familiar enough. The theme of March's and Simon's chapter is that 'the basic features of organisation structure and function derive from the characteristics of human problem-solving processes and rational human choice' (169), and that many aspects of what in other branches of the literature are thought of as the results of the different aspirations and drives of the several persons involved may to some extent always, to a large extent often, and sometimes wholly, be results of the limits on intellective capacities, of perception differences and of communication channel capacity.

The last contribution we should note (out of a veritable largessse of novel or freshly presented ideas) is their treatment of how the boundaries of programmes are arrived at and how programmes are linked.

The organisation depends to a great extent upon the training that employees bring to it – training acquired by apprenticeship or in schools. Hence the boundaries of specialisation of individual jobs tend to be determined by the structure of trades and professions in the broader social environment. (*March and Simon, 1958, 161*)

Such a sociological factor was accepted by Gulick as one of the limits of division of labour: 'the technology and custom at a given time and place' (Gulick 1937, 4). But specialisation of task can proceed within a given trade or professional competence; the further specialisation of programmes goes, the more interdependent the units embodying these programmes (159). Interdependence is no problem if the pattern of interdependence is stable; the necessary meshing of output can be built into the programmes. If the pattern varies in an imperfectly predictable way, co-ordination is required to act between the programmes, switching or modifying.

> Thus we predict that process specialisation will be carried furthest in stable environments, and that under rapidly changing circumstances specialisation will be sacrificed to secure greater self-containment of separate programs. (*March and Simon, 1958, 159*)

The most common way of linking programmes with a degree of interdependence so as to ensure co-ordination of output is the plan or schedule: a statement in advance that determines which programmes will follow which and when. (If everything were predictable and standardised, the plan itself would be a programme.) Where contingencies arise, or are expected to arise, that cannot be anticipated in the plan, means must be found of reading off from the real situation what they are when they occur, and determining what modifications to programmes or assemblies of programmes will regularise the situation, or minimise the difference from the desired outcomes. Such a deriving of information from the actual situation to compare with a desired situation is called 'feedback', and hence March's and Simon's names for the two methods of co-ordination: 'The more stable and predictable the situation, the greater the reliance on co-ordination by plan; the more variable and unpredictable the situation, the greater the reliance on co-ordination by feedback' (March and Simon, 1958, 160). An important note follows:

> Insofar as co-ordination is programmed and the range of situations sufficiently circumscribed, we would not expect any particularly close relation between the co-ordination mechanisms and the formal organisational hierarchy. That is to say, schedul-

ing information and feedback information required for co-ordination are not usually communicated through hierarchical channels. Hierarchy may be important in establishing and legitimising programs, but the communication involved in the execution of highly programmed activities does not generally follow the 'lines of command' (Bakke, 1950). (*March and Simon, 1958, 161*)

This is one of the few times that March and Simon use the word 'execution' in a context of organisational activity rather than the activity of an individual or unit 'executing' a programme – when what may be involved in doing this is nowhere specified. It is also one of the few places where programming and formal hierarchy are brought together. We will have to glean a lot from the hints in this passage.

Let us, then, try to put together from all this material a coherent account of what March's and Simon's assumptions about the process we are interested in might be – that is, an account not inconsistent with what they do say, but couched in the terms we have been using.

First: implementing a plan, or executing a policy, or carrying out a command, or what-have-you must not be thought of as inevitably involving a movement from top to bottom of a formal hierarchy. It is more fruitful to think of an order given to an organisation as being like the customer's order to a steel manufacturing concern, for example. In a specific sense, executing an 'order' means assembling or reassembling an organisational pattern out of the 'bits' the organisation comprises – unless, that is, the 'order' (or policy, command, etc.,) is already such as to match a pattern within the organisation, so that it becomes the equivalent of putting a coin in a slot-machine and accepting what comes out. In either case, the process is begun wherever the order is received.

Second: on receiving an 'order' (we shall assume that it *must* be obeyed, or fulfilled), the organisation either recognises its type and, as it were, clicks into action of its own accord, the receiving unit's recognition triggering off a performance in that and in one or more other units, who in their turn activate other procedures, and so on – much like a steel ball flashing its way down the pin-table; or else the receiving unit is unable to process the 'order' as it is, and either itself must resort to non-programmed activity (search, innovation, problem solving) or must transmit the 'order' as it is to another unit for the purpose. The task is then to search among the available resources of packaged skills and specialised experiences, memories, equipment of all sorts, for a way of transforming the unfamiliar 'order' into one that can be 'recognised'; or, if that fails, to search for the least disruptive modification of existing programmes, or the least expensive acquisition of new, that will enable the organisation to accept the 'order'. The more unfamiliar 'orders' an organisation receives (assuming it cannot reject them), the less like a pin-table or slot-machine it is or becomes.

But even the most 'slot-machine-like' organisation is not *very* like such a thing, because (quite apart from its being 'made up of people', as it is so often put – meaning that they all have their own reasons for joining the organisation, looking for promotion, acquiring power and so on) the links between the separate programmes of routinised or specialised or professionalised activity, by which it does anything of what it does, are subject to communication imperfections much more significant than anything that might go wrong with a pin-table or slot-machine.

The signals (messages, stimuli) that trigger off a performance programme are *perceived* only under certain conditions: most readily if they are in (or, presumably, are immediately translatable into) the language and the technical concepts the unit embodying the programme is used to working in. If they are not, the message may be received but it cannot be 'recognised'.

Again, when work is performed on raw material so as to transform it into something 'recognisable' by the next unit in a chain or assembly of programmes, information on what it was like on entry is removed. When the raw material is information itself, the same applies; what comes in may be various forms of guesses, what is sent on is a conclusion or inference which is then regarded by other units as *their* raw material, a usable 'fact'. Information about the outside world, about operating processes and conditions and about outcomes or results of operations is heavily subject to 'uncertainty absorption' as it moves inward and upward in the organisation.

Executing an order, then, may be like throwing a switch, or it may be a very complex process requiring much planning and organising (or reorganising), before actual operations can be performed; even then, the linking of programmes may have to be monitored as the process proceeds, the 'plan' supplemented by control through 'feedback'.

Let that suffice for the moment. This is clearly a very different sort of account even from that of Bernard, or the early Simon of the 1944 article. It is highly sophisticated, using concepts from psychology, engineering and sociology, in particular, to illumine an area not previously studied so directly: the *cognitive* aspects, the information-processing and pattern-recognising aspects of communication in an organisation. Here March and Simon were not just pioneers; they were pioneers who have not yet been superseded and in many respects not even followed up. As we elaborate our own theory of the execution process in later chapters, it will bear many similarities to this one.

Two American scholars who were not really in the same tradition of organisation theory at all, but who dealt more specifically with the execution process and added to our understanding of it, were the economists Gordon Tullock and Anthony Downs.

Tullock and Downs

Tullock's *The Politics of Bureaucracy* (1965) is an odd book, at once curiously ignorant of preceding work, and full of enlightening and penetrating originality. There are extremely few references; the 'evidence' is culled from ancient China, Ibn Khaldun and similar unspecified sources and novels, but above all (and, in one sense, exclusively), from Tullock's own experience in the US State Department. The only book by an acknowledged organisation theorist that is quoted is *The Dynamics of Bureaucracy* (1955) by Peter Blau, and there is much internal evidence that Tullock was not aware of the work of Barnard or of March and Simon, for example. Nevertheless, there is a great deal to the present point in Tullock.

The approach is that of the economist. If the extracts from March and Simon stress the cognitive difficulties of internal relationships in an organisation, Tullock is almost exclusively concerned with the motivational aspects. Every man in an organisation is a subspecies of 'economic man', assumed to be concerned first and last with his own interest; an organisation is regarded not as a co-operative enterprise, nor as a structure of command and sanctions, but as a species of market, where, instead of being conceptually equal to one another in their transactions as in the familiar trading market, men are placed one over another, so that one has the power of rewarding another.

Tullock keeps saying that although this is only a formal and logical scheme, it also is a fair representation of reality (32, 119, etc.). He makes no pretence at scientific objectivity; he does not mind having it both ways:

> Most civil servants, especially at the higher levels, are, therefore, committed to a career of finding out what their superiors want (frequently not an easy task) and doing it, in the hope that these superiors will then reward such behavior with promotions. . . . (*12*)
>
> The problem is to so arrange the structure that the [subordinate] is led by self-interest into doing those things that he 'ought' to do. . . . (*119*)
>
> The [superior] should so attempt to organise the hierarchy that its members act, in a sense, as his proxies. He should attempt to make inferiors reach decisions that are in accord with his own wishes without the necessity of issuing specific orders in each case. . . . (*132*)
>
> It will be more important to [an expert adviser] to appear to be right than to be right. Unless the superior is very careful, he may find that experts are devoting their effort to developing rationalisations for opinions that they think that he holds, rather than producing independent expert advice. . . . (*52*)
>
> The [superior] will not usually have perfect knowledge of the subordinate's 'division' of the total organisational task. A [subordinate] may be able, therefore, through deliberately misrepresenting the facts or through carefully choosing the facts presented, to control the [superior's] decisions so as to make them favor the objectives desired by the subordinate. . . . (*65*)

A rather lengthy extract will establish perfectly Tullock's general position and also illustrate his method. (In all these extracts, the words 'politician' and 'sovereign', which Tullock sometimes uses for 'subordinate' and 'superior' and sometimes not, are substituted by the latter words.)

> The discussion here may be summarised by putting the matter symbolically. Let us say that a superior knows facts A, B, and C. The subordinate, due to his more intimate contact with the problem, knows facts A, B, C, D, E, F, G, and H. On the basis of facts A, B, and C alone, action X would be indicated. On the basis of the more inclusive set, action Y would be suggested. The situation is complicated further by the recognition that there will surely exist facts I, J, and K that are unknown to both the

superior and the subordinate. These other facts can never be known, however, and, in normal cases, the greater information possessed by the subordinate implies that policy Y will be more successful than policy X. Nevertheless, the wise and efficient [subordinate] will tend to recommend X rather than Y. He will back up this recommendation by reasoning from A, B, and C, and if he is artistic will bring in, say, G, which will reinforce the argument.

The result of such recommendation is that the [superior] will be impressed with the soundness of the [subordinate's] reasoning. If, by contrast, the [subordinate] should recommend policy Y, this would involve a lengthy and involved effort to educate the superior on the additional facts D, E, F, G, and H. Even if he is successful in convincing the superior of the appropriateness of Y, this behavior is not likely to endear the subordinate to his superior, who in any event may not have sufficient time to undergo the educational process. As there are usually several subordinates reporting to a single superior, the next promotion is likely to go to the man who has reached 'correct' decisions, not to the one who has come up with 'peculiar' solutions backed up by a long list of 'facts' which appear dubious to the superior.

This analysis suggests that, in a bureaucracy, factual information tends to flow from the top down instead of from the bottom up. This conclusion is contrary to the normal assumption that subordinates in a bureaucracy collect and winnow information and pass on only the most important parts of it to their superiors. This is what 'should' happen in the ideally efficient organisation, and it is also what would happen if men were machines. Departures from this 'ideal' become especially significant in poorly organised hierarchies. In a badly run bureaucracy, the information that is really important to the subordinate does not concern the real world, but rather his superior's image of the real world. As a result, almost no new information that will be relevant for policy, will enter the organisational machine at the bottom tier. The typical method through which such an organisation adjusts itself to new and changed conditions is through external sources acting on the man at the top, and, subsequent to this, his inferiors finding out from him. In the Department of State, Walter Lippman, the *New York Times*, and the *Washington Post* are, I am sure, the primary sources of information upon which the foreign policy of the United States is based. (*Tullock, 1965, 69–70*)

Much could be said about the logic of this passage, about the idea that 'facts', however numerous, 'indicate' action, and so on. Let us just note that Tullock, in his own words, is talking about 'a badly run bureaucracy', and that a great deal of what he has to say about bureaucracies in general, and about the people in them, perhaps is really to be understood as applying to those specific bureaucracies and processes to which it applies, particularly the Department of State in Tullock's time. On the other hand, it is fair to note that much the same analysis can be found in other and earlier books, such as Simon's, Smithburg's and Thompson's textbook *Public Administration* of 1950:

> Status differences exert a considerable filtering and distorting influence upon communication – both upward and downward. Upward communication is hampered by the need of pleasing those in authority . . . Subordinates . . . want to tell him the things he would like to hear. Hence, things usually look rosier at the top than they really are. . . . Information going downward in the hierarchy is often distorted also. . . . In the struggle for position on the status ladder, the suggestions and other statements of those higher up are often given more weight as guides to decisions than those who made the statement actually intended. (*Simon, Smithburg, Thompson, 1950, 236–7*)

That book is full of insights which are highly suggestive for the present discussion, and the temptation is to quote much more. The unfortunate fact is that nowhere in a large book do the three authors specifically advert to the 'execution' process as we are considering it: 'execution', as already noted, means for them the tactics of gaining acceptance for a plan so that it become adopted, and what is necessary after any plan has become adopted is not gone into in anything approaching our terms.

Tullock's evidence of motivational constraints on the rationality of the execution process, then, is in a recognisable tradition of American writing, even if he does not know it – a tradition that possibly tells us more about American public administration than it tells us about public administration 'as such' – if such an animal is conceivable. The Bryson (1951) article quoted earlier was another example of the genre.

In a later section, Tullock turns to 'cognitive' aspects, but in much the same manner and without himself making the distinction. He quotes an 'experiment' used in training by the army, where a dozen soldiers are strung around a large circle, out of earshot of one another: the officer in charge gives, in front of the remainder of the class, an oral message to the nearest soldier, with orders to repeat it to the next man on the circumference, and so on. When the message gets back to the class, it is, of course, usually garbled. Tullock's 'lesson' is this:

> All of this may appear to have little relevance for our subject of hierarchical organisations. In fact, the experiment does have little or no relevance for the way in which hierarchies actually operate. The experiment is useful in refuting the popular view of the way in which a bureaucracy works. The 'normal' or standard version of bureaucracy seems to be something like the following: the lower levels of the structure receive information from various sources. This information is then passed along upward through the pyramid. At the various levels, the information is analysed, collated, and co-ordinated with other information that originates in separate parts of the pyramid. Eventually, the information reaches the top level where the basic policy decisions are made concerning the appropriate actions to be taken. These decisions on policy are then passed down through the pyramid with each lower level making the administrative decisions that are required to implement the policies set from on high. This descriptive scheme has not, to my knowledge, been used by any serious student of bureaucratic hierarchies, but it does seem to be the version held by the 'average man', and by most bureaucrats themselves. (*Tullock, 1965, 138*)

It is not clear what descriptive scheme Tullock thought that serious students of bureaucratic hierarchies did use, or if he meant that he did not know of any respectable academic source for his own account. As we have seen, he might have cited Barnard, surely serious enough: Barnard postulated that 'the organisation for the definition of purpose' (the structures and processes through which top-level decisions are prepared) is also 'the organisation for the specification of work to do' (the same structures and processes go into reverse, as it were, to produce the 'administrative decisions' Tullock refers to, turning 'purpose' into job cards, time schedules, and the like). Tullock might have used the insights of an even more prescient practitioner, the Colonial Office civil servant Sir Henry Taylor, writing a hundred years before Barnard:

> It is not only necessary that the legislature should make provision in the laws for their due execution; it is also desirable that

the executive agency should work towards new legislation on the same topics. For the execution of laws deals with those particulars by an induction of which the results to be aimed at in legislation are to be ascertained; and the generalisation from those particulars can only be well effected when the lowest in the chain of functionaries is made subsidiary to the operations of the highest in a suggestive as well as in an executive capacity – that is, when the experience of the functionary who puts the last hand to the execution of any particular class of enactments is made available for the guidance of the legislature.

But in most cases this cannot be accomplished to any useful purpose otherwise than by a system of filtration. The lowest classes of functionaries, whilst they may be assumed to have the largest knowledge of facts, must also be taken to have the least power to discriminate and to generalise. They cannot be expected to distinguish barren from fruitful facts; those which are mere specialties from those which lead to general conclusions. What is wanted is that the crude knowledge collected in the execution of the laws should pass upward from grade to grade of the civil functionaries entrusted with their administration, more and more digested and generalised in its progress; and lastly, should reach the legislature in the shape of a mature project of law, whereby what was superfluous in the legislation in question might be abrogated; what was amiss might be amended; what was insufficient, enlarged; what was doubtful, determined; what was wanting, added. (*Taylor (1836) 1958, 128–9*)

It is not worthwhile to dispute with Tullock that his account of the assumptions of the average man and most bureaucrats concerning the way a bureaucracy works is the true one: proving otherwise would be an enormous undertaking. We are more interested in Tullock's 'corrections' of the popular stereotype, the way *he* thinks it

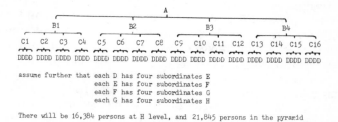

assume further that each D has four subordinates E
each E has four subordinates F
each F has four subordinates G
each G has four subordinates H

There will be 16,384 persons at H level, and 21,845 persons in the pyramid

Fig. 4 Tullock's pyramid

works. The army experiment, he says, 'disproves this theory of bureaucracy'. If we take a hierarchy ascending from H on the bottom level to A at the top, the information reaching A must be 'materially different from that which H perceived'. The order which A then issues will also undergo 'major changes': 'Consequently, H will receive from his superior, in final consequence of his original observation, a distorted version of an order based on a distorted version of his original observation' (Tullock, 1965, 138). It might be otherwise if all the bureaucrats between H and A were mere postmen, simply transmitting reports and orders verbatim, but:

> The members of a hierarchy do not, in fact, think of themselves as mere messenger boys, faithfully transmitting the reports of their subordinates. G would, in our example, not be likely to simply pass along H's report accurately. He would consider it a part of his duty, because of his superior experience and training, to extract the fundamental aspects of the information from H's report, and to add some comments of his own. In addition he could be receiving, at the same time, information from the peers of H that would have to be co-ordinated with that of H before the preparation of G's report to F. As a result of this structure, reports are transmitted upward under what may well be the worst possible of circumstances. (*Tullock, 1965, 139*)

'Mere messenger boys' is not possible in any case (from the 'army experiment'); but Tullock has slipped over into affective arguments again (superiors putting in comments of their own to show their superiority). The same general conclusions, he goes on, hold with respect to an order:

> B is, presumably, only one of several direct subordinates to A. B will then have to decide what parts of the general policy directives issued by A affect his particular division of the hierarchy. He will prepare orders and pass along to his inferiors, C_1, C_2, and C_3, only those parts of A's overall directive that he considers relevant. But to this directive he will add his own detailed administrative instructions. C_1 will do likewise with regard to passing the orders to D_1, D_2, and D_3, When it finally reaches H, at the lowest level, the order will have undergone significant changes. Note also that, in the case of orders, issued from the top, the distortion is likely to vary within the organisation. Thus, an order received by B_1, B_2, B_3, from A will be passed on in slightly different form by each of them. By the time the general

directive reaches the lower levels, there might be major differences among the versions received by comparable bureaucrats
in different parts of the same organisation. Uniformity could
not be expected from a bureaucracy that attempted to operate in
this fashion. (*Tullock, 1965, 139*)

Again, the analysis of what happens level by level is acute; the air of
exposing an obvious absurdity, and the conclusions, are odd indeed.
Tullock has articulated the *double* interpretation that Simon, in the
1944 article, left a little obscure. On receiving an order, B has two
decisions to make: what parts of the order affect his division; and
what orders and 'detailed administrative instructions' to prepare and
pass on. Even after one level, A's order will take several different
forms by the time it reaches the Cs. In a hierarchical organisation of
the kind we are dealing with, where there is horizontal specialisation
at each level, it would be strange if it were not so, if the same words
could convey meaningful instructions to professionally distinct
units, for example – unless in some uninteresting matter like the
sounding of a fire alarm, or the date of the annual Christmas party.
Only in some such matter could 'uniformity' of response be
intended. The implicit condemnation in the final sentence is inex-
plicable. We should, perhaps, give the author credit for what he
reveals of the process we are pursuing, and leave aside his reasons for
doing so.

The same might be charitable in respect of his conclusion that,
because enough information to keep six hundred men busy is collected at the base of an organisational pyramid, and two-thirds of it
'discarded' at each level as it is 'winnowed down' to enough information to occupy one man at the top,

the great bulk of the field information originally collected is
discarded and no use is made of it. This, quite naturally, raises
the question as to the wisdom of collecting this excess information in the first place. (*Tullock, 1965, 141*)

Nowhere does Tullock allow for the possibility that the information
gathered at any level is *summarised* before being passed on, rather
than that some of it is selected and the rest discarded.

The piece of 'arithmetic' for which the book is best known is
Tullock's analysis of the consequences of imperfect understanding
of, or wilful disobedience of, a superior's wishes by a subordinate. A
has four assistants, B_1, B_2, B_3 and B_4.

. . . for purposes of analysis, let us assume that for each three actions that B_2 takes that are strictly in accord with A's wishes, there will be one action that will go contrary to that which might have been desired by A. This allows us to divide B_2's activities into three sets: first, he will spend, as we have assumed, one-fifth of his time 'receiving supervision' from A. Second he will spend three-fifths of his time carrying out A's wishes. Third, he will spend one-fifth of his time doing things which are not really desired by A at all. Extending this same numerical calculation to all four assistants, the total organizational group of five men, A and his four assistants, will really devote two and two-fifths man days each day to carrying out activities in the external world that are consistent with the purposes for which A established the organisation. Four-fifths of a man day each day will be devoted to activities that A is either unconcerned with or would be opposed to. (*Tullock, 1965, 144*)

Extending the hierarchy to three levels (sixteen Cs) and then four (sixty-four Ds), and retaining the same assumptions, Tullock shows that since what he is still calling the 'distortion' of subordinates (since they are not postmen) is compounded by the number of levels, the amount of the total man days spent on doing things in the world is about fifty-one (for a total force of eighty-five persons), of which about twenty-two are spent on actions desired by A, while twenty-nine are spent on actions on which A is neutral or to which he is actively opposed.

Also, note that the total time that the organisation is spending on matters purely internal to the hierarchy is expanding more rapidly than the increase in personnel. The number of activities undertaken with respect to the outside world that are not within A's desires, too, is increasing more rapidly than the other magnitudes. While I make no claim that the numerical values in this model are more than very rough approximations, the model does, I think, represent a reasonable description of reality. (*Tullock, 1965, 159*)

Tullock is effectively presenting the problem of how to bring a large organisation under control 'from the top'. But, from his basic premise that all members are pursuing their own self-interest, he quite mis-states the nature of the problem. What Barnard and the early Simon saw as an absolutely necessary 'interpretation' function, in an organisation specialised vertically and horizontally, Tullock sees as a 'distortion'; and since he cannot imagine a cure for self-interest, he has no real recommendations to make on organisational control beyond 'control by statistical method' or sample checking, or by limiting size drastically: in bureaucracies 'which have greatly exceeded the limits of control and which, consequently, are not really performing the functions for which they were organised', he says, there will be two types of behaviour, 'bureaucratic free enterprise' and 'the imperial system':

> Think of a very large administrative structure or pyramid, with say, ten steps or levels between the apex and the men who are on the 'firing line', that is, the men who carry out the organisation's functions with the external world. The single individual or group at the top will surely have little or no control over those at the bottom if we accept, as a rough approximation, the quantitative estimates introduced in Chapter XV. In a large organisation of this type, each link in the 'chain of command' will introduce some modifications and changes on the order received from above, and as a result of the series of these changes, which compound each other, central control will be eliminated.
>
> It can only be concluded that, in a very large organisation of this type, for the greater part of its specific activities, the bureaucracy will be 'free' from whatever authority it is allegedly subordinate to. 'It', the bureaucracy, will do things, will take actions, not because such actions are desired by the ultimate authority, the center of power, in the organisation, but because such things, such actions, develop as an outgrowth of the bureaucracy's own processes. (*Tullock*, 1965, 167–8)

And the illustrations come once more from the US Department of State. The 'imperial system' turns out to refer to the British Empire, where colonial governors were known since school days to all members of the Cabinet in London (170).

Of course, if it really were the case that the price of having a hierarchy of ten levels were as high as this, there would have been many fewer such hierarchies even by 1965. It is possible that Tullock's model has some parts missing.

Anthony Downs, in a book of very wide scope and prolific conceptualisation (*Inside Bureaucracy*, 1967), somewhat bridges the gap between Tullock's fertile naivety and the sophistication of March and Simon, as well as taking into account a great deal of other scholarship in organisation theory and neighbouring fields. He echoes Tullock in his 'central hypothesis' which, he says, follows the tradition of economic thought from Adam Smith forward. Men in organisations choose rationally; that is, they weigh up costs in terms of time, effort, or money: 'Every official is significantly motivated by his own self-interest, even when acting in a purely official capacity' (Downs, 1967, 2). But he considerably extends the idea by a typology of goals and of officials: five types of official – climbers, conservers, advocates, zealots and statesmen – each type pursuing a different set of goals (Downs, 1967, 88), the list of which comprise power, income, prestige, security, convenience and so on (Downs, 1967, 84). Goals are also ranked in a hierarchy for each official: *ultimate*, to do with the meaning of life; *social conduct*, rules about society; *basic political action*, policies for governments; *basic personal*, ambitions; then some bureau-oriented goals, *social function*, *bureau structure*, *broad policy* and *specific policy* goals (Downs, 1967, 85). Organisations, too, have 'different structural depths':

> Our analysis recognises four 'organisational layers'. The shallowest consists of the specific actions taken by the bureau, the second of the decision-making rules it uses, the third of the institutional structure it uses to make these rules, and the deepest of its general purposes . . . change can occur at any depth without affecting layers of greater depth, though it will normally affect all shallower layers. Thus, a bureau can change its everyday actions without changing its rules; it can change its rules without shifting its rule-making structure; and it can alter its rule-making structure without adopting any different fundamental purposes. But if it adopts new purposes, all the other layers will be significantly affected. (*Downs, 1967, 168*)

(This is definitionally so: no evidence is given.)

This theory is not worked through as meticulously as could be; indeed, it is but incidental to the main development of the book, which is concerned less than was Tullock's with 'power struggles', more with the nature of control and communication in 'bureaus', and the process of search and selection in decision making, as were March and Simon.

In his account of communication problems, Downs relies heavily on Tullock's model, including the two types of 'distortion' inevitable in a hierarchy of authority. The first, the 'winnowing process' in upward transmission of information, he specifies as 'screening' level by level, following Tullock, rather than 'summarising' as in March and Simon: officials merely 'select' what to pass on and what to omit, and if there are six such 'filters', 'only about 53 per cent of it will express the true state of the environment as A would have observed it for himself' (Downs, 1967, 118). The second is the 'leakage of authority' involved in downward passing of orders (Downs, 1967, 134). But Downs explores these processes in considerably greater detail than Tullock: for example, by noting 'anti-distortion forces' at work on information transmission upwards, the use of redundancy of information and several channels, competition among subordinates, the neutralisation of known biases by 'counter-biases' and so on, and by relating biases to uncertainty:

> . . . the more inherently uncertain any information is, the more scope there is for distortion in reporting it. Inherent uncertainty means that the range of values variables may assume cannot be reduced below a certain significant size. The greater the uncertainty, the wider this range, and the more latitude officials have in emphasising one part of it without being proved wrong. They tend to designate one part as most probable not because it really is, but because the occurrence of that value would benefit them more than other possible outcomes. This amounts to uncertainty absorption based upon self-interest or advocacy rather than objective estimates of real probabilities (March and Simon, 164–8). (*Downs, 1967, 121*)

The problem for the counter-biaser, then, is to 'recognise whether the estimates of his subordinates are really based on relatively certain information', to which they add their characteristic bias, 'or whether they embody false resolutions of uncertainty' (122). It is a subtle analysis. Distortions can be cumulative:

> Consider the case of the combat capabilities of certain aircraft used several years ago. These capabilities involved, among other things, radar bombing scores. Naturally, each bombardier was motivated to get as good scores as possible, and some even cheated to do so. Squadron commanders were motivated by competition to report the scores of their squadrons as favourably as they could; hence they did not inform their superiors that many of their most impressive scores were run on sunny days with no strong winds and lots of optical assistance. Similarly, the wing commander knew that he was competing for money with other types of weapons (such as submarines); hence

he summarised the scores reported to him as optimistically as possible before forwarding the summary to his superiors, minimising such qualifying facts as the percentage of air aborts. Cumulative distortion resulted, and the top men in the hierarchy received a report of capabilities grossly exaggerating the real situation. Such exaggeration need not result from any overt falsehoods, but simply from selective suppression of qualifying information. (*Downs, 1967, 123*)

Other ways of tackling distortion are the use of the by-pass (skipping from high to low echelons without going through the intervening levels), developing methods of making messages distortion-proof by coding or by direct transmission of raw data (television pictures of a battlefield available by satellite in the Pentagon, etc.,), and so on.

In utilising Tullock's theory of distortion in 'command', Downs introduces certain differences of emphasis:

. . . insofar as A is concerned, controlling the bureau means getting its members to achieve his own goals to the greatest extent possible. Looking at the information available to him, he decides to implement a certain policy. Since he has to consider a great many policies, he must formulate each one in general terms, and has no time to work out the details. These he is compelled to leave to his subordinates, even if he retains the right to review their plans. Therefore, the orders of top-level officials to their subordinates are always relatively broad in nature.

When B_1 receives this order, he begins translating it into more specific directions for lower-level officials. But B_1 also has limited time for this task; hence he too must delegate the details to his C-level subordinates, and so on down the hierarchy. Finally, the general policy issued by A becomes transformed into specific actions performed by G-level personnel. (*Downs, 1967, 133*)

Then appears this footnote:

In reality, there are many feedbacks from lower levels to upper ones in this process, so that the downward-flowing orders are often modified in response to suggestions from lower levels. Nevertheless, the basic structure of the process is the same as that described in our analysis.

The main text continues:

In this process, orders from the top must be expanded and made more specific as they move downward. There are a number of different ways in which these orders can be made more specific at each level, and each official has some leeway in selecting the one he will follow. Even if his superior has merely ordered him to propose a set of alternatives, an official exercises discretion in designing the choices he will present.

The result is that the policies of any organisation are defined at all levels, not just at the top, as Chester Barnard has pointed out (*The Functions of The Executive*, 231–2). At every level, there is a certain discretionary gap between the orders an official receives from above and those he issues downwards, and every official is forced to exercise discretion in interpreting his superior's orders. These orders are a form of information flowing downward through the hierarchy, just as reports are a form of information flowing upward. In passing information upward, intermediary officials must translate data received into more general and more condensed form. In passing orders downward, they must translate commands received into more specific and expanded form. This symmetry occurs simply because there are many more people at the bottom than at the top. (*Downs, 1967, 134*)

Several points here are worthy of note. If there are 'many feedbacks' from lower levels to higher in the implementation of policy, it surely cannot also be the case that it is 'lack of time' that prevents a superior from working out the details for himself. Secondly, a structure containing feedback is *not* the same basic structure as a linear up-and-then-down one. Thirdly, Downs's insight that orders are 'expanded' on the way down and 'made more specific', and his odd statement that an official is 'forced to exercise discretion in interpreting his superior's orders', assort ill with the continued use of the term 'distortion' to label such indispensable activities. Important though this function clearly is, Downs does not go further into it, or into precisely how the trick of transforming the policy issued by A into specific actions at G-level is done; he falls back on Tullock's more general formulation, under the term of a 'leakage of authority', with only a hint that there is something to be investigated further:

Whenever rational officials have the power to make choices, they will use that power to achieve their own goals. . . . Because individual officials have varying goals, and each uses his discretion in translating orders from above into commands going downward, the purposes the superior had in mind will not be the precise ones his subordinate's orders convey to people farther down the hierarchy. The resulting diversion constitutes a leakage of authority.

Such leakage is not caused by delegation *per se*, but by the fact that such delegation is accompanied by variances in officials' goals. Delegation of discretion without goal variance would not result in leakage of authority (except through unintentional errors). Hence goal variance among officials is the crucial cause of authority leakage. However, since goal variance itself is caused by technical factors (such as differential information) as well as conflicts of interest, this conclusion does not mean that authority leakage results solely or even mainly from self-interest. (*Downs, 1967, 134*)

Here once more we have the unsatisfactory mixing of cognitive and motivational elements in the *analysis*. Although a very great deal of Downs's hypothesis about the causes and consequences of communications problems in hierarchical organisations can stand, this central reasoning of 'distortion' and 'leakage' implies the possibility of a distortion-free and leak-free process, an ideal type which can only be Tullock's 'average man' model where all intermediate ranks are mere postmen — while the rest of the analysis requires a much more complex ideal type with feedback, with an intriguing symmetry between condensing information on the way up and expanding it on the way down, and other features that are imperfectly articulated. We may, for instance, beg leave to doubt whether the explanation of the symmetry is as simple as Downs says — 'because there are many more people at the bottom than at the top' (Downs, 1967, 134). We may find that, in such a vertically specialised hierarchy, the same phenomenon would have to occur in a purely linear hierarchy, with only one person at each level.

There is much else in Downs's book, such as his 'laws' of Imperfect Control, Diminishing Control and Decreasing Co-ordination (Downs, 1967, 143), and his descriptions of a seven-step 'basic control cycle' (Downs, 1967, 144), counter-control devices (Downs, 1967, 147) and other inventions, whose fuller appreciation must be left for another occasion.

Without referring to the work of Tullock or Downs at all, Herbert Kaufman and Michael Couzens have more recently examined the problems of communication in government agencies, and the risk of subordinates' non-compliance going undetected, in a short book for the Brookings Institution, heavily oriented towards headquarters/ field offices relationships, entitled *Administrative Feedback: Monitoring Subordinates' Behavior* (1973). It has no explicit theory of the implementation process we are considering here, however.

Pressman and Wildavsky

Finally, in this survey of present theories of the execution process, Pressman and Wildavsky's *Implementation* (1973). I have already quoted their observations about the literature. In their own bibliography, footnotes and appendix on 'Use of "Implementation" in Social Science Literature', they do not refer to any of the classic administrative management writers, or to Barnard, the March and Simon book, Tullock or Downs. If they had done so, they might not have been able to say, 'not enough is known about the subject to develop appropriate categories, and there is no previous literature on which to rely for guidance' (Pressman and Wildavsky, 1973, xiii). Many of the definitions (of 'policy', for instance) and categories (of internal conflict, for instance) that they felt obliged to develop for themselves were already to be found (in Downs, for instance), for use or adaptation at worst.

As noted earlier, Pressman's and Wildavsky's book is really to be considered as belonging in a different tradition, that of policy implementation studies and programme performance accounting. They used a tracer case-study, a 'one-off' series of events rather than an ongoing routine, whereas most of the case material used in the literature we have been surveying is cross-sectional, revealing structure or role relationship rather than dynamic process, even where the analysis is concerned with process. Again, Pressman and Wildavsky deal with a story that crosses a continent and involves several different *types* of organisations; theories heavily oriented towards a top-to-bottom process in a single organisation are not directly applicable. Third, they focus their attention neither on an ideal type of an authority or communications structure, nor on the organisational psychology of personal motivation (though they have a place for both), but on the analysis of a stochastic decision process – the calculation of the probability of 'what happened' actually happening, the isolation of influences, the values attached to different vectors as the action moves from stage to stage, place to place, one set of actors to another. Much of this analysis would clearly apply similarly to execution processes wholly within one large organisation: accordingly, the book has a place in the present survey.

The book is about an urban aid programme in the United States, set up by the Economic Development Administration (EDA) of the Department of Commerce (and not the seemingly more appropriate Department of Housing and Urban Development), to pump massive sums into a single city area in an attempt to create jobs for the unemployed – mainly black – and hence reduce the risk of urban unrest. Thus the programme was avowedly 'experimental', and the book could have been an analysis of the conditions of success of a social experiment rather than a study of the process of implementation in general, except that, as the authors show, the programme lacked almost every element of a true experiment in any scientific sense. The city chosen was Oakland, California, part of the San Francisco Bay metropolitan region (and neighbouring city to the University of Berkeley which already had in being a policy research and action programme, the Oakland Project, Wildavsky its director).

On 29 April 1966, Eugen P. Foley, the 'enthusiastic, restless and imaginative Assistant Secretary of Commerce', as the *Wall Street Journal* called him, announced the programme at a press conference. After discussing Oakland's unemployment rate – more than twice the national average – he unveiled the scheme: grants to public works projects, and loans to individual businesses, amounting to around $25m dollars, which he said would provide some 3,000 new jobs. To make sure the jobs would go to the people for whom they were intended – 'inner city' unemployed, mainly black, the source of the feared race riots if nothing were done – and not to the white unemployed who would otherwise get preference, grants or loans would be given only against an 'employment plan' prepared by the employer, committing himself to obtaining his labour, if at all possible, from the approved supply. A locally representative review board would approve each plan and receive a monthly report on hiring thereafter. In 1968 things seemed to be going well, according to a book by Foley's special representative in Oakland; but the truth was apparently otherwise, for in March 1969 the *Los Angeles Times* reported that only twenty jobs had so far materialised and the programme was 'bogged down in a bureaucratic fight'. An official EDA report the same week said that an investment of over $1m in business loans had created only forty-three jobs. As time passed, the pessimistic view became dominant:

> Four years after the initiation of the program, few jobs had been created and the major public works projects – the marine terminal and the aircraft hangar – had not been built. If despair and disillusionment in the minority community were in any way related to EDA activities in Oakland, these conditions would only have been worsened by the gap between promise and performance. (*Pressman and Wildavsky, 1973, 5*)

It was not, Pressman and Wildavsky say, their goal to be 'Monday-morning quarter-backs', dissecting mistakes with the clarity that only hindsight can give:

> After tracing the tortuous course of the program from the time of its inception, we will examine those factors that lay behind the program's frustrations: the difficulties of translating broad agreements into specific decisions, given a wide range of participants and perspectives; the opportunities for blockage and delay that result from a multiplicity of decision points; and the economic theories on which the program was based. (*Pressman and Wildavsky, 1973, 6*)

The 'technical details' of implementation of this agreed programme proved more difficult than anyone had imagined, leading to disillusionment: the authors' hope was that, if there is more understanding of what causes such difficulties, fewer promises may be made, but more of them would be kept (Pressman and Wildavsky, 1973, 6).

We can leave to the other tradition of implementation studies (that of 'programme pathology') the task of evaluating and comparing Pressman's and Wildavsky's diagnoses with others. If Pressman and Wildavsky are pathologists, we are concerned with a logically (but not necessarily historically) prior study, the physiology of the normal process. So we will pay attention only to their account of what they understand this to be, or assume it to be.

Beginning (as already noted) with the axiom that if there is implementation to study, there must be a complementary concept, that which is to be implemented, they choose to name the latter 'policy' (we need not go into some rather confusing complications they discover about different usages of 'policy'). But Pressman and Wildavsky are not so clear as Van Meter and Van Horn about the distinction between 'policy impact' and 'policy implementation' studies. Implementation is used in both senses, without distinction:

> Let us agree to talk about policy as a hypothesis containing initial conditions and predicted consequences. If X is done at time t_1, then Y will result at time t_2 . . . Implementation would here constitute the ability to achieve the predicted consequences after the initial conditions have been met.
>
> Implementation does not refer to creating the initial conditions. Legislation has to be passed and funds committed before implementation takes place to secure the predicted outcome. (*Pressman and Wildavsky, 1973, xiv*)

'Predicted consequences' and 'predicted outcome' could refer either to the action the agency or agencies take, or to the consequences of that action, the results. But the authors seem to clear up that ambiguity by designating the first as 'program':

> A program exists when the initial conditions – the 'if' stage of the policy hypothesis – have been met. The word 'program' signifies the conversion of a hypothesis into governmental action. The initial premises of the hypothesis have been authorised. The degree to which the predicted consequences (the 'then' stage) take place we will call implementation. (*Pressman and Wildavsky, 1973, xv*)

This seems to be the 'policy impact' or 'performance measurement' meaning of implementation. Yet the very next sentence is: 'Implementation may be viewed as a process of interaction between the setting of goals and actions geared to achieving them' (xv) – which is surely a succinct statement of implementation in its 'operationalisation' meaning. On the same page:

> Programs make theories operational by forging the first link in the causal chain connecting actions to objectives. . . . Implementation, then, is the ability to forge subsequent links in the causal chain so as to obtain the desired results (*Pressman and Wildavsky, 1973, xv*)

– which is even more explicitly 'operationalisation'. There are several other places where implementation means the organisational process, or multi-organisational process, mediating between goals and substantive outputs, actions geared to achieving them, and *not* to measuring what results have been achieved. Indeed, the word in the book's title and subtitle is at least ambiguous as between these two senses: or perhaps ambivalent.

Using the same word in two, or even three, distinct senses without noticing is not an unusual feature of discussions on themes like this. If 'implementation' is the name of what follows the setting of goals – the choosing of action, the moving into action, and the effect induced by action – the same applies to 'execution'. It is the arranging for the death sentence to be carried out, the carrying out of the death sentence and the death-sentence-having-been-carried-out. The synonyms for each word also (curiously) bear the same ambiguity: consider words like completion, fulfilment, and accomplishment. One word stands for process, output and outcome.

Thus, 'failure of implementation' may mean any one of the following:

(a) undeniably, the outcome was other than predicted (and desired), although the actions intended and taken were such as might have been (by a reasonable man) predicted to produce the desired outcome;
(b) the actions intended to be taken were not taken (because of *force majeure* of some kind, let us say), although the intended actions were such as might have been (by a reasonable man) predicted to produce the desired outcome; and either no action at all was taken (and so no outcome), or unintended actions were taken;
(c) the actions intended and taken were not such as might have been (by a reasonable man) predicted to produce the desired outcome.

Either (a) the reactions of the environment to the action taken had been misapprehended by all concerned, or (b) the capability for action had been misjudged, or (c) the implementer was a fool. Obviously, it matters which, if you want success in implementation.

Pressman and Wildavsky saw their purpose as to teach policy makers to put more of the real world into their initial conditions, policy implementers how to estimate capabilities for action more realistically, and both to cease, in designing their programs, to rely on a mere means–end analysis – that is, a demonstration that the means chosen *could* lead to the end given (but will not necessarily do so). In their usage (a common one in government), a 'program' is a complex of ongoing actions by different agents with some common goals (as in 'the urban aid program'). But the word can also refer to a *plan* for such a complex of actions, so that 'a program for urban aid' might exist before any action was actually taken on it. Yet again, 'programming' means the activity of 'gearing' agents and actions into such a complex for the achievement of a goal or goals. This sense matches that of March and Simon (see p. 41 above), and is implicit in a somewhat obscure discussion which follows the discussion of 'policy' and 'implementation':

> Considered as a whole, a program can be conceived of as a system in which each element is dependent upon the others. Unless money is supplied, no facilities can be built, no new jobs can flow from them, and no minority personnel can be hired to fill them. A breakdown at one stage must be repaired, therefore, before it is possible to move on to the next. The stages are related, however, from back to front as well as from front to back. Failure to agree on procedures for hiring minorities may lead the government to withhold funds, thus halting the construction. Program implementation thus becomes a seamless web. (*Pressman and Wildavsky, 1973, xv*)

The 'chain' that is forged is apparently not a linear one, and not uni-directional in time even if in logic. The passage of time, they say, wreaks havoc with efforts to maintain tidy distinctions. People alter their objectives as circumstances change; money and staff and other resources are subject to slippage; the actual implementers find themselves involved in sustaining the 'initial conditions', in assembling fresh political support. The longer the 'chain of causality', the 'more numerous the reciprocal relationships among the links' – a difficult metaphor, meaning presumably that as the system becomes more complex, uni-directional linearity is lost:

> The reader . . . should . . . be conscious of the steps required to accomplish each link in the chain. Who had to act to begin implementation? Whose consent was required to continue it? How many participants were involved? How long did they take to act? Each time an act of agreement has to be registered for the program to continue, we call a decision point. Each instance in which a separate participant is required to give his consent, we call a clearance. (*Pressman and Wildavsky, 1973, xvi*)

This approach to the consideration of the execution process, or what Pressman and Wildavsky are calling the 'causal chain linking actions to objectives', is distinctively multi-organisational.

Tullock and Downs spoke of 'distortion' and 'leakage of authority', but they assumed that the chief at the top did have the authority to command. Barnard and Simon, though using a different understanding of what authority is, took it for granted that the 'loading' of authority a top-level decision acquires there will carry it through the hierarchy to operating level. In the multi-organisational context, in contrast:

> actions cannot be commanded. There is no hierarchy of officials in a single line of command who can be directed toward a set of predetermined objectives. In such cases the careful specification of plans and objectives by a public agency will not suffice to guarantee effective programs. (*Schultze, 1969, 202; Van Meter and Van Horn, 1975, 467*)

Into the activity of interpretation (of instructions received into instructions to be given), there is injected a new element, a decision about whether or not to comply or co-operate with what are, effectively, the wishes of someone in another organisation – someone else's boss, with other interests, other political supports, other constraints on resources – as well as the common aims that are the ground of the program. (In passing: the books are legion which take the 'realistic' view that, in this regard, *all* bureaucracies are 'multi-organisational'.)

When an ongoing program comes under challenge, Pressman and Wildavsky say, the 'initial conditions' may have to be re-established. The point of the program, why it was begun, may have to be thrashed out again: as time goes on, the original point may become obsolete, or lose its political backing, but other reasons for the program may have emerged. Difficulties of getting agreements in the implementation stages (of forging the later links in the causal chain) may weaken support. Lack of positive outcome, or the pattern of results actually achieved, may alter the pattern of support or aspiration levels. So the logically 'later' stages get mixed up with the logically 'initial' stages – there are what they call 'reciprocal relationships among the links'. It is not the case that goals are established once and for all in the beginning, or that all-round agreement on the 'initial conditions' will ensure implementation in any of its senses. And those already engaged in the implementing process, far from being merely 'interpreters' of higher policy, will often be expected to defend and make the case for the program, as if *they* had initiated it. Many others

(Simon-Smithburg-Thompson, Tullock, Downs and a host of commentators in newspapers and elsewhere) have noted the persistence of bureaus through apparent changes of goals and programs, and usually put it down to the bureaucrats' interest in keeping their jobs. Pressman and Wildavsky are pointing to a contrary phenomenon: the pressures on officials towards commitment not to bureau but to program and program goals (especially in multi-organisational settings). For without a widespread measure of such commitment, programs would not ever be implemented or kept going once launched. Again, it is perhaps not otherwise within the 'single' bureaucracy.

The concepts of 'decision point' and 'clearance' are used in a later chapter of Pressman's and Wildavsky's book to quantify these considerations and portray them in tables and diagrams. One table (95) lists the organisational participants in the EDA–Oakland Program – the EDA Oakland Task Force, the headquarters departments of EDA in Washington DC, the EDA regional office in Seattle, the regular Oakland office of EDA, the several other US Federal Government Departments including the US Navy, the various City of Oakland and Port of Oakland agencies, citizen groups and so on. It describes their connection with the programme, their objectives and perspectives on it, and gives a rating on their 'sense of urgency' (commitment). Another table lists the decision points with dates (thirty of them), at all of which, by definition, a 'renegotiation' of some degree of importance was required, resulting in one or more 'agreements' at each point, amounting to seventy agreements (101). Playing mathematically with such a network suggests the following:

> In order to get by all the decision points, the program required dozens of clearance actions by a wide range of participants. In situations of high controversy and mutual antagonism, the probability that these actions would be favorable or taken in a reasonable time might be quite small. But we have ruled out this kind of drama. Instead, we shall assume the best. We shall deliberately err on the side of assuming more agreement and good will than might actually have been the case. We shall load the dice in favor of keeping the program going. Suppose, then, we take a spread of probabilities on the high side that each participant will take a favorable action at each decision point. We can try four: 80 per cent, 90 per cent, 95 per cent, and 99 per cent. (*Pressman and Wildavsky, 1973, 107*)

The computations follow, showing that on an 80 per cent assumption, the probability of eventual success after 70 clearances is 0.000000125, probability of success having been reduced below 0.5 after only four clearances. On a 99 per cent favourable assumption, the probability of success after 70 clearances is still less than 0.5 (0.489), having dropped below 0.5 after 68 clearances. (The intermediate figures are: <0.5 after 7 clearances on a 90 per cent assumption; <0.5 after 14 clearances on a 95 per cent assumption.) The authors, conclude, modestly enough, that

> the probability of agreement by every participant on each decision point must be exeedingly high for there to be any chance at all that a program will be brought to completion. . . . The high probability of agreement at each step required to produce a modest probability of successful completion makes it unnecessary to know the precise probability for any particular one. No doubt the probabilities vary from one participant and organisation to another, over time within the same organisation, and between different levels of government and private *versus* governmental actors. But if one assumes the best – and 99 per cent for each and every clearance point appears to be about as close as one can go without assuming away the problem entirely – the odds are still against program implementation. *(107–9)*

A program requiring 70 sequential favourable decisions (after it has been completely authorised) for it to be put into action for the first time stands less than an even chance of ever going into action, even when one assumes only one chance in 100 that each particular decision maker will be unable to assent.

That conclusion, of course, is mathematically entailed by the assumptions: but they are not unreasonable assumptions, and the programme was a real enough programme. The main point is that general acceptance of programme goals, magnanimity, lack of 'personal' opposition, and so on, were all assumed to be present. Where they are not, probabilities of favourable decision at clearance points can be expected to be much lower than 80 per cent. Moreover, there are of course many other kinds of thing that could go wrong, unrelated to human opposition: accidents, bad weather, failure in supplies, etc.

On the other side of the balance, it is true that the participants in the decision points are not all equal and substitutable: clearance by one person could increase the probability of clearance by some others. But, say Pressman and Wildavsky, given the American context of fragmented power, the difference in the public objectives of the participants and the federal/local angle, independence of the participants is a realistic assumption and influenced the designation of decision points in the first place. Therefore:

> Our normal expectation should be that new programs will fail to get off the ground and that, at best, they will take considerable time to get started. The cards in this world are stacked against things happening, as so much effort is required to make them move. The remarkable thing is that new programs work at all. (*Pressman and Wildavsky, 1973, 109*)

'Clearance', of course, is not necessarily a yes/no affair. Programs can be delayed, modified, scaled down, distorted, adapted in various ways. And if a programme requires two or more 'action paths' to be travelled simultaneously (in the EDA case, construction of public works and creation of employment possibilities including training programmes), there is the likelihood of the two (or more) paths getting out of kilter, generating a number of unexpected decision points and new alternative paths or links, setting up goal displacements, and other difficulties, the 'end of the line' where the paths should converge again seemingly receding over the horizon. Instead of a simple model of the 'causal chain' kind, Pressman and Wildavsky have arrived at a model of a programme surviving in an environment, being adapted, altered, its origins forgotten:

> Appearances are deceiving. Looking back at the very array of government programs that are in operation, we conclude that they must have been implemented. Why, then, should our new program fail in implementation when so many others that fill the landscape have evidently succeeded? It is easy to forget (perhaps because we never knew) about their initial difficulties. The years of trial and error that led to the present state of operation are lost from view. The huge amount of resources that may have been poured into different alternatives before one caught on is conveniently part of past history for which we are not responsible. Programs that started out to accomplish one set of objectives end up accomplishing another for which, long after the fact, we give undue credit for implementation. . . . Adaptation to the environment must have been achieved; otherwise, by definition, programs would not exist. No genius is required to make programs operative if we don't care how long

they take, how much money they require, how often the objectives are altered or the means for obtaining them are changed. Indeed, the law of averages would suggest that, given sufficient new initiatives, some of them must grow and prosper. . . . (*Pressman and Wildavsky, 1973, 116*)

The idea of the 'survival of the fittest programme', the one that can continue to find its niche in changing conditions – indeed, the idea of programmes struggling with one another – is one that possibly comes more easily to American readers than to British, though the latter are fast learning: the 'TSR2 programme', the 'school milk programme', the 'rail modernisation programme' and a number of others that had to fight for existence in recent British history provide examples enough. One may yet demur at the notion of a 'programme' whose objectives are frequently altered, and whose mechanisms for achieving them are also changed now and again. One is reminded of the proudly displayed 300-year-old axe that had had five new heads and ten new handles in the period. Perhaps what is persisting is not a 'programme' at all, but something indistinguishable from a bureau or an organisation. And at that point the concept ceases to tell us anything more about implementation.

There are many other insights in the Pressman and Wildavsky book to which we can come back later. Perhaps one more thought is relevant here. Implementation can be made easier, they point out, if the number of clearances and decision points can be reduced. This can be done to some extent by setting up new agencies for each new programme, or by reorganising the existing pattern of jurisdictions in favour of a new programme. But there are limits:

No matter how the federal government is organised and reorganised, virtually all social programs will cut across the jurisdiction of different bureaus, departments, and overhead agencies. While the number of clearances could be cut down by organising with a single set of programs in mind, there is no organisational arrangement that will minimise clearances for all programs, past and future. New entrants are likely to find, as did the EDA in Oakland, that they must fit into arrangements that have been made with other purposes in mind. (*Pressman and Wildavsky, 1973, 162*)

This is reminiscent of March's and Simon's 'recombination of existing programmes' to meet new demands raised to 'macro'-level: for organisation read government. It is cheaper to recombine existing programmes, and it is not a strategy that can ever be completely avoided; but where existing organisational units have their own legitimacy, their own 'sovereignty', their own goals and their own traditions and customs, 'recombining' is not a mere exercise of hierarchical authority and is a task that may be more likely to fail than to succeed. And if this is true of implementing a Pressman and Wildavsky programme, through several organisations, should we not look again at the possible problems of recombining March and Simon programmes within the single organisation?

Pyramid and network

What can we say we have learnt from this survey of the literature of implementation?

First, perhaps, that there are two distinct literatures; one, promising great theoretical richness as it develops, concerned with studies of substantive government policies, evaluating performance, measuring outcomes and accounting for discrepancies between intentions and results in the real world; the other, older and narrower, concerned with the elucidation of the operationalisation process, the transformations in organisations whereby ideas become actions, plans become performance, high-level policies become the day-to-day work of low-level personnel.

Second, that much confusion can be avoided by recognising what is mere semantic entailment and what is not. It may well be true that 'implementation does not commence until goals and objectives have been established (or identified) by prior policy decisions' (Van Meter and Van Horn, 1975, 448). But you are not saying anything about the real world when you hold that implementation must be preceded by policy making: you are only saying something about the word. To implement, to execute, to complete, to fulfil, to accomplish and so on – these are transitive verbs.

It is not (that is to say) implicit that an activity in real life which we might wish to label 'implementation' is necessarily preceded in time by an activity which we might wish to label 'policy making'. We would be making the assertion about precedence true by our labelling. Actions are not either policy making or implementation, save as we so classify them. 'Real life' does, presumably, have its dynamic logic: that is what we should be trying to elicit. To describe real life we have to name things, categorise them; but we need not make the mistake of asserting that a semantic relationship between our labels 'ought' to represent a relationship between the things we tie them on to, that nature should follow our scheme, rather than vice versa.

A *fortiori*, the semantic relationship between words cannot imply anything at all about the respective jurisdictions of real-life persons we might wish to call 'implementers' and 'policy makers', let alone 'civil servants' and 'politicians', or the like.

This is not to say, of course, that the eliciting of such logical relationships, the spelling out of the implications of the terminology and categories habitually employed in speaking about a real-life process, is pointless or without merit. An economist's 'model' is the product of such an exercise; and that is the path we shall be following.

A third lesson from the implementation literature might be, however, that it is not always wise to try to proceed from simple models to more complex (more 'lifelike') ones. It has obviously been tempting for writers to present the 'basic relationships' with as few terms as possible, and then go on to larger generalisations (Haas and Drabek, 1973, 183–4). So both Mooney (1931) and Simon-Smithburg-Thompson (1950) begin their expositions by picturing two men joining their efforts to roll away a stone, and others (cf. Barnard, 1938) have people banding together to get some changes made in local affairs. The common goal or aim comes first; the organisation of resources and factorisation of task to match the skills available follows; the newly formed enterprise begins to decide on its strategy and tactics and to put policy into effect. It is simply entailed in the construction of such a model that such a group's 'actions' can be traced back through apportionment of task to determination of policy and sharing of goals.

But that model of 'implementation' would not explain the process in the kind of large-scale, ongoing organisation that would have to be the subject of empirical study for most purposes. Its people cannot be said to have 'banded together to do something'. If there is a goal they all share, it may be no more than the continuance of the banding together – for whatever purpose. More likely, there will be a veritable host of purposes – manifest, latent, formal, informal, collective, individual, public, private – shared in different proportions. Organisation structure cannot be seen to match purpose, one to one, as in rolling away stones; rather is the structure (in the short term) a *given*, and anyone with a job he wants doing must adapt purpose to structure rather than the other way about.

Such a man could, however, learn from a less simple model of the implementation process how he might go about it. He could be advised to find out what people in the organisation actually did (ignoring entirely anything said about their purposes), work out whose services would be necessary in getting his job done and in what order, make some contacts and slip in his materials with the rest. Plotting these key workers ('key' for *his* purpose), planning the path connecting them and channelling the job along it would for him be 'implementing his policy' or 'executing his intention'.

Such an understanding (or model) of the implementation process is not semantically entailed, and could not have been deduced from any statement of the goals of the organisation or of the people in it. What our well advised friend would have to do is quite distinct from the meanings of any terms or labels he might use to describe what he had done: his 'forging of the links in the causal chain so as to obtain the desired result' (in one of the formulations of Pressman and Wildavsky, 1973, xv) would be a piece of empirical engineering depending on practical knowledge of the way that particular organisation was made and working. He could well be successful even if his behaviour were entirely 'without authority', provided his knowledge of the technical and organisational requisites was adequate. The function of the model might be only to 'put him up to it'; but success – and especially repeated success – would help to validate the model, to show that it was indeed a good ('fruitful') model of the implementation process in such organisations.

That might be our fourth lesson from the survey of literature: that we should not confuse the 'P/Q relation', as we called it earlier, with the 'authority relationship', or explain the policy/action transformation in terms of command and compliance, orders filtering down, and the like. The nexus between superior and subordinate does not by itself tell us anything about the nature of the 'interpretation' process noted by Barnard, the early Simon, Tullock and Downs: March and Simon considered the processes of uncertainty absorption and so on quite separately from their consideration of hierarchical authority. But much remains unclear about just what the 'P/Q relation' is.

At least it seems established that there is not (in a real-world process) a single point of transformation, a saddle before which everything is describable as 'P' (whatever 'P' stands for), and after which all is 'Q'. The process which turns policy into action, or whatever the favoured phrase is to describe the implementation process, has not one such 'hinge' but several. That was perhaps what was wrong about such formulations as 'the politics/administration dichotomy': not that they were dichotomous, but that they divided only once. Appleby showing that what is 'policy' depends upon where you are looking from; Tullock and Downs holding that whatever happens between the *A* level and the *B* level also happens between *B* and *C* and so on; Barnard and the early Simon equating the structure (though not the content) of the general/chief executive's interpretations with that of the division head/captain's interpretations – these are all indications that the 'P/Q relation' is generic not only in the sense that a large number of words can be used as the respective terms of the relation, but also in the sense that it describes what occurs at all stages of the process. This is expressed in the metaphor of the 'chain', which in a way has 'hinges' all along its length. But what 'hinge' means, and what the 'relation' is, we must explore later.

A discovery of another kind arising out of our survey of the literature might be that there are two different appreciations of the nature of organisational relationships: one that stresses hierarchy, and is conventionally portrayed by the pyramid image; and the other implying a 'system', usually pictured in a network image.

'Hierarchy' need not mean only a gradation of authority, rank, or status: it can be applied to any ordering in steps or grades from low to high, as measured along some single scale. 'System' has many connotations: but at its simplest, it denotes a pattern of links between individual entities by which each can affect and be affected by the others. 'Hierarchy' is usually depicted on a piece of paper as running from bottom to top (or top to bottom) in horizontally-ruled lines. 'System' is usually depicted as a number of circles connected by lines in an irregular reticulation (not a rectangular grid), with neither top nor bottom in principle.

The classical administrative management writers, along with Barnard, Weber, the early Simon, Tullock, and Downs (from among the writers quoted here), worked with a pyramid image. Much of the approach of March and Simon, on the other hand, and of Pressman and Wildavsky, can be represented only by a network image.

Notions of uncertainty absorption points and decision points, of communication barriers and causal chains, and a hundred other such ideas where 'hierarchy' is not at all prominent in the conceptualisation, lend themselves easily to 'system thinking' and the network image – though it is correspondingly difficult then to 'map on to' understandings of implementation processes that crucially depend upon rank and hierarchy (say, Tullock's).

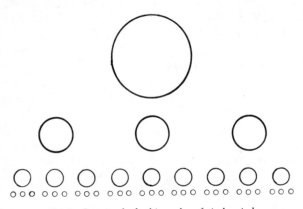

Fig. 5   Portrayal of a hierarchy of circle triads

For such reasons, although it is comparatively easy to place Downs on top of Barnard, as it were, and make a composite theory out of all the 'pyramid model' writers, it is not easy to add Downs to March and Simon or Pressman and Wildavsky. Let us, therefore, elicit separately the assumptions about the implementation process of each conceptual framework.

Although precise formulations differ, the 'pyramid model' writers are the more given to designating 'stages' of the process by which ideas are turned into action. The accounts of the process contain assumptions about the *number* of these stages; assumptions about the *ordering* of the stages – linear, cyclical or some other; assumptions about the *characteristics* of each part of the process, how it is different from other parts; assumptions about the relationship of one stage or level to the next, how the *transition* is made; and assumptions (the earliest, these) about how the stages of the process are related to the levels of an organisational hierarchy of *authority*.

In the literature from which we have quoted a doctrine of implementation stages is not well worked out, and most of the

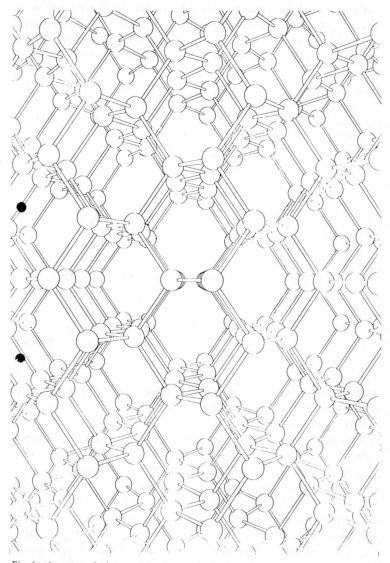

Fig. 6   A portrayal of a network of spheres (actually of atoms in a diamond crystal –
acknowledgements to *Scientific American*, August 1974)

accounts (as in the administrative reform literature) seem to rest on a three- or four-stage version of the Dewey 'thinking' sequence or on Talcott Parsons's ordering of societal change. Only in Downs does an explicit 'hierarchy of goals' (with assumptions about the process embedded) appear, although there is a considerable separate literature on organisational goals without other relevance to the present theme (Perrow, 1961, 1968, 1970; Simon, 1964; Hall, 1972, 79–96). Urwick's hierarchy of job gradings, in the same way, might be translated into the stages of a process. Assertions about the number of stages in the process vary from three to seven or eight.

A doctrine of 'stages' usually assumes a linear ordering: movement begins at the first stage and 'develops' to the last. Litchfield incorporated a series of cycles, each including other cycles, so that movement through the process was not linear but 'wheels-within-wheels'. Tullock and Downs conceive of episodic movement, each 'case' beginning at operating level, working its way up to the top levels and then back down again.

There is remarkable consensus to report on how the stages differ from another, what the characteristics (or 'qualities', in Urwick's phrase) of each are. There is complete agreement that the 'work on the world' – that which alone actually makes real changes and not mere proposals for change – is done at the bottom, at operating level, the last stage in the process of execution. Most agree, too, that operative work is responsible work and that those at operating level are far from bereft of discretion. The most common way, however, of describing the progression from setting goals, deciding strategy, and so on, to working at operating level is a progressive 'narrowing of discretion'. The early Simon, and to a lesser extent Tullock and Downs, are careful to point out that discretion is, as it were, 'complete' within its scope at each stage; but the scope gets more circumscribed. March and Simon, and Barnard in another way, make the point in reverse: the less activity is programmed, the more 'search' is involved, the more discretion is enjoyed; the farther away from operating level one rises, the greater the range of interrelated matters that come into one person's purview, the more complex the problems he has to deal with, the greater the number of his options, the larger the consequences of error, and so on: a 'pyramiding of the formulation of purpose' that becomes more and more general, as Barnard puts it.

The process of implementation, then, is seen as a progression from the general to the particular, a narrowing of the field of view or of thought, a limiting of choice and discretion. It is a progression, also, from the abstract and metaphysical towards the concrete and physical, each stage more pragmatic than the preceding stage, closer to the hard facts of the real world. Wisdom may reside at one end, but knowledge comes from the other; policy is blind if not led by operation.

The next component of the 'pyramid model' is concerned with what we have been calling the 'P/Q relation': assumptions about how material moves from one stage to the next. For most of the earlier authors, the transition is mediated by the giving of commands, instructions or orders. That is to say, the concept of the process, 'implementation', is closely tied to the concept of the organisational structure, 'hierarchy of authority'; and so we find an assumption that there is a change in state of the matter of the process at every change in authority status in the organisation. The identification is clearly seen in the early Simon article, where successive army ranks are used in the illustration, and in Tullock (followed by Downs), where a diagram of seven or so grades in a superior–subordinate relationship to one another (distinguished by successive letters of the alphabet), with the base line officers said to be 'in the field', is the main representation of the process.

There is, however, general agreement among later writers that orders given 'at the top' cannot usually be merely 'passed down the line'. Barnard, the early Simon, Bryson and Downs all agree that 'interpretation' must take place: the command given at any level must be intelligible to the subordinate, must be in terms of his specialised concerns, and so must be, in Downs' words, 'expanded' as it descends towards operating level, while being made more 'specific' at the same time, as Simon shows. Illustrations are not given, and understanding of how precisely this is done is befogged by Tullock's and Downs's equation of the operation with 'distortion' and 'leakage of authority' owing to the ambitions of subordinates; whereas it is clear even from their own accounts that there is a 'cognitive' as well as a 'motivational' aspect to whatever is happening as orders are 'interpreted'. Indeed, the interpretation function may have little to do with the superior–subordinate relationship: it can well be imagined as necessary between persons of *equal* rank but different specialist function on the same 'level' of an organisation, if messages of certain kinds are to be exchanged (as Downs notes (1967, 116)).

We may well conclude that, although Downs's account is the fullest, it contains several inconsistencies, and that this element of the model would bear further development.

The 'pyramid model', it may be, *derives from* the identification of the stages of the process with the gradations of an official hierarchy of authority, and identification of the transformation mechanism with orders passing from superior to subordinate. One would expect a 'non-pyramid model', accordingly, to differ in those respects. Before moving to consider the 'network model', however, it is fair to note that, in practically all cases, the accounts of the implementation process ascribed to the various authors quoted here have been *constructed* by the present writer: that is to say, extracted from their context and presented in a way that the original authors may well not have intended. Since most of the books used are about organisations, organisational hierarchies or bureaucracies, it is perhaps inevitable that these identifications found should have been found; there is both explanation and warrant for these accounts of implementation to be based on the most salient facts of the situation surrounding most actual occurrences of the phenomenon, viz. organizational hierarchy, or bureaucracy.

Yet two books, one the earliest textbook of organisation theory as such, the other the only one avowedly about the process under study and nothing but the process, are not based upon the 'pyramid model', and do not depend upon the identifications just noted in the other books. Their reasons may be different: in March's and Simon's case, possibly because they began from a strong analogy between individual behaviour and organisational behaviour; in the case of Pressman and Wildavsky, possibly because the actual historical events which they sought explanation for did not occur within one organisation (or even two or three), and the salient features of these events appeared not to be influenced strongly by an organisational hierarchy of authority. In each case it was possible to give a satisfying explanation, to make sense out of the observations made, without using the relationship of superior to subordinate as a key element.

The assumptions of the 'network model' of the execution process are, perhaps, only subtly different from those of the 'pyramid model' taken one by one. The development of 'stages' of the 'pyramid model' is replaced by a 'chain' metaphor; there are assumptions about the ordering of the 'links', about the nature of each, about the transition from one to another and about how the process is related to legitimate authority, just as before.

But the basic assumption is that the process under study is one of creating and establishing links between separate bodies – *making* a chain, not just using one; a chain which, in principle, might be made up of different sets of bodies for each implementation exercise, though the more often a chain is 'forged' the more easily it is 'forged' the next time, until it may be virtually permanent. There is also an assumption that the chain is made up of bodies which, whether or not they belong to a single organisation, exhibit a degree of independence, a relative 'autonomy' as among themselves: either because they are specialised, by skill and equipment or by jurisdiction, and so not substitutable for one another, or because they have their own 'legitimacy' or lines to the outside.

The ordering of these linkages, the assembling of a particular manifestation of the process, is seen as a technical matter primarily. Each 'body' or 'unit' (or 'programme' in March's and Simon's sense) is a place where work is done on the material being processed, and it can accept the material only in a certain form, it can do only certain things to it, and it can put it out again only in a certain form. The task of implementation, therefore, is to design a sequence in which each unit will be able to accept the output of the preceding unit (preceding output form must be compatible with succeeding input form), and transform it in ways that will *cumulate* to the overall transformation desired – ideas turned into corresponding actions.

The assumption is that the 'organisation-as-a-whole' (or, in the case of governmental activity extending over several organisations, the 'government-as-a-whole') is a dynamic complex of such more or less permanent chains, and that the greater part by far of the demands made upon it can be met by 'switching-in' one or other of these chains, combining parts of one chain with parts of others or, in relatively unusual cases, making up a new chain entirely from individual links. Sometimes there will be accepted a demand which cannot be met in any of these ways; in that case, new units must be formed, or existing 'programmes' broken up and reformed (relearned). Another part of the working theory assumes that the further one moves from simple 'switching-in', the stronger will be resistance to change. Pressman and Wildavsky, dealing almost exclusively with new 'programmes' (and at a much more 'macro' level than March and Simon), show how improbable implementation is even when the forging of a new chain is *not* fought all the way.

The transition between links of the chain is a subject of great interest both to March and Simon and to Pressman and Wildavsky. There are clear parallels between the former authors' concept of 'uncertainty absorption points' that endow discretion and the latter's concept of 'clearance'. The stress laid by March and Simon on the purely cognitive aspects of communication difficulties inside an organisation, as against the assumptions that such difficulties are mainly motivational, is matched by the stress laid by Pressman and Wildavsky on 'loading the dice in favor of keeping the program going' by assuming a 99 per cent favourable clearance rate, which over seventy clearances still produces less than one chance in two of success. March and Simon note that perception and communication inside a unit are in terms of a special in-language: accordingly, some information entering a unit will not be understood because not properly perceived; other information will be translated at the threshold so that it can be internally used. (This adds to Barnard's point about intelligibility of orders, and Downs's concept of 'interpretation' between superior and subordinate.)

Hierarchical authority, to March and Simon, is a source of legitimisation of programmes and of change in programming. But authority as such plays little part in the execution process as they see it – not even in co-ordination. For Pressman and Wildavsky, concerned with a number of hierarchies and not one, it plays an equally small part.

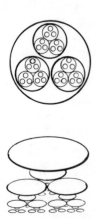

Fig. 7   Alternative portrayals of a hierarchy of circle triads (see *Fig. 5*)

Status authority is involved in a minor explanatory role at some points.

Both books, however, use the concept of hierarchy as defined earlier and as distinguished from status hierarchy or organisational hierarchy of authority. For instance, March's and Simon's concept of general programmes that select or modify more specific programmes, while the more specific programme thus selected or modified may in its turn stand in a similar relation to a more particular programme still: that is a hierarchical structure of 'levels' of programme, moving from the general to the particular, each level *including* the more specific levels below it. Pressman's and Wildavsky's concept of decision paths that have to branch to take care of *subsidiary* problems is similarly hierarchical. (A pictorialisation might not look like a hierarchy, since it might run from left to right rather than from top to bottom, but that is a mere device of presentation (see Beer, 1966, Chap. 9).)

What is interesting is that there are several features of the treatment of the process by Barnard, by the early Simon, by Bryson, and by Tullock and Downs, that would more comfortably fit into a 'network model' than the 'pyramid' one. There are obvious similarities between Pressman's and Wildavsky's arithmetical presentations of the likelihood of a programme's survival through a large number of clearances, and Tullock's arithmetical presentations of the likelihood of a piece of information's survival undistorted as it passes up through a hierarchy, or of the intentions of a superior surviving unscathed as they are dealt with by a succession of subordinates. Mathematically they are both *catastrophes*, and the presence of an authority relationship is not an essential part of the argument in either case: opportunity or occasion to introduce 'distortion' or require 'clearance' is all that is necessary. Gulick, Barnard and March and Simon all agree that the basic specialised skills of which 'operations' are composed are imported whole into the average organisation from the society outside; Barnard suspected that nine-tenths of all organisational activity is specified and authorised by, and done on the personal responsibility of, 'those who make the last contributions', the men on the shop floor or 'in the firing line': 'There is no meaning to personal specialisation, personal experience, [etc.] if this is not so' (Barnard, 1938, 23). Compare this with Simon's quotation from US Army Field Regulations to the effect that an order should not 'trespass upon' the province of a subordinate, or with Bryson's quotation of Shen Pu-hai's maxim that the skilful ruler 'does nothing' in order to allow his subordinates to develop their own ideas. In each case, the concept is that of the essential autonomy of the specialist, the trained man, the man who knows how, the man close to the action; and Gulick, among the classic administrative management writers, accepted that the *raison d'être* of an organisation is the assembly and integration of sufficient numbers of such specialists, trained men and skilled operatives to 'perform the tasks of the organisation'.

Autonomy, of course, is not complete: it is always relative autonomy, within the system; often substantive autonomy within procedural rules – as when Simon speaks of the 'tactical doctrine' and 'accepted tactical principles' which the subordinate army officer must follow. Tullock adopts exactly the same illustration at the end of his book and notes that, when actually in combat, the patrol commander cannot *either* simply obey his orders specifying his mission, for they are not detailed enough, *or* simply follow his 'general instructions' about how to carry out patrols, for the circumstances are always special: these are only the guides – or, perhaps better, the limits – within which the commander decides (Tullock, 1965, 179 – my language, not Tullock's). The concept central to Simon's own thought about the decision maker is that he sits in the centre of a web of influences upon him – some of which are authoritarian. It would not need much rewriting of Downs to produce very similar images: the whole purpose of authority structures, he says, is to 'reduce conflict to an acceptable level' (Downs, 1967, 50) – or, even more strangely in a hierarchical context, it is for 'adjusting inconsistent behavior patterns among the organisation's members to an acceptable level of complementarity' (51). These are reticular rather than pyramidal concepts, as are the concepts of a communication network cutting across the authority hierarchy (55) and of every member of a bureau having different goals.

To some extent, therefore, the choice of image – pyramid or network – is a dilemma; neither will adequately portray all the relationships one observes or wishes to present. Pressman and Wildavsky could not have conveyed their 'programme survival' ideas without implying an 'ecological' or 'market' model; Tullock and Downs could not plausibly discuss 'bureaucracy' (their subject, after all) without relying on a pyramidal framework. The network image more easily accommodates notions of 'influence', 'relative autonomy', 'communication nets', 'feedback', and so on. The pyramid image more easily accommodates notions of 'narrowing discretion', 'increasing generality', 'pyramiding of purpose', and the like. A scholar seeking to set out what the current theory of the implementation process is, as established in the literature surveyed, would have to do more or less what we have done – switch from one image to the other as the topic altered.

Let us leave it at that for now, and begin from this point, in Chapter 4, to see how far these ideas can take us in explaining, or making sense of, the narrative which now follows in Chapter 3.

CHAPTER 3

Closure of a Railway Branch Line

Not far from where I write, in the early morning of a January day a dozen or so years ago, a nearly empty two-coach diesel train made its last passenger-carrying run over a rural branch line. There were no fanfares, no coach-loads of enthusiasts; it was not, on the whole, a much-lamented line, though its closure removed all rail services from the brewery town (and road traffic bottleneck) of Tadcaster. By now, almost every vestige of the line, which in its heyday carried crack London to Harrogate expresses, has disappeared – except for the tell-tale horizontal straight lines in fields where the embankments were, and the wide grassy cuttings where wild flowers grow. At two or three points road widenings have cleared away level crossings or bridge abutments, and white-painted platform seats and lamps decorate gardens. Most people have simply forgotten about the trains that used to run there, and none of the local schoolchildren ever saw one.

Branch line closure is an emotive subject: but its inclusion in this book has nothing to do with that. The case history will serve to provide writer and reader with a common stock of illustrations, a set of known reference points in an abstract argument.

A single case history is evidence of a negative kind: if this happened, then a proposition which says it cannot happen is disproved. The arguments and assertions later in the book are not based on the material in the case-study: they stand or fall on their own evidence or plausibility. but the 'closure' narrative may show what sort of situation an assertion is intended to apply to.

A case-study is never written up simply because it happened and is 'true', but because it is a case of something the writer wants to demonstrate. Its conclusions are built into its selection in the first place. This case-study is designed to illustrate the relationship between the realm of high public controversy and the daily work of men with no stake in the controversy who are yet its agents. It is a case-study of implementation, in the 'policy operationalisation' sense.

It is not, therefore, a case-study of the relationship between government agencies, or of the roles of Ministers and civil servants, or of the social effects of governmental decisions upon communities or groups, or of the effects of national-level decisions upon the morale of local-level employees, or of the role of personality in interaction among officials, or of any of a number of other themes which the subject matter (the closure of a railway branch line) could have been made to illumine. For all its circumstantial detail, it is not, either, a study of a particular decision, since it makes no attempt to explore the mind of any decision maker before and after any of the choices made, nor does it lay out in systematic fashion the pros and cons or the influences brought to bear. Nor is it at all concerned with the rightness or correctness, or the effectiveness or efficiency, of any of the actions it describes.

What we have is a straightforward, rather old-fashioned description, of legal setting, formal duties and official communications, and a chronology of major events that could be tabulated in a list of dates. This unsophisticated formula was chosen because it is all that is needed for the purpose.

The word 'closure' is defined in the Transport Act, 1962, Section 56(7), thus: 'Where the Railways Board or London Board propose to discontinue all railway passenger services from any station or on any line (hereinafter referred to as a closure). . . .' The closure of a railway branch line, therefore, legally refers to the complete withdrawal of passenger services over that section or sections of track. It would be, therefore, possible to run goods trains over a line already closed in this sense. The following narrative, however, takes the story further than 'closure' to the abandonment of the line, the taking up of the track and the disposal of the land.

Historical background

The background will be familiar enough to most readers. The Victorians of the Railway Age laid down a dense network of lines linking virtually every centre of population with its neighbours, sometimes two and three times over by rival companies. Many companies obtained powers of compulsory purchase from Parliament, and Parliament did not deal with railway matters in *laissez-faire* fashion, but regulated rates and charges and discriminatory facilities on the one hand, and operations in the interests of safety on the other hand. Some companies went bankrupt soon after formation; some lines that were begun were never finished; some duplicated services were discontinued, on takeover by a rival company, and lines closed. There has always been the problem of the unremunerative branch line, and competition from motor road services was serious even in the 1920s. *How To Make The British Railways Pay* (Farrar, 1931) is the title of a book published during a period of particular crisis and numerous closures. But the withdrawal of a service was a matter for the railway company only.

Part of the intention behind nationalisation in 1947 was the amelioration of the rural transport problem, just as it was intended to solve the problem of rural electrification by deliberate cross-subsidisation. Costs would be spread over a larger system, and the criterion of social need was to have priority over commercial accounting (see Section 3(4) of the Transport Act, 1947).

This was, perhaps, a perfectly feasible policy in 1946–7; the war had in some respects helped the financial position of the railways as a whole, since it checked competition from the roads, and the railways did in fact 'pay their way' until 1952. From then onwards, as the *Reshaping* report puts it, 'the surplus on operating account declined progressively. After 1953 it became too small to meet capital charges, after 1955 it had disappeared, and by 1960 the annual loss on operating account had risen to £67.7m' (Beeching, 1963, 3.) As the overall surplus diminished, the amount available for cross-subsidisation of unremunerative services diminished with it: this plank of the nationalisation platform was giving way.

There was still hope in 1953 that freeing the British Transport Commission (BTC) from some of the shackles of the 1921 Act on its rates and charges, reorganising the management structure and embarking upon massive expenditure on modernisation would in due course enable losses to be turned into profits, while maintaining social responsibilities. But how much social conscience should the railways allow themselves in the light of their statutory duty to make their costs meet their revenues? How did one measure social needs?

It was the rural branch line that pointed up this dilemma most sharply in transport, as it was the plight of the mining village whose coal seams were running out which focused attention on the social factor in the case of the National Coal Board.

There was nothing at all in the 1947 Transport Act about branch line or station closures, and no one had thought much about it. It had not been a problem for government or any national body before. The railways were to all intents and purposes nationally operated all during the war; but the 1947 'nationalisation' – meaning their being taken into public ownership – raised public consciousness; even by 1949 there was a certain amount of newspaper and Parliamentary unease about the rights and wrongs of a public body being able to withdraw services when it chose. It would clearly be better – if only for cosmetic reasons – for the railways to have to 'make their case' to someone. That someone must surely be the Minister; yet there was nothing in the Act. Civil servants in such a situation look for precedents in analogous legislation. The closest any transport legislation came to providing for the new problem was in the procedures for abandoning a *canal*, which needed the authorisation of the Minister (which he could not give unless he was satisfied the canal was no longer necessary), and involved public notices, final dates for the lodging of objections and other formal proceedings of the kind.

But supposing this were used as a model, on what grounds might the Minister intervene in what was seen as a commercial decision for the British Transport Commission to make? And if, nevertheless, it were thought that for the quieting of public unease it was desirable that the Minister should have a role, by agreement with the Commission even if not statutorily, by what means might he be enabled to satisfy himself that a branch line was no longer necessary? There were no 'courts of inquiry' in the Act, no inspectors on his staff, except for accidents, safety and the like. But there was in the Act a power for the Minister to refer a matter 'affecting the services and facilities provided by the Commission' to the Transport Users' Consultative Committees (TUCCs) for advice. Just right, it may have seemed.

When the Committees were included in the Act, it was certainly not envisaged that closures would become their main business. They were intended to be a representative group of railway users like the other Consultative Committees in other nationalised industries, a gesture towards consumer participation in decision making, but appointed, not elected; available for consultation, but with little power to initiate business; set up at a regional level, covering quite a large area, so that they were remote from ordinary domestic consumers and travellers. In the first year or two neither the Minister nor the Commission could think of anything to consult them about. Perhaps it was convenient all round when in 1950 the Minister and the Commission came to an agreement that proposals for station and branch line closures should be approved by the appropriate Area Transport Users' Consultative Committee (ATUCC).

The agreement did not specify how the ATUCC was to set about the task; so each Committee tackled each case as it came, 'on its merits'. Some thought site inspections appropriate, some received deputations, some added to their own numbers for the occasion. In 1953 the chairmen of all the ATUCCs met to consider their procedures together for the first time and agreed on a measure of uniformity of practice, so as to avoid anomalies. From this point on there began the apparently inexorable development of a process that might be called 'creeping judicialisation'. The ATUCCs, from being ordinary committees, meeting in a committee room with an agenda and so on, became a species of public inquiry; then – since this was the decade of 'Crichel Down', when 'use of land' inquiries into compulsory purchase orders and the like were also becoming more and more judicialised – they were turned into a species of administrative tribunal, protesting all the while (it is true) that they were no such thing, but certainly being taken to be so, and in the end (until the new legislation) acting as if they were so. Their procedures grew more complex, more standardised and more formalised; they printed a single handbook of guidance for objectors; they took care over legal niceties and 'due process'.

Then, for reasons we need not go into, the Transport Act, 1962, while legitimising and regularising a great deal of all this pragmatic development of procedure, the fruit of a ten-year alliance of civil servants, railway administrators and provincial gentlemen engaged in tackling problems on their merits as they arose, pulled the rug from under the ATUCCs by taking away their decision-making power. Henceforth they were to 'report on hardship', not 'approve': and all opposed closures were to be subject to the consent of the Minister of Transport.

Very few people, in all probability, were aware that the detailed rules set out in the 1958 Central Transport Consultative Committee Handbook, for instance, had no statutory basis; nor that the powers of the Minister, before 1962, rested on no specific authority over closures of branch lines (as with canal abandonments in an earlier Act) but merely on an agreement with the BTC, backed by his quite general powers to give directions. Very few people understood, immediately, the difference in the role of the Consultative Committees after 1962: that they were now on the sidelines, and that real decisions had been centralised in the Ministry. They went on being regarded as a form of 'Railway Court', with the fate of local travellers in their hands; they had become a necessary institution.

A new chairman of the Railways Board had been appointed in June 1961, Dr Richard Beeching (now Lord Beeching), formerly technical director of ICI. One of his first acts was to commission a series of studies of railway traffic and the profitability of the several parts of the railway system. In March 1963 the Board published *The Reshaping of British Railways*, known popularly as 'The Beeching Plan', in which was envisaged a reduction of total railway route mileage from about 18,000 to about 13,000, and of stations from 7,000 to about 4,000. Among the branch lines named in the plan were two in Yorkshire, known as 'Crimple Junction to Cross Gates via Wetherby', and 'Wetherby to Church Fenton'. (For general accounts of this history, see Bonavia, 1971; Allen, 1966; Parris, 1965; Reid and Allen, 1970; Ellis, 1959; Hanson, 1961; Coombes, 1966: for 'closures' in particular, see Mills and Howe, 1960; Howe and Mills, 1960; Howe, 1964; Howe and Else, 1968; Beeching, 1963; and the Annual Reports and Handbooks of the Central Transport Consultative Committee.)

Machinery in the Ministry

We now move towards the particular decision in the case of these two lines. But an account in some detail of the machinery and procedures developed in the Ministry of Transport to advise the Minister on these decisions will be relevant.

The change from the possibility of ministerial intervention under the 1957 Act to its inevitability under the 1962 Act, in connection with any closure proposal to which formal objection had been made, necessitated staffing changes in the Ministry to handle the volume of work foreshadowed by the *Reshaping* report. Railways matters became the exclusive charge of an Under Secretary for the first time, with two Assistant Secretaries heading Railways A Division and Railways B Division, and the Railway Inspectorate, whose main duties were safety and the investigation of accidents. Railways B Division dealt with 'Section 56(8) decisions' on closures, needing the full time of about twenty-five people. (For the relevant sections of the Transport Act 1962, see Appendix.)

The Minister's specific power under the 1962 Act arose in respect of representations about 'hardship' made by a user of the service or facility whose withdrawal was proposed, and his letter of consent to or rejection of the closure carefully referred only to the report of the ATUCC and his conclusions on it. But in exercising this power the Minister was not himself limited to considering only the report from the ATUCC against the case made by the Board. In practice, although it would be extravagant to regard a decision of this sort as implying collective responsibility, the decision of the Minister would justifiably be regarded as the decision of the Government. A prime necessity therefore was the institution of a 'clearance' procedure with other government departments, who might have information relevant to future developments or intentions in their own sphere of responsibility, which it might not be possible to make public but which ought to be weighed against the past experience of the Railways Board in respect of a particular service.

Secondly, although the Government had not accepted in full the recommendations of the Select Committee on Nationalised Industries in 1960 that the responsibilities of the Railways Board should be strictly 'commercial', and that any modifications of their proposals on 'social' grounds should be placed fairly and squarely on the shoulders of the Minister, the mere fact that the Minister would now be intervening in perhaps the majority of the more important closures greatly increased the likelihood of pressures upon him to take into account factors other than either the railways' estimates of the savings that would flow from the closure or the hardship to users strictly considered: for example, the effects upon employment or rural depopulation, the effects of the transfer of traffic to the roads in terms of congestion and accidents and other such 'social' factors. Avoiding the ambiguities of the word 'social', the Ministry agreed with the other departments concerned a procedure enabling local authorities and other public bodies (such as River Boards, the Coal Board and other public corporations), and responsible persons such as Members of Parliament, to make representations on 'nonhardship' grounds, or the wider issues of a closure, not directly to the Minister of Transport, but to the department to which they would normally go on such a ground or issue (HC *Deb*. 15 May 1963, col. 1318; and 31 July 1963, col. 446; Howe, 1964, 53).

This procedure worked as follows. Although under no statutory obligation to do so, the BTC before 1962 had been in the habit of making the Ministry and the Consultative Committees fully aware of their general plans for closures and withdrawals. Section 54(1) of the 1962 Act enabled the Minister to direct the Board to make such plans public. For the two branch lines in question, this requirement had been met by their inclusion in the *Reshaping* report. After a Section 54(1) publication of a plan, the Railways Board were statutorily free to give the formal Section 56(7) notice of a total withdrawal of passenger services from a station or on a line whenever they were ready to do so. The Board agreed, however, to notify the Ministry each week of closure proposals of which formal notice would be posted in the following week. This enabled the Ministry to prepare its own list for circulation to other departments within a few days of the formal notice having been given. Each month, the Ministry sent round to departments a cumulative and consolidated list, including all closures to which the Minister had already given his consent since the 1962 Act, with the dates, and those which he had refused; and all proposals under consideration by the Minister, with columns for number of stations, date of publication of S.56(7) notice, date of ATUCC hearing, date of receipt of ATUCC report and the decision of the Minister with its date. Some of the columns on any monthly list would, of course, be blank, and would be progressively filled in as a case proceeded month by month. At the end of the document came new proposals to which objections had not then been received by the ATUCC, divided into those for which the time limit for objections had not yet expired and those for which it had.

The circulation was:

Ministry of Defence
Ministry of Defence – Army
Ministry of Defence – Navy
Ministry of Defence – RAF
Treasury
Home Office
Scottish Development Department

Ministry of Labour
Ministry of Agriculture, Fisheries and Food
Ministry of Housing and Local Government
Ministry of Power
Department of Education and Science

Ministry of Public Building and   Ministry of Health
  Works   Welsh Office
Ministry of Social Security   General Post Office
HM Customs and Excise   Department of Economic Affairs
Board of Inland Revenue

The same notice was circulated widely inside the Ministry of Transport: the other Railway Divisions, the two Nationalised Transport Divisions, Inland Transport Planning Branch, Statistics Division, the Highways Divisions, Road Passenger Transport Division, Ports Division, General Division and Regional Development Division; and also to each of the Ministry's Divisional Road Engineers in the field and to the Chairmen of the Traffic Commissioners in each Area.

The second main element in the new machinery in the Ministry was a Working Party, comprising officials from Transport and other interested departments, and for which Railways B Division acted as secretariat. This Working Party met as necessary and might consider several closures at a session, at the stage between the receipt of the ATUCC report and the Minister's decision. For each, it would have before it all the information available to the Minister: the financial and economic information supplied by the Railways Board in support of their proposal; the ATUCC report on hardship, and any suggestions for alleviating it; the report from the Ministry's own Divisional Road Engineer on road capacities and journey times by alternative transport, parking problems, effects on road transport operators, needs for road improvements and, on the other hand, benefits from the avoidance of bridge works and the like that closure might bring; the views of other government departments on defence, employment, town and country planning and other implications; any representations made by local authorities and other bodies on 'non-hardship' matters, together with the comments upon these of the appropriate department; and a brief from Railways B Division on precedents or any other relevant consideration not mopped up by all the rest.

The Working Party might have to consider a particular closure more than once and could ask for more information from any of the bodies concerned, including the ATUCC. When the Working Party had come to its own conclusions, papers would be sent up in the normal way to the Minister for his agreement to the recommendation (which might, of course, involve further meetings and consultations in difficult cases).

Under Section 56(11), the Minister in granting his consent might attach such conditions or give such directions to the Board as he thought fit, and where he attached conditions he could vary them from time to time. Directions were not used in this connection under the 1962 Act; and about the only condition the Minister placed upon his consents concerned the character and adequacy of alternative means of public transport. (In one case where he refused consent, he was influenced mainly by the high cost of bringing alternative road routes up to the standard needed for a bus service (Howe, 1964, 53; *Guardian*, 25 July 1963.)

In the two years up to the end of 1964 there were 317 Section 56(7) notices published. Five proposals gave rise to no formal objection; the Minister gave consent to 173 and withheld it from eighteen, and 121 cases were still under consideration – sixty-six by ATUCCs and fifty-five by the Minister (BRB Annual Report 1963 and 1964; Howe and Else, 1968, 132). Among the consents – indeed, the very first to be given under the 1962 Act procedure – were those in respect of the two Yorkshire lines.

The Wetherby closures: the proposal

The branch lines in question formed links between one main line and another: that from Harrogate to Leeds and that from York to Leeds. The present railway line south out of Harrogate curves south-east for two miles and then, at a point near Crimple Beck, bends very sharply right to head south-west in the general direction of Bradford. From Crimple the line used to continue in this south-easterly direction through Spofforth to Wetherby, dividing just before the town into two lines, one continuing through Thorp Arch, Newton Kyme and Tadcaster to join the York main line at Church Fenton; the other turning south through Collingham, Bardsey, Thorner, Scholes and Penda's Way stations to join the same York–Leeds main line at Cross Gates. The two lines were properly known as Crimple Junction to Cross Gates via Wetherby, and Wetherby to Church Fenton: the passenger services involved were Leeds–Harrogate via Wetherby, and Church Fenton–Wetherby.

The Church Fenton branch was the older, having been opened in 1848 by the York North Midland Railway Company, control passing to the North Eastern Railway Company (NER) in 1854. In 1866

the North Eastern Railway Company (Leeds and Wetherby Branch)
Act gave powers for the construction of a single line from Cross
Gates to join the Church Fenton branch at Wetherby, but work was
suspended in 1867 for fianancial reasons, and the line was not
opened until 1876. In 1901 the track was doubled in order to provide
a route for NER expresses between Leeds and Harrogate that did not

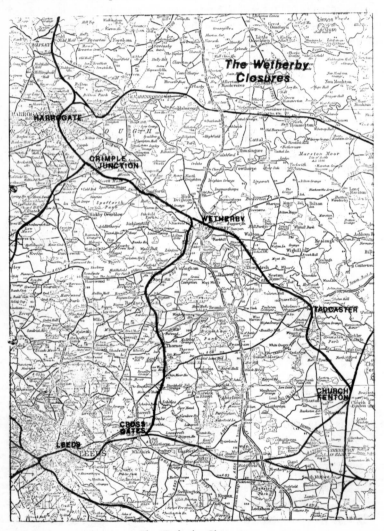

The Wetherby Closures

involve running over the Midland Company's line through Holbeck. In 1903 both companies commenced through services from London to Harrogate, the Midland from St Pancras via Leeds and Holbeck, the Great Northern from King's Cross via Doncaster, Church Fenton and Wetherby. This competition ceased some time before the 1939–45 war (Brock, 1958).

The services running over the two branches appeared in the list of services proposed for withdrawal that was published in Appendix 2 of the *Reshaping of British Railways* report in March 1963. But it had been common knowledge well before this date, among both railway staff and many of the regular passengers, that closure was being considered.

At this time these lines were in the North Eastern Region of British Railways, with its headquarters in York. The Region was divided into four operating Traffic Divisions, centred in Leeds, Newcastle, Hull and Middlesbrough: the two lines were in the Leeds Division.

Regional headquarters at this time contained a number of functional departments, grouped under four Assistant General Managers who themselves reported to the General Manager. The departmental heads who played principal parts in the narrative were the Chief Civil Engineer (CCE), the Chief Signal and Telecommunications Engineer (CS & T), the Chief Mechanical and Electrical Engineer (CM & E), the Chief Accountant, the Stores Controller and the heads of the Commercial Department and Movements Department who were themselves respectively Assistant General Manager (Commercial) and Assistant General Manager (Movements).

In each of the four Traffic Divisions, this departmental structure of the traffic departments Movements and Commercial was partly repeated, but the engineering side was not 'divisionalised' in the same way.

The initiative for a process of closure rested, in the North Eastern Region, with the Divisional Office in Leeds. But matters of this kind do not come out of the blue. The future of these services and lines, amongst others in the Division and in the Region, had been a subject of discussion for years, had been mentioned at the Monday 'management meetings' of Assistant General Managers with the General Manager in York, and had been in the minds of various people at Division and at Region concerned with locomotive and rolling stock deployment, passenger and freight traffic planning, and so on – in particular, the Movements Assistant and the Technical Assistant who worked directly to the General Manager as part of his long-term planning staff. It might be arbitrary, therefore, to give a date to when awareness of declining ticket sales and traffic on the lines through Wetherby turned into an intention to begin the process of withdrawing the services.

The North Eastern Region was accustomed to taking a traffic census on two occasions each year, one in July and one in October, for the purpose of identifying lightly used trains in a service. (Such a census generally involves the counting of the number of passengers joining and alighting from each train at each station on each day in two separate weeks, one during the summer service period and one during the winter service period: for each period a representative weekday (Mondays to Fridays) is chosen, the figures for Saturday and Sunday being shown separately.) In these instances the surveys were taken in the weeks of 8–14 July and 21–27 October 1962, and it was the information provided by this census that appeared in the Heads of Information in the closure procedure for the use of the Minister, the ATUCC and the objectors.

An extract from this information will illustrate its form. The number of passengers joining and alighting at each station on the Leeds to Harrogate via Wetherby journey, on the Monday of the October week selected, for each of the four trains which constituted the daily service (with the total for the day), can be seen in the table below. This pattern, of a reasonably heavy traffic only between Leeds (City) and Cross Gates, along the main line from Leeds to York before the branch line proper began, and of empty trains at off-peak hours, was typical of the other days and of the traffic in the opposite direction.

Divisional Office was, of course, well aware of this aspect of the Leeds–Harrogate via Wetherby service, and of the need to retain as much as possible of this heavy commuter passenger traffic for the railways. Accordingly, Division's planning for the closure included the proposal that certain trains between Leeds and York should stop additionally at Cross Gates.

Another feature of railway operation over the Crimple Junction to Cross Gates line had to be taken into account. Through trains from Newcastle to Liverpool via Harrogate and Leeds used the Wetherby line instead of the alternative line via Arthington, no longer because of inter-company financial considerations but so that when they entered Leeds (City) station they would be facing west, and avoid

Time dep. Leeds	7.26am			12.20pm			4.17pm			5.35pm			Total		
	J	A	LS	J	A	LS	J	A	LS	J	A	LS	J	A	LS
Leeds (City)	16	–	16	38	–	38	38	–	38	213	–	213	305	–	305
Cross Gates	2	4	14	1	29	10	12	20	30	7	119	101	22	172	155
Penda's Way	2	12	4	–	8	2	1	11	20	2	49	54	5	80	80
Scholes	–	2	2	–	1	1	2	8	14	–	22	32	2	33	49
Thorner	1	–	3	1	1	1	–	3	11	1	5	28	3	9	43
Bardsey	–	2	1	–	1	–	–	1	10	2	5	25	2	9	36
Collingham Bridge	1	1	1	–	–	–	–	1	9	–	10	15	1	12	25
Wetherby	–	1		–	–		–	9		2	13	4	2	23	4
Spofforth										1	2	3	1	2	3
Harrogate										–	3		–	3	

J = joining   A = alighting   LS = leaving station

having the locomotive 'run around the train' before it could proceed. With diesel locomotives, whose controls are duplicated at each end, this is no longer the expensive and time-consuming operation it was under steam; but passengers who came into Leeds sitting 'back-to-engine' would find themselves going on to Liverpool 'facing-the-engine'. This situation did obtain for a short time after the closure of the Wetherby line. However, since the closure also of the line from Northallerton to Harrogate through Ripon, all through trains between Newcastle and Liverpool now travel via York. On the other of the two lines, between Church Fenton and Wetherby, there was but one train a day, on weekdays only, leaving Church Fenton at 7.44 am. On the Monday of the census week, it carried seven people, four of whom got off at Tadcaster.

Formal discussions with the trade unions and with staff had begun earlier in 1962 at Leeds, in order to ensure that employees were fully informed and to invite their suggestions on postings, regradings and the other effects of a closure on the locally employed railwaymen. Fairly detailed negotiations had taken place with the Traffic Officer of the principal bus undertaking running services in the area. The area was, in fact, densely covered by bus routes, operating at hourly or half-hourly intervals; and it was agreed between Division and the several undertakings that there appeared to be no need for any additional bus services to be offered in connection with the proposal for closure.

The assembling of this data for presentation in the Heads of Information was centralised at Regional Headquarters, and was the responsibility of Traffic Facilities Investigation subsection, in Movement Department in York. The subsection organised the taking of the census, prepared the statement of the comparative cost to passengers and the comparative time taken by rail and by alternative public road services (simple extracts from the published time-tables and fare schedules), and the statement of estimates of financial savings. In the form agreed at this time, the statement for these two services said, *in toto*:

Annual earnings	£9,200
Annual direct expenses	£57,700

Planning to cater for the consequences of the closure on the operation of the rest of the system proceeded into 1963 and it was not until 2 June 1963 that the decision to publish the formal notice of intention to withdraw these services was taken at a 'management meeting' of heads of Departments, and notification of the decision given to Divisions and BRB headquarters. The advance notification under the procedure agreed at this period was received in the Ministry of Transport on 7 June, and the formal S.56(7) notice was first published on 14 June 1963.

Under S.56 the Railways Board was required to give at least six weeks' formal notice of the intention to withdraw services in two newspapers circulating in the area affected for two successive weeks, as well as to send copies of the notice to the Area Transport Users Consultative Committee. The promulgation of the formal notice in practice was much wider than this: in the North Eastern Region copies were habitually sent to Members of Parliament for the constituencies affected, to the Traffic Commissioners for the area, to all local authorities in the area and to other public bodies and large industrial firms as users of the service; to the Trade Union Congress, the National Parks Commission, the National Farmers' Union, the Commercial Travellers' Association, the General Post Office in London and the Regional Director of Postal Services in Leeds, and to Union International (for international freight traffic). Posters of the formal notice were displayed on every railway station directly affected and some others.

The formal notice is reproduced as an appendix to this volume. Its significant dates were 9 September 1963 for the proposed withdrawal of passenger services and 3 August as the last date for objections to be lodged with the Secretary of the ATUCC. The Secretary of the TUCC for the Yorkshire Area, whose office was in

York, in fact received the first objection on 20 June and notified the Regional Railway Board and the Ministry that an objection had been received on the same day, adding in his letter to the former a request for the Heads of Information in respect of these proposed closures. On 11 July he received this document, some forty foolscap pages, and sent copies of it the following day to the Chairman and members of the Consultative Committee, to the local MPs, the Traffic Commissioners, the bus companies, the Central Office of Information (Leeds) for transmission to the national press and to the objectors who had by then made themselves known and others as they appeared.

Twenty-two objections were lodged before the period expired, fifteen of which would appear to be from private persons and seven by representative bodies: Barwick-in-Elmet Parish Council, Tadcaster Rural District Council, City of Leeds Labour Party, a body of 113 users of Scholes Station, the Amalgamated Engineering Union (Leeds District), Leeds Corporation and Harrogate Constituency Labour Party.

As objections came in they were allotted a number by the Secretary of the ATUCC, and a full copy of each objection was sent to the Regional Board with a request for their comments. A copy also went to each member of the ATUCC. As soon as the last date for objections was past, a Summary of Written Objections was prepared by the Secretary, taking the form of broad parallel columns. In the first column were listed a number of 'Grounds for Objection' found to be common to several objectors, grouped under headings: 'Buses General', 'Bus Services', 'Railways', 'Use of Private Cars' and 'General'. The second column gave the reference number of the objections in which a particular 'ground' was mentioned, and the third, 'British Railways' Comments'.

Twenty-seven distinct 'grounds' are listed. The first, under 'Buses General', is:

Bus services not a satisfactory alternative to rail for distances of 15 miles and above. Reasons – frequent stops; not possible to read; uneven temperatures due to doors being frequently opened and closed; vibration; smoke-laden atmosphere; overcrowding; unreliability in snow and fog.

British Railways' comment is:

Not sufficient people are prepared to pay for a higher standard of comfort to make rail travel profitable. The standard provided by buses is comparable to that in other parts of the country but it is not possible to guarantee any passenger a seat. Problems of peak periods are common throughout the country. Trains as well as buses suffer delays in bad weather. The Railways contend they should not be expected to maintain uneconomic services merely because rail travel is safer and more reliable in adverse weather.

Under 'Bus Services' there are a number of objections to the adequacy of the alternative means of transport suggested, in that on many journeys changes of bus or detours are necessary. British Railways do not deny this, but point out that in some of the cases mentioned *bus* routes have been withdrawn and licences surrendered because of lack of support. Under 'Railways', there are objections on the ground that the *existing* service was in itself unattractive; that more frequent and more comfortable trains would have attracted enough traffic to make them pay; that rail buses and unstaffed halts should be tried; that since through trains to Liverpool use the line, keeping local stations open would help to cover expenses; and there are proposals for new trains and new timings. It is unnecessary to quote the Railways' comments; they can be imagined. To objections that withdrawing the rail services would increase congestion on the roads and in Leeds, the Railways offer no comment.

Since the ATUCC was not *required* to hold a hearing (though if it heard oral evidence at all it had to do so in public), it was necessary for the Chairman to decide formally that there would be a public hearing. Its date was fixed for Tuesday, 20 August 1963, in the ballroom of the Old Swan Hotel, in Harrogate. The objectors were individually advised of its date and place, and invited to state whether they would be present or represented. A list of persons who might be expected to be present and to speak, and on whose behalf, was prepared by the Secretary for the use of the Committee.

The hearing was neither protracted nor very lively. It began after morning coffee and was all over by lunch-time (11 am to 12.30 pm). Forty people attended, besides the members of the ATUCC, twenty men from Press, radio and TV, and nine representatives of the railway and road service undertakings. Here is a local newspaper's account of the proceedings:

FIRST RAILWAY CLOSURES COURT

Objections heard at Harrogate.

'Our duty is not to see that lines are closed as quickly as possible, but to be quite sure, if and when closures are decided upon, that the public are reasonably protected and have adequate facilities.'

This was stated by Gen. Sir Roy Bucher, former president of the British Legion, when he opened in the ballroom of Harrogate Old Swan Hotel, today, the first 'railway court' to hear objections to proposed rail closures.

It was convened by the Yorkshire Area Transport Users Consultative Committee, and concerned the proposed withdrawals of the passenger services between Church Fenton and Wetherby, and Harrogate to Crossgates, Leeds via Wetherby.

Soon similar hearings will be held throughout Britain as 11 other Area Committees sit to sift protests against line closures.

So far, 97 cases have been listed for hearing between now and Christmas.

British Railways gave the following statistics about the two lines under consideration today: total yearly running expenses, £57,700, total takings £9,200. The first line carries two trains a day – one passenger, one goods. The second carries six passenger trains up daily, five down, and four through expresses plus goods trains.

Sir Roy Bucher, who is chairman of the committee, said it was their task to hear objections and report direct to the Minister on any hardship they considered would be caused by the withdrawal of the services, in the light of alternative services available or proposed.

One objector to the proposed closure of the Church Fenton–Wetherby line was Coun. A. J. Dyer (Knaresborough) who is prospective Labour Parliamentary candidate for the Harrogate division.

He said the train journey took less than half an hour, whereas by bus, it would take 90 minutes.

'Rattle-Traps'

One objector, Mr Frank Biller, 61, a brewery taxation adviser, of Kirk Deighton, said that for three years he travelled daily from his home to Leeds by bus.

'After three years I decided I had had just enough of it. I found the journey tiring and monotonous. There was no opportunity to wile away the time by reading and, in the early days, the buses were rattle-traps.

'No bus company has yet found a way of heating a bus properly in winter. I consider the double-decker bus is an anachronism, a leviathan on the road.

'After three years I decided to travel by train. I did not get as good a service, but I did achieve a comfortable, pleasant journey, so that when I got to the office I was in a position to start a day's work feeling refreshed after the journey.

'Stops and Starts'

'The bus is not a suitable alternative service, but only one as can be regarded as a proper means of travel for short journeys.

'All the stopping and startings get on one's nerves.'

After a number of other people had objected to the withdrawal of trains or the modification of services, the chairman said the committee's report would go to the Minister of Transport. (*Yorkshire Evening Press*, Tuesday 20 August 1963, p. 5)

Immediately after the public meeting, the Consultative Committee met in private and arrived without great difficulty at the broad conclusions of their report. A draft was drawn up within two days by the Secretary of the ATUCC and sent to the Chairman and members; the report was signed by the Chairman and Secretary on 6 September 1963 and transmitted to the Minister of Transport on 9 September. Copies of the report were sent to British Railways Board headquarters in London, to the Regional Board, the Central Transport Consultative Committee and the secretaries of all the other ATUCCs. The actual report of the Consultative Committee to the Minister must remain confidential, but a Press statement released on 12 September to the Central Office of Information, the principal objectors, and those who had spoken at the hearing, said that the Committee had reached the conclusion on the Harrogate–Leeds via Wetherby service, that

the proposal would cause hardship to the few regular rail users from Harrogate and Spofforth, but in view of the small numbers concerned, they were unable to suggest means of alleviating this hardship if the railway service was withdrawn.

The Committee also considered representations that the proposal would cause hardship to people now using other stations on the line, but they were of the opinion that this could not be fully substantiated except perhaps as being minor hardship. They have, however, drawn the Minister of Transport's attention to undoubted inconveniences which, in their opinion, could be caused by the withdrawal of the passenger rail service.

On the Church Fenton–Wetherby service, the Committee could find no evidence that the proposal would cause hardship.

Because of the Official Secrets Act, and because communications between Government departments on such matters should remain confidential, it is not possible to say what observations were meanwhile being received by Railways B Division in the Ministry of Transport from other departments, including those collected by other departments from local authorities and other bodies on 'nonhardship' grounds; or what advice was tendered by the Divisional Road Engineer in Leeds or other officials of the Ministry.

To some extent, it can be conjectured. There was a well-known RAF airfield at Church Fenton and other defence establishments at Harrogate and elsewhere in the area. There was a Royal Ordnance Factory at Barnbow near Cross Gates and a former Ordnance Factory (now a Trading Estate, but containing the British Library Lending Division) at Thorp Arch near Boston Spa, served by the Church Fenton–Wetherby line. Bardsey, Collingham and other villages are rapidly being developed with well-to-do housing for Leeds commuters: the area is not one subject to rural depopulation. The A1 dual carriageway trunk road, and the main road traffic routes from the West Riding conurbation to Teesside, Tyneside and the coastal resorts at Scarborough and Bridlington run through the area, are already heavily loaded and are programmed for improvement – to which railway bridges and level crossings are notorious obstacles. There are no places served by these lines which were due for industrial expansion and only Harrogate is a notable resort, continuing to enjoy rail service by other lines. It seems unlikely, on the whole, that there could have been any strong case, on defence, employment, industrial location or town and country planning grounds, for keeping the lines open.

The consent

The Minister's consent to the withdrawal of services on both lines was not, in any event, long in coming. It was conveyed in a letter signed by the head of Railways B Division on the direction of the Minister, addressed to the Secretary of the British Railways Board, dated 18 October 1963: the letter is reproduced in an appendix to this volume. BRB Headquarters sent copies of the 'consent' letter to York, under a covering letter of 20 October which formally asked the General Manager of the North Eastern Region to arrange to keep the Secretary informed of any proposal for altering any of the existing or additional bus services, so that he might notify the Minister as required by the conditions attached to the consent.

On 22 October Assistant General Manager (Movements) at York sent a preliminary advice of the consent, promising later advice of the date of implementation, to the following:
Assistant General Manager (Commercial)
Chief Civil Engineer
Chief Signal and Telecommunications Engineer
Chief Mechanical and Electrical Engineer
Chief Accountant
Estate Surveyor
Public Relations and Publicity Officer
Internal Auditor
Treasurer, Cash Section, York
Establishment and Staff Officer
Stores Controller
Paper and Printing Officer, Eversholt House, London NW1
Divisional Manager, Leeds
Divisional Manager, Newcastle
Divisional Manager, Hull
Divisional Manager, Middlesbrough
with copies to other sections in York HQ, e.g. Local Passenger Services Section, Timetable Section, Works Section.

Although a date for the withdrawal of the services had been, according to the statute, included in the original formal notice, the first objection had invalidated it. Once consent had been received, therefore, the first major decision to be taken by Regional HQ was the date for actual withdrawal of passenger services. This might depend primarily on the problems involved in providing additional alternative services where these were a condition of the consent; or, if no additional services were required (as in this case), it might depend mainly upon the introduction of necessary amendments to published timetables. (In one case closure has followed consent within two weeks, and several within a month, but the average is two to three months.)

For the Wetherby services, it was agreed between the responsible sections under the Assistant General Managers (Movements) and (Commercial) that passenger services could be withdrawn on 6 January 1964; and this date was confirmed at a Monday 'management meeting' at York HQ in November. British Railways Board were informed accordingly and an advice was sent to all Departments and Divisions on 27 November 1963 by the Assistant General Manager (Movements); in practice, by the head of Traffic Facilities Section on his behalf. Traffic Facilities Section then initiated procedures to inform all UK railway stations and booking offices, the General Post Office, the ATUCC and the addressees of the original formal proposal for closure notice.

The operation

From about this point onwards, the story begins to fragment and ramify too much to be continued as a single narrative: and for the main purpose, it would contain much redundant detail. The layman, by a small exercise of imagination, can envisage some of the consequences of a decision to withdraw services on a railway branch line and close its stations, from the obvious, concerning the redeployment of locomotives and rolling stock, the retirement or transfer of staff, the amendment of timetable and fares handbooks and station posters, to the perhaps less obvious, including the reallocation of leave rosters, the reorganisation of parcels and postal services, the rerouting of signal and telecommunications circuits, the effects (immediate and long-lasting) upon the railway police, advertisement hoarding contracts, the printing of tickets, and a host of other such details. It might not occur to the layman (unless a railway enthusiast) that one of the people to be informed is the Keeper of Historical Records, and that one of the actions to be taken in advance of the published date for the final services to be run is to send a stock inspector along the line to spot items of high value (intrinsic and extrinsic) and have them removed to safe keeping as soon as possible. Among items of high intrinsic value is copper wire; the main items of high extrinsic value are the collectors' items (lamps, nameplates, etc.) which may later be sold at auction.

It will have to suffice to say that each of these matters, and the hundred other such not mentioned, fell to be dealt with as they arose by the section of the appropriate HQ Department and of Divisional Office in Leeds that was accustomed and equipped to deal with it, having been alerted to the possibility by the advice circulated on 27 November 1963. Shortly after the date of ending of service was known, the head of Traffic Facilities Section called a meeting of representatives of the interested internal sections – Local Passenger Services, Timetables, Rolling Stock, Works and others – and of Leeds Divisional Office, which was attended also by a representative of the GPO Parcels and Mails service. This meeting was not for the purpose of giving instructions to each section on the actions to be taken, for the sections were relied on to be aware of what needed to be done, but to spot snags and unusual features of this particular operation that might produce a need for positive co-ordination.

The case history will be continued by following the action taken in one particular Department; and the Department chosen is that of the Chief Civil Engineer, since its action produced effects perhaps more overtly manifest to the outside observer. The Chief Civil Engineer was responsible for the recovery of the physical assets: track, equipment and buildings. To narrow it down further, the story of only one of the sections of line involved in the closure, that between Crimple Junction and Cross Gates, will be told.

The last passenger train ran on the line, as scheduled, on 6 January 1964. However, the line remained open for freight traffic. The decision concerning whether to keep the line open indefinitely for freight traffic only was a wholly commercial one: was business enough to warrant it? At a meeting of the Works Progress Committee (chaired by Regional Planning Manager, containing representatives of Movements, Commercial and Technical Departments) on 9 March 1964, Commercial Department indicated that there was no case for retaining the line for freight traffic only. It was agreed at that meeting to submit proposals for the abandonment of the line, and that the date for withdrawal of freight service would be 27 April 1964. This date was published to customers – mainly coal merchants, timber dealers and the like – by direct communication and by notices at the stations, and freight service was indeed withdrawn on 27 April 1964.

The work of recovering track and the demolition of buildings, and so on, required expenditures and allocations of labour and equipment of an order greater than could be absorbed in the cost limits up to which each principal officer was allowed to authorise work. It therefore needed North Eastern Regional Board authorisation. On 22 April 1964 Chief Civil Engineer received from Movements Planning Manager a formal request for an estimate of costs for the work of recovery of track and demolition of buildings, with drawings; this letter was copied to all interested departments. At the same time, Estates Surveyor and Chief Signal and Telecommunications Engineer received similar requests for estimates; and at a meeting of the Works Planning and Progress subcommittee on 1 May 1964, Movements Planning Manager was instructed to prepare the physical programme of the abandonment.

During June the Chief Civil Engineer's Permanent Way Adviser carried out an assessment of the track, listing the dates of laying of the various sections, the type of rail and sleeper, its condition – whether re-usable and if so, on what category of line it could be re-used – with total mileages in each category tabulated. Chief Civil Engineer asked Estate Surveyor to indicate which assets (station buildings, weighbridges, coal cells, etc.) he wished to retain for sale or lease; and Bridge Engineer was consulted as to whether metallic bridge superstructures should be regarded as scrap or could be considered for re-use. (Masonry and concrete slab bridge decks are not usually considered for recovery because of the high cost of demolition.)

Drawings and estimates were sent to Movements Planning Manager by Chief Civil Engineer on 11 June, and Estates and Rating Surveyor replied on 15 June, listing his requirements for the removal of buildings and other recoverable assets, and listing also fencing works required at the junctions. A few extracts will illustrate:

Cross Gates East Junction: fence to be erected across closed Branch opposite Marshall Avenue.
Penda's Way: total removal. Station access hand-gate to be secured.
Scholes: no demolition or works required.

Collingham Bridge: the following to be removed:
Down side platform and waiting shed
Footbridge No. 39
Station coal house and lamp room
Make good with post and rail fencing after removal of foot-
bridge. Secure gates at Station Level Crossing if not already
secured.
Prospect Tunnel (*Bridge No. 34*). Tunnel ends to be bricked up
and access doors formed in new end walls.

This letter also deals with signal boxes, bridges and level crossings
on the whole length of the two lines. Similar documents were pre-
pared by Chief Signal and Telecommunications Engineer; and on 16
June Movements Planning Manager submitted the works project to
Assistant General Manager (Technical), with copies to interested
Departments.

On 27 June a memorandum summarising all this information and
recommending the recovery of the track and other assets was submitted to the members of the Regional Railway Board; and at their
meeting on 3 July 1964 the Board duly authorised the work.

Meanwhile, Assistant Engineer (Permanent Way) had on 14 May
1964 recommended the use of 13,000 yards of track from the
Crimple Junction–Cross Gates branch for use on the relaying of
track north of Newcastle, and Chief Civil Engineer had informed
District Engineer, Newcastle. On 18 June Chief Civil Engineer asked
General Manager for advance authority to recover this amount of
track and this was given on 19 June. A meeting took place on 3 July
between Chief Civil Engineer and District Engineers (Newcastle) and
(York) at which arrangements were made for the recovery of this
length of track to be treated as a separate exercise, beginning on 9
August and finishing by 13 December 1964. District Engineer (York)
was advised by Chief Civil Engineer on 10 July regarding the programming of this work, and District Engineer and District Manager
(York) met on 15 July to settle arrangements for the provision of
engine power, manning, and so on.

On the same day, as it happened, 15 July 1964, the main Works
Order was issued by General Manager to Chief Civil Engineer, with
copies to Chief Accountant, Estate and Rating Surveyor, Chief
Signal and Telecommunications Engineer, Movements Planning
Manager and Chief Mechanical and Electrical Engineer. The Order
is a printed form, headed by the printed words: 'I hereby give

authority for the work described below to be carried out:', and under 'Nature of Work' there was typed: 'Recovery of redundant track and other assets between Cross Gates Junction and Crimple Junction'. The Order also gives the book value of the railway formation for transfer from Operational to Non-operational account, and the net estimated cost of the work.

The work thus authorised, however, was not the subject of a single works programme or contract, which might be followed through the documents from this point to its completion. The lines, as it were, began to lose their identity and became a quarry first of recoverable assets and then of disposable assets, including scrap, and finally (in logic though not always in time) of land and remaining buildings, each asset tending then to be associated with other assets of a similar type from other locations, rather than with assets of other types at this location, and its recovery or disposal fitting into a programme or contract determined by convenience or by the most economic use of resources, rather than by a timetable concerning the Crimple Junction to Cross Gates line specifically. This pattern was in no way peculiar to this closure: it is the regular pattern. The Works Order has an accounting and budgeting significance more than a works programming significance.

So it was Chief Civil Engineer's responsibility, following the Permanent Way Adviser's assessment of the line, to decide how and when any part of the track would be recovered or disposed of. Mention has already been made of the recovery of track for use north of Newcastle, which proceeded as arranged. As another illustration, in January 1965 Chief Civil Engineer received a request from District Engineer (West Riding) for the recovery of crossings ('points') for use in his district. This was authorised, but it was not programmed until June 1965; on 8 June District Engineer (York) was advised of the date for the recovery of named points and crossings from the branch and asked to supply the necessary manpower.

Estate Surveyor, having been supplied with precise details of the property to be abandoned, had the responsibility for the management and maintenance of the lengths of disused railway and station sites until they were sold. It was consequently his interest to see that such sites as could be sold should be disposed of as soon as practicable. Meanwhile, however, certain assets – mainly ballast – attracted the interest of potential purchasers, who did not wish to buy the land but only to enter on it and remove what they wanted. Contracts of this kind were negotiated by Chief Supplies and Contracts Officer at British Railways Board in London, on the advice of Estate Surveyor at York; and on 21 January 1965, for instance, Estate Surveyor wrote to Chief Supplies and Contracts Officer about several such possibilities on three distinct disused railway lines in the vicinity of Leeds, including a part of the Wetherby branch line, mentioning the names of the firms interested, and mentioning also that terms of sale had already been agreed for the land and buildings in a particular area (at one of the stations on the Crimple Junction–Cross Gates line, coloured red on a plan accompanying the letter), and that that area must be excluded from any extraction activity and entry on it forbidden.

The letter goes on, in paragraphs that were common to several such letters, to remind Chief Supplies and Contracts Officer that it would be undesirable to allow arrangements for retrieval of ballast that could endure for long periods without provision for termination, since this might inhibit sale of the sites; and that contracts should include provision for site restoration and making good of any damage to fences, culverts, etc., compensation for injury or inconvenience of adjoining landowners, and the protection of pipes, wires or cables on the site. Extraction of ballast is assessable for local rating, and the party given the permission to extract should be made responsible for making any such payments. Planning permission was also required, and the Minister's consent was required before any part of the formations were sold. Estate Surveyor asked, finally, that he be given an opportunity for comment before any arrangements with firms were concluded, and that he be supplied in due course with full particulars of the arrangements and the precise extent of railway property which they covered.

The disposal of remaining removeable assets (after usable track, crossings, bridge superstructures, signalling equipment, buildings and so on, have been recovered by works programmes of Chief Civil Engineer and other Departments at Regional HQ, and subject to any contracts for the removal of ballast, etc., concluded by Chief Supplies and Contracts Officer) became the responsibility of Scrap Sales Controller at British Railways Board HQ in London. On 29 July 1965 Scrap Sales Controller inquired about the position on the Crimple Junction–Cross Gates section, and asked for a schedule of materials remaining, with a view to the letting of a single contract for their 'uplifting'.

This schedule was prepared by Chief Civil Engineer and sent to London on 8 September 1965, requesting that an uplifting contract be arranged. The items included 45,000 yards of track, concerning which detailed advice was given on how access could be achieved, as well as details of its type; demolition and removal of eighteen bridge superstructures, with the aggregate weights of the several materials involved; about 300 timber telegraph poles; concrete platform supports, buildings including signal boxes, waiting sheds, cabins, weigh offices, etc.; mile posts, to be recovered where still *in situ.*. Copies were sent to General Manager, Stores Controller, Estate Surveyor, Chief Signal and Telecommunications Engineer and Chief Mechanical and Electrical Engineer, all at York, and to District Engineer (West Riding).

This contract was, in fact, let on 2 November 1965, and by March 1966 it was two-thirds completed. Day-to-day supervision of the work of the contractors, ensuring that the contract was being satisfactorily carried out, was the responsibility of District Engineer (West Riding), through his Permanent Way Inspector. The certificate of completion of this contract was dated 22 March 1967.

Recovery of the remaining ballast was not, however, included in this contract. On 3 March 1966 District Engineer was asked for a schedule of the type and quantity of ballast available for sale, and sent this information to Scrap Sales Controller on 12 March, indicating that ballast recovery should begin on the competition of the track, etc. recovery contract. The sites were not declared 'non-operational' (allowing Estate Surveyor to sell any land and buildings left at the best advantage he could obtain) until the very end of 1967. The pattern of actual sale and conversion was not determinable for some time after.

CHAPTER 4

Models and Sequences

So ended the railway age in Tadcaster and Wetherby: a finite, relatively brief and now completed part of their considerable history as route staging posts. But this is not a book about the history of railways or of Yorkshire towns. Let us see what the narrative can tell us about the implementation process in bureaucracies.

Building models

When reviewing the literature of implementation in Chapter 2, we saw that each of the treatments by different authors had an underlying model (mainly either pyramidal or reticular in conception) made up of assumptions about a number of elements. First, about the nature of the process of implementation – a number of stages of development or an assembled chain of events; second, about the ordering or sequence of such stages or events; third, about the character of each stage or group of events (the way in which it was taken to differ from the others in the same process); fourth, about the nature of the transition between stages or links in the chain (how progress is made); and fifth, about the relationship of the process of implementation to 'authority'. Differing assumptions about each element created the different accounts of the implementation process.

Most of us, it is safe to assert, whether we are authors of books about implementation or utter laymen in these matters, have some notion in our minds of what this process must be; what the connections are between the realms of high public controversy (say, the argument over whether running a railway is to be a commercial business or a social service), and the ordinary tasks of the workaday world (including loading ballast from a disused railway track into a lorry, perhaps). From a myriad of snippets of experience we have derived enough understanding of the nature of these connections to enable us to make sense not only of a narrative like the case-study, but of our everyday life. Indeed, we need some such method of handling our experiences before we can learn anything from them, and if we do not find ways of learning from our experiences we are pretty helpless. But it is not at all necessary that we should be able to put such ideas into words or even to think thoughts about them:

> Having a particular way of dealing with the world is not, of course, the same thing as being able to make verbal statements about it. People who are highly skilled, physically or socially, are often quite incapable of formulating why they do certain things when. Being adapted to one's environment does not pre-suppose being able to describe it. (*Berger and Seaborne, 1966, 65*)

Where a 'particular way of dealing with the world' is nevertheless widely shared, so that most people can communicate through it, we might call it the 'common sense' of the matter. If, now, we were to interrogate a respectable sample of Europeans and Americans using a suitable series of questions to elicit whatever 'common sense' there is on how high-level decisions are linked with ordinary everyday work activities, it seems very likely that what would emerge would be an assumption that the high-level decisions somehow *contain* the lower-level activities, that the latter are derivable from, or follow logically from, the former; and secondly, a not-too-explicit assumption that the gap between high-level decision and low-level work is bridged by a succession of relatively small transformations, so that the earlier decision develops bit by bit into the later actions. The 'common sense' account, that is, sees the process as one that goes from the general to the specific, from the broad to the narrow, as, indeed, a processing of the general *into* the specific, each step or stage a little more pragmatic than that preceding. Some respondents might identify the stages with the ranks of an organisational hierarchy of authority – the general at the top, the 'real work' at the bottom. Some would assume that the process involves a progressive narrowing of the horizon of choice, or discretion, with the 'top' being virtually unlimited, the 'bottom' having very little discretion or freedom of action.

Some particularly thoughtful respondents might qualify the 'common sense' notion in various ways, noting, for instance, that account has to be taken of the fact that people can learn from their earlier mistakes, that it is necessary to find out whether a proposal 'will work' before deciding on it, and so on. They will want to incorporate the idea of 'feedback' from the 'bottom' modifying the decisions at the 'top'. Or they may note that the 'higher' realms are not just different in degree of discretion from the 'lower' realms, or earlier in time, but are of a different *kind* (quality, character) and need different orders of skill, experience and material attributes.

These ideas, it will be clear, are not, in fact, taken from any such public opinion survey, but from some of the writers discussed in Chapter 2, in particular, those who adopted a 'doctrine of stages' within a 'pyramid image'.

What we would not expect to hear from the man in the street would be the kind of answer produced by March and Simon, or Pressman and Wildavsky: that the process of connection is one of assembling a number of *given* actions or groupings of actions, one of constructing a 'chain' from elements that are not in themselves derived from, or contained in, or do not follow from, the particular decision or policy to be implemented. Such an understanding is not contrary to reason but it is not 'common sense' either.

Let us see which of these two major sets of assumptions – that the process of implementation is developmental or that it is aggregative – is the more enlightening, or fruitful, when applied to the case study material.

Development

It is undeniable that there was a connection, a relationship of cause and effect, between the activity which could have been observed at one of the stations on the former Crimple Junction–Cross Gates line in May 1966, when a team of workmen belonging to a contractor were loading ballast on to a small fleet of lorries, and the decision of the Cabinet in 1960 that the railway system 'must not be allowed to become an intolerable burden on the national economy' and that, accordingly, a programme of branch line and station closures was necessary. The men would not have been shovelling ballast unless the rails themselves had been removed; the rails would not have been removed unless it had been decided that no trains would ever again run over that track; that decision would not have been made unless the Minister's consent to closure had been received; the Minister would not have consented unless he had been satisfied that the hardship likely to result from closure did not outweigh the financial saving; he would not have been so satisfied unless the Area Transport Users Consultative Committee had advised as they did; the ATUCC would not have been consulted unless there had been objectors to the Railway Board's proposal to close the line; the Railway Board would not have made the proposal in the way it did had not the line been scheduled in the Beeching report; the Beeching report would not have been commissioned and made in the absence of the political climate engendered by the Cabinet decision.

That is to say, each event in the sequence was a condition of the succeeding event's taking place. But this does not imply that it was either a *necessary* or a *sufficient* condition, that a succeeding event of another kind might not equally well have satisfied the condition, and so extended the sequence in a different way from what actually happened, or that a later event that actually happened might not have happened anyway following another kind of prior event. We can be sure neither that these precise later events *had to* follow these earlier events, not that precisely these earlier events *had to* precede these later events. Although one can trace backwards in the way described above once the events have occurred, that is not at all the same as describing the process as it rolls forward, much less being able to predict from knowledge of the process what event will occur next, before it does occur.

Nor, even if an event is a necessary condition of a succeeding event, is it entailed that it is a substantive influence upon, or a limitation of or constraint upon the *content* of, the succeeding event. The relationship might merely be that the later event cannot occur before the earlier event has occurred; that is, the time order is fixed, but otherwise the events may be independent of each other.

The 'developmental assumption' implicit in many of the accounts of the implementation process postulates a good deal more than the fixed time order of a series. It says that the *nature* of a succeeding step is uniquely determined by the nature of the preceding step. It could not, in the circumstances, be other than it is. Perhaps the analogy (conscious or unconscious) is with the way a single-cell egg develops into a full-term baby, chick or whatever.

The fertilised human egg, it is fairly well established, begins to divide immediately on conception, forming two cells, then four, then eight and so on, until by the time the 'blastocyst' is ready to implant itself in the uterus wall it is a hollow sphere of many cells, only some of which become the baby. Cell division continues and some of the new cells become the sites where, for example, the left leg will develop. The question is, how is this differentiation engineered?

It is comparatively easy to grasp how the first cell (the egg) can do nothing but divide. It contains within it the two sets of parental genes, the entire instructions for developing not only the baby but also the child and the adult, with all his or her inherited characteristics of appearance, gait and many other idiosyncrasies. Perhaps the chromosomes that carry the genetic code also carry the instructions on the 'order of development'? But we are assured that the chromosomes do not differ from cell to cell in the developing embryo: they are coded into not only the fertilised ovum but every cell in the body, at this and all later stages including the mature adult – and also into the cells of the blastocyst which do *not* become any part of the embryo. So the differentiating mechanism is not in the chromosomes themselves or even in the cells as such.

Transplanting experiments (not on human embryos) suggest that, in a very early (or 'young') embryo, cells from the site of the future leg will, when transplanted to the site of the future arm, become arm. But in an 'older' embryo, where the leg is already developing, cells transplated from it to the developing arm will not become arm but will continue to become leg. The number of cell divisions since ovum (the 'age' of the embryo) is apparently significant in determining what a particular cell population will become. (If the reader can bear with the biology a bit longer, the relevance will be explained.)

The differentiating mechanism is part age (time), part location (space). In amphibians, the lining tissue of the mouth site forms the teeth, but it does so only if it is in contact with neighbouring cells of the mouth. At the due time the chemical signals from the underlying cells, as they divide, trigger a chemical response in the cells above that leads them to develop as teeth. Once that response has been triggered, teeth is all they *can* become. And whatever the chemical trigger is, it is apparently not species-specific: it will trigger teeth development in different species. Cells from the teeth site of a frog (which has horny teeth), transplanted under the right conditions to the teeth site of a newt (which has bony teeth), will be triggered to become teeth, but they will be frog teeth, not newt teeth.

'Young' embryo cells retain the capability of becoming either leg cells or arm cells, depending upon where they find themselves; older embryo cells do not have this option – though leg cells, up to a certain age, can still become either ankle cells or toe cells, as it were; but the time comes when the new generation of cells at the leg site finds things already too far gone for such 'choices'. 'Development' is a process of the actualisation of one set of possibilities at each place, at the expense of the shutting off of all the other sets of possibilities. The set that is actualised at each stage of cell division is determined by the development that has already occurred: no new cell population can become what another cell population is becoming. As the embryo approaches full term, for each new cell population practically the whole of the blueprint of potentialities that each cell carries in its complement of chromosomes is already shut off: only a few possibilities are left.

This process of development of differentiated organs out of originally undifferentiated material is named by the biologists the process of 'organisation'. A three-month embryo displays 'more organisation' than an egg. The term can also be used phylogenetically: mammals are 'more highly organised' than molluscs. (For non-specialist further reading: Comfort *et al.*, 1964; Kennedy, 1965, 1967.)

The 'developmental assumption' about the nature of the implementation process cannot, of course, be supposed to entail all of the biologist's understandings in detail. Yet the analogy is close and suggestive. The egg is the original policy decision which, it is held, somehow contains the blueprint for the many different activities of the final stages of implementing the policy. Implementation is a progressive 'pragmatisation' of the general into the specific – from the undifferentiated and abstract to the highly differentiated and concrete; from the broad, all-encompassing beginning to the several specialised actions – in a series of stages marked by the passage of time (no reversal) and by descent through a hierarchy, each stage a little more clearly defined than that preceding, the realm of what could be done reduced, stage by stage, to what shall be done at the next stage. And by the time operating level is reached, very little discretion remains. It surely is an analogy for the beliefs about the implementation process held by such as Barnard and the early Simon, by Tullock and by Downs, that fits at many points.

Its main flaws as an explanatory model for the process of branch line closure have been hinted at already. The 'pure' developmental hypothesis assumes that each stage is a necessary condition of the succeeding stage, and that each stage is a sufficient condition of the succeeding stage. You don't acquire teeth except at teeth sites; and when you have teeth-sites, all you can acquire are teeth. But it is not true that you cannot find men shovelling ballast unless the rails have been removed or that you will always find men shovelling ballast once you have removed the rails. Men shovel ballast every day on still active lines, taking it away and putting new ballast back down; and similarly, men remove rails to lay down new ones, without triggering off other men to cart away the ballast. At a less trivial level, perhaps, it is not true that you would never have got a line closure proposal unless there had been a mention in the Beeching report, nor that, provided there was a mention in the report, a line closure is all that could have resulted. It is not true that unless the Cabinet had decided against cross-subsidisation the Board would not have set out on a reduction of route mileage (it might well have done so for its own reasons); nor that, as soon as it *had* decided against cross-subsidisation, the Board's only feasible means of implementing that decision was a reduction of route mileage. One can repeat the little analysis for every stage. The pure developmental assumption does not make enough sense, on this material.

Aggregation

Maybe it would, if 'this material' had concerned the development of an organisation to carry out the purposes of the Cabinet. A salient characteristic of the material is that several existing organisations are involved. It is 'multi-organisational', and each organisation is already there. The existence of an organisation implies two things, in particular, for the analysis: first, a large number of goals or purposes or objectives (including survival); and second, a certain division of labour already established.

In a real organisation, in a real society, the division of labour (at least at final operating level) cannot derive from some stated purpose alone; it is (at least to some extent) determined by the structure of trades and professions in the society, what people are in practice trained for and habilitated to (although some educationists would wish to point to the reciprocal of this as the true relation: that does not actually matter for our analysis). There was general agreement in the implementation literature that (in military analogy) all the strategic planning and staff work must reduce, if battles are to be won, to the skills of the man with the gun. Neither strategies nor tactics, however superior, may bring victory except through the way they deploy troops and armour and their equivalents in other services; what troops and armour are capable of is a *given*, within very narrow limits.

It is common form the world over for the 'front line troops' and their civilian counterparts (lathe operators, bookkeepers, men with shovels, teachers) to regard those above them in the organisation as parasites on their labour, pushing paper around as distinct from working. Sour grapes apart, the perception has this merit. Prudentially, tasks and policies had better be tailored to the skills and equipments that are already available in the organisation – which gives their custodians considerable power. As Gulick (1937, 4) pointed out, tasks which depend for their achievement on the use of equipment that has not yet been invented, or on manual skills that, although perhaps theoretically possible, are not in practice possessed by anyone, or on a distribution of knowledge and experience which is not the distribution that prevails – such tasks are not achievable, except after an interval of time and expenditure of resources on invention, training and reorganisation.

The number of conventional 'trades' that there are – rifleman, engine-driver, plumber, typist, and so on – although large, is still much smaller than the number of organisations there are in the country, and infinitesimally small in relation to the number of different 'tasks' that can be accomplished using only combinations of those trades and occupations.

This is a key element in the 'aggregative' assumption in modelling the implementation process. Getting something done is seen as a matter of putting together a number of discrete units – *making* a chain, each part of which will contribute some necessary operation or make some necessary transformation in the 'raw material', each unit accepting as its input the preceding unit's output and the various types of work cumulating to the desired change. In principle, each unit can be included in many different chains and there may be as many different chains as there are kinds of product, or policies. Each unit, therefore, has its own function, or *raison d'être*; it is specialised by skill or knowledge or equipment or some combination of these, and is not substitutable by another unit (unless by deliberate duplication to cope with workload). The designing of the sequence of such units in assembling a chain is a technical matter, a selection and ordering of elements from the 'stock' under the simultaneous constraints of appropriate transforming capabilities and compatibilities of outputs to inputs – the latter a little like playing dominoes, matching a left-hand side's spots against the right-hand side spots of the next counter to be played, or vice versa.

If the pure developmental model of the implementation process assumed that the nature of the activity at each succeeding stage is determined uniquely by the nature of the activity at the preceding stage and had an organic-growth analogue, then the pure aggregative model assumes that the nature of the activity at each succeeding stage is wholly independent of the nature of the activity at the preceding stage and has a machine analogue.

'Theory of machines' or of 'automata' is derived from information theory and cybernetics rather than mechanical engineering or the like, and we shall neither need or be able to go very far into it; but a few elementary principles, as in the embryology illustration, will elucidate the applications.

The 'intrinsic variety' of a system is a measure of its complexity, which is a statement of how many different parts it has and how many ways they can be independently connected and switched in or out – made operational or not. The more complex the system, the greater the number of different 'states', or arrangement of parts in relation to one another, in which it can be found. This number is its 'variety'.

This number can be very high with only a small number of parts. Imagine a closed system with only seven parts, where each part can be connected with every other part by a channel in each direction, with a single on/off switch in each channel. Such a system generates a variety of 2^{42}, or well over a million million different states.

If there are constraints on which parts can be linked with other parts (as in dominoes), variety is reduced; similarly, if 'feed' can be only one-way. Under whatever constraints may operate, the greater a system's variety, the more ways it has of transforming an input to the system into an output from the system – the greater the range of its 'products', the variety of its responses. The set of the permutations of inputs–connections–operations–outputs actually designed into a machine, the number of states of its system, intended to be used to produce outputs from inputs, is the 'specification' of the machine.

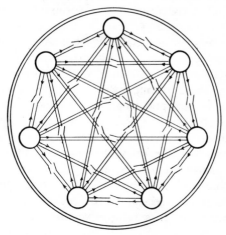

Fig. 8 Variety of closed system of seven parts fully interconnected and switched (*Beer*, 1966, 251)

If we now imagine a machine whose parts are themselves little machines, with inputs and outputs and work done between, the general picture remains. The specification of the larger machine is the number of different ways its component machines can be coupled together; this gives the list of the things that can be done with all the possible inputs to the larger machine, and of all the different outputs that can result. An 'automated' factory is a familiar enough example of a machine made of component machines. But any of the complex machines in such a factory is likely itself to be a 'machine made of machines', by these definitions.

Some machines have a very simple specification: one kind of input, transformed by a fixed set of internal relationships into a single, invariable output – a simple switch, a torch, a door lock, a postage stamp vending machine (all of these actually have more than one input but we will pass over such refinements of description). Slightly more complex machines – for instance, a chocolate machine, a cold drink vendor with an array of buttons to press, perhaps accepting several coins and even giving change, or the clockwork representations of the universe (an orrery) and other 'automata' beloved of the eighteenth-century philosophical iconoclasts – can be rather impressively complicated and 'marvellous'. But in such machines the structure of the input determines the structure of the output, via fixed internal relationships. The clockwork is all a matter of mechanical gears, pawls, triggers and so on. Nothing truly surprising can happen.

A television set is considerably more complex than an orrery, because it meets a much more sophisticated requirement: that the output (in certain particulars) should remain constant under conditions of varying input. It contains several devices designed to 'read' characteristics of the input signal, measure deviation from a standard and lop off excess – 'smooth out' random fluctuations in picture brightness, for example, or volume. The structure of the input does not wholly determine the structure of the output but it activates mechanisms that select among the characteristics of the signal and inhibit some of them. (A television set has a 'higher' specification than an orrery in many other ways.)

A still higher specification results from the capability required of computers, for example, to read inputs and not just measure them against a norm but 'follow instructions', selecting items of 'knowledge' from its 'memory' stores and associating them, or performing calculations with them, in one or more of the ways in which it has been programmed, or pre-set, to do; and producing an output or result which may well be 'surprising' to its minders – not only because the computer is capable of more 'ruthless' logic, but because a large one is capable of 'mental' operations of a scope and at a speed which outstrips the capabilities of its designers' own brains. (For non-specialist further reading: Wiener, 1950; Grey Walter, 1953; Sluckin, 1954; Beer, 1966; von Bertalanffy, 1968.)

The 'performance programmes' of the March and Simon version of the aggregative model are analogous to relatively simple, low-specification machines (routines) which nevertheless have fairly sensitive 'reading' or sensing devices (filters, in-group perceptions) that select between instructions and do their 'smoothing' of inputs in ways that do not show up in their outputs (uncertainty is absorbed; discretion is exercised). Such low-level performance programmes, in the March and Simon model, are enclosed in larger systems ('higher-level programmes') which, in turn, read their own inputs and make judgements about which combination of lower-level programmes is called for (co-ordination by plan), monitor the outcome and match it against the input, recombining performance programmes in alternative sequences as indicated (co-ordination by feedback). The analogies can be refined and extended much further; but perhaps that is enough to go on with. The source of the conceptual framework, the terms and the assumed dynamic relationships between elements of the model is surely unmistakable; the thinking is derived from the theory of machines, or from understandings themselves derived from it.

The feature of this model of the implementation process which most clearly distinguishes it from the developmental model is that the 'stages' or 'programmes' (or whatever one calls the clusterings of activities that are the medium of the operations or transformations that constitute the process) *pre-exist the process* and can be combined in different ways, and possibly in different orders or sequences, provided only that the output of one can be 'plugged into' the input of the next. Each cluster is, therefore, seen as an independent unit, with activities that can be triggered off, wholly or selectively, by the input from the previous cluster, but which are not specified by that input. And the same input from any other cluster that happened to become the previous stage would have the same effect.

This model makes better sense of some of the case-study material than the developmental one. The ballast loaders on the abandoned railway track are clearly an 'independent unit', added on to complete a fragment of the process. The ATUCC hearings are intelligible as a 'plug-in attachment' to take care of a certain part of the process in the middle. Much of the 'lower-level' process consisted of the people in certain units – say, Traffic Facilities Section – diverting their attention temporarily to some aspect of the Wetherby closures, as part of their normal day's work; a phenomenon for which the idea of their being 'switched into' the process for a time, and switched out again, is a fair representation.

But the aggregative assumptions seem perhaps less fruitful for the higher levels, or 'earlier' stages. It was not true that a 'programme' of branch line and station closures existed, that could simply be included in the implementation of the Cabinet's 1960 decision; it had (as we would quite naturally say) to 'be developed'. Again, the time of certain groups of civil servants and Railways Board officers – those concerned with consents and with the 'reshaping' of British Railways – was wholly given over to these questions, and the nature of their activities was by no means independent of the nature of the activities at preceding 'stages': they could not be 'switched into' any other implementation processes; their outputs were compatible only with their respective 'next stages'.

However, if we go 'higher' or 'earlier' still, we find the agggegative assumption making some sense again. Consideration of the needs of the national economy lends itself to the image of allocating resources from a certain total, or requiring retrenchments amounting to a certain sum, and deciding what combination of spending programmes will produce the desired result, railway finance being one of the elements to be switched in or out, or modified. The 'ideological' conflict over nationalisation, or over cross-subsidisation, which can perhaps be seen as 'higher than' or 'prior to' the Cabinet decision, would respond to the same description.

This is an interesting suggestion. Some 'stages' or groups of 'stages' of this process, as seen in the case-study, are apparently different in kind from other stages or groups of stages. The 'aggregative' assumption makes sense of some; the 'developmental' assumption makes better sense of others; and by and large, the earliest and the latest stages are 'aggregative', the middle ones 'developmental'. Why should this be? Would it apply to all cases of the implementation process, or is it a peculiarity of the material we are using?

Here are the apparent clusterings. There is, earliest (or logically most prior), a group of issues concerned with nationalisation and the 'commercial or social service' controversy. There is a group of issues concerned with railway cross-subsidisation and the need for 'reshaping'. There is a group of issues concerned with the mechanics of 'reshaping', the selection of lines for closure and the authorisation of closure in particular cases, with safeguards of the interests involved. There is a group of issues concerned with the running of the railway, de-scheduling trains and redeploying rolling stock and manpower, utilising track and other fittings. And there is a group of issues concerned with demolition, disposal of scrap and sale of land. Other clusters, or clusterings within these clusters, may be detectable, but we can make do with these five.

The 'aggregative' assumptions seem to apply best to the final two, and possibly the first, and less well to the second and third. There is, perhaps, a clue to the reason in the words themselves. 'Railways' are not mentioned in the first and fifth, and 'closure' is mentioned only in the third ('reshaping', however, in the second). What one can infer from this (and it has been confirmed by the fuller narrative) is that although the whole process is concerned with a 'closure', only at the middle stages are the activities described entirely concerned with closure. At the 'higher' or 'earlier' ideological level, nationalisation and the 'commercial or social service' controversies are about other public services than railways. At the level of railway operation, the activities described are often empirically indistinguishable from similar activities occasioned by other kinds of event. The redeployment of rolling stock, for instance, goes on all the time.

At the level of scrap disposal, the same effect can be seen – and when it comes to ballast lifting, it wasn't even a railway staff activity but a contracted-out job. Now these effects *may* be merely the result of the particular material of this case, and we could not be sure without looking at other cases. Still, we could form the hypothesis for testing from what we know about the present material, and it would surely be this. If a case-study is designed to examine the implementation of policy X, then the descriptions will take the following form:

'anterior' clusters of activities in which X appears as a possible policy
'central' clusters of activities concerned almost entirely with X
'posterior' clusters of activities in which the implementation of policy X is to some degree integrated with the implementation of (possible or actual) policies Y, Z, etc.

'Aggregative' assumptions will make more sense of the observed activities in the anterior and posterior clusters, and 'developmental' assumptions will be more appropriate for at least some aspects of the central clusters.

Time, logic and organisation

One or more 'anterior' clusters of activities, a central cluster, one or more 'posterior' clusters: this assumes a 'time order' of activities. There is also a 'logic order' implied in the assumption that what we are looking at is a *process*: a proceeding by incremental change from one state of affairs to another. Then there is in the record an assumption that the case moves through an organisation, and from one organisation to another; it has a 'trace', or dynamic path, that can be followed physically from one location to the next – or perhaps, from one 'office' to the next, from jurisdiction to jurisdiction, or 'province' to 'province', in Simon's term. The activities that together provide the case material can be laid out, as it were, in three conceptually distinct orders: a time sequence, a logic sequence and an organisation sequence.

We are turning now to the second set of assumptions from which the two main models we discerned in the implementation literature were built up: that concerning the ordering or sequence of the elements of the implementation process.

The simplest model would be one where it is taken for granted that all three types of sequence coincide: the steps of the logical order are in a fixed time order and move in an ordained path in organisational space. The process simply unrolls steadily, from the earlier events (which are at the 'policy' end, or the 'higher' level, the 'more general' scope, etc.), towards the later events (which are at the 'operational' end, the 'lower' level, the 'more detailed' scope, etc.), and this is a progression from top to bottom of a hierarchy in an organisation or organisations. In such a linear progression, if you knew the date on which a particular initial decision was taken, and the rate at which matters of that kind normally progress, you could tell where to find the case being dealt with on any later date.

By the nature of the literature, there is no clear example of such a model being consciously adopted by a writer, although it seems implicit in certain remarks of Gulick's and in Urwick's scheme, and is all but explicit in Le Breton and the 'administrative reform' writers (see Chapter 2, pp. 26ff.).

One alternative understanding was that the process was less a straight line than a sine curve of a sort beginning (e.g., for Tullock and Downs) at the operating level with an input of information from the outside world, processed up through the hierarchy to the point of decision, and then, on the 'implementation' side, down through the hierarchy again to the operating level. The Litchfield cycle was similar, beginning with decision and moving to implementation, but then back through 'reappraisal' to 'decision' again – presumably on a succeeding 'cycle'.

'Feedback' is also a cycle. A feedback circuit is overt in March and Simon, but they specifically dissociate the implementation process from the formal organisational hierarchy. In Pressman and Wildavsky, time sequence and logic sequence are specifically dissociated: 'The steps are related', they say, 'from back to front as well as from front to back', and in the terms we are using they appear to allow for a 'posterior' event to occur before an 'anterior' event. The process, they say, may have to retrace its steps and re-establish an 'early' stage. The longer the logical 'chain of causality', the more numerous these 'reciprocal relationships' – not a feedback phenomenon, more a kind of running repair while the process is still in motion.

However we disentangle the Pressman and Wildavsky categories, they certainly alert us to the possibility, and perhaps the desirability, of keeping separate (a) the notion of hierarchy of authority and the notion of the implementation process, and (b) in our understanding of the implementation process, the time sequence, the logic sequence, and the organisation sequence.

Now, without attempting to apply the very simplest assumption – that of straight time-sequence linearity, coinciding with logic sequence and a known organisational path – to the whole material of the case-study, it seems to make immediately recognisable sense of certain parts of the narrative at least. The length of time it took the Ministry to make a decision on consent to a closure proposal, for example, from receipt of a S.56(8) notice until the issue of the 'consent letter' (where one was issued), was broadly calculable; and where matters stood at any one point in time could be predicted with reasonable accuracy. The same would be broadly true of such a sequence as that at regional Railway Board level, between Works Progress Committee agreement to submit proposals for the abandonment of a line, the requests for various estimates, the drawing up of work schedules and authorisation of the work. The absolute length of such a process might vary quite a lot, but the knowledgeable observer could weigh up the special features of a particular case and make allowances for these in estimating the rate of progress; then, knowing 'who does what' in Ministry or Board offices, the relative invariability of the procedures involved might enable him to make a good guess as to where to find the papers.

But supposing one had actually done this for the papers about the Wetherby closures; supposing that a knowledgeable observer had gone into the Ministry or the Regional HQ, discovered his 'starting date', made his prediction and gone to the indicated office – he might indeed have found some papers to do with Wetherby there. But there would have been a number of other offices where there were also papers to do with the Wetherby lines. A number of alternative predictions would also have been borne out. In order to have made *all* the correct predictions the observer would have needed a rather more complicated model than a linear one.

Let us see what kind of model would meet the conditions; that is, offer a good chance of predicting the number and location in organisational space of all the offices where a given case was being considered, given a known 'rate of progress' from a starting date and assuming no accidents or delays, deviations due to 'personality' or motivational factors, or other disturbances of that sort. Let us assume, also, a single organisation of the 'bureaucratic' type, such as the Ministry or the regional Railway Board headquarters.

Feasibility and clearance

The following account of how a case is dealt with in such an organisation is an analytic and 'idealised' one, generalised from the author's experience and from a number of case histories and textbooks (e.g. Brittan, 1964; Rhodes, 1965; Chapman, 1969; Brown, 1970; Garrett, 1972; Hill, 1972; Heclo and Wildavsky, 1974), as well as from the books already discussed in Chapter 2. It is an inductive ideal type and not an empirical description; alternatively, it is a hypothetical model, the validity of which readers can test for themselves against reality as they know it. It purports to be a purely general account of the way *any* matter is considered in *any* British ministry, give or take an idiosyncratic peculiarity here and there, or, with obvious allowances for differences in nomenclature and style, in an organisation outside the civil service but of the same broad type, like a railway regional HQ.

Let us use the following terms to denote the organisational hierarchy: agency or subdepartment, branch or group, division, and section (see Fig. 9). We can assume, further, that there are several such 'agencies' in a ministry, and that each 'section' comprises a head, with, under him, two or more supervisors and, under them, a number of operatives. Let us then assume that the head of one of the sections wishes to initiate consideration of a case which requires for a satisfactory settlement a change in agency policy.

The section which has become convinced that a change of policy would be advantageous will produce a minute or memorandum setting out the difficulties ascribed to the existing practice, making a proposal for (usually) the minimum alteration that will obviate these difficulties and listing what the section sees as the implications of its suggestion, in terms of effects upon other policies, of additional costs (or savings) and of disturbance of present activities. This memorandum will be addressed to the head of division, the section head's immediate superior.

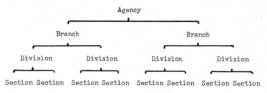

Fig. 9   Ministry jurisdictions

The division head will probably have been informed previously about the problem; he may have asked for the memorandum. He may or may not have his own ideas about a solution, but at this stage he is unlikely to commit himself, and he may not even devote much of his time to personal study of the matter. Unless the memorandum is obviously silly, or unacceptable on some other quite general ground, he will probably merely ask a few questions to clear up specific points and then 'adopt' it, by either writing a brief covering minute or having his own version drafted. Then he will send copies to the heads of all other divisions which, it appears to him, might be affected by the proposal, asking for their views.

Receipt of the paper in each addressed division sets off a standard procedure. Either by simply reading it through, or by a more laborious inspection, the head of division first scans the proposal and its justification for 'engagement' to see whether he recognises the matter as one in which his office has a responsibility. If no 'hooks' can be seen on which his responsibilities might be caught, the division head might take a second opinion by showing the paper to one of his section heads, and then dispose of the memorandum by returning a brief annotation or minute of the 'noted with thanks' variety.

The reverse may happen: an office to which a copy of the memorandum was not initially sent may see one incidentally, or hear tell of it, and spot 'hooks' that the originating office had missed which, willy-nilly, involve the affairs of the omitted office. The latter is expected to make this known and to ask for a copy of the memorandum, or ask to be kept informed.

If an addressed division finds itself engaged in one or other aspect of the proposal, the memorandum (copied if necessary) will be sent to heads of sections within the division, possibly also to supervisors, with or without a minute specifically requesting 'views'. These persons will, in turn, consult their own subordinates as necessary, until the operatives (those who apply the ultimate 'front-line' skills or routines of existing practice) have been heard, at least by proxy, wherever the proposal may seem to involve changes at their level.

What each person does when confronted by such a memorandum (or extract or other version of one) can be described analytically as follows. The memorandum's statement of the current situation is inspected for accuracy and completeness, as seen from the office of the person considering it. Its identification of the difficulties that current practice leads to is tested against the knowledge and experience of the office consulted and agreement, dissent, amplification, etc., noted. The position to which the memorandum proposes the agency should move is examined to see whether it is, for the consulted office, a *possible* state of affairs; if it is not, the differences between the proposed position and the closest approximation to it the consulted office sees as a possible one are noted. Even if *possible*, the proposed position might not be a desirable one from the consulted office's point of view; it might conflict with their customary policies or modes of operation, or introduce uncertainty. It might also be seen to conflict with existing *agency* policies, instructions or practices, in ways not noted in the originating office's memorandum, or with the policies or modes of operation of another division or agency not on the circulation list – in which case the consulted office noting this will either itself inform the omitted office or suggest that it be informed.

If the proposed new state of affairs is, in the eyes of the consulted office, a possible one and not an undesirable one, then the proposed route to or method of reaching the new state of affairs (the actual changes proposed) will be inspected to see whether, if put into practice by the consulted office, the changes proposed would in reality transform the present state of affairs into the desired state of affairs. If it would not, the crucial factors producing the discrepancy are, if possible, identified, and the nature of the state of affairs that would, on the consulted office's predictions, be the actual result of implementing the proposed changes is indicated. They might, for instance, suspect an overshooting or undershooting of the mark aimed at, or unmentioned side-effects, or considerably greater implementation costs or disruption than estimated, and so on. The consulted office might or might not then go on to suggest alternative changes from present practice which would, in their view, achieve the stated desired result within the stated margins of costs and disruption, avoid the foreseen side-effects, etc.

Each consulted office, having thus examined the originating office's statement of the problem and of the solution proposed, prepares a statement of its views. A 'consulted office' is to be taken as referring to anyone consulted and replying in his official capacity, or 'ex officio', using the resources of his post, information and experience recorded in the files, for example, rather than 'personal opinion', whether he be division head, section head, supervisor, operative or other.

Any proposal of this kind – for a change in agency policy – will, thus, be considered in a number of divisions of the agency and at a number of levels in each division; possibly in partial form, parts of the original memorandum having been abstracted; possibly in an aggregated form, parts of *different* proposals having been considered together as they affect a particular consulted office. When consideration has been given, and each 'consulted office' has prepared its view, the process of collating all these views begins.

A supervisor may collate the views of several operatives. A section head will collate the comments of the several supervisors under him (some of which, of course, may be of the 'noted – no comment' kind). The division head will put together the 'divisional view' of the original proposal and send it back to the originating division – unless the proposal is seen as conflicting with a major interest or responsibility of the branch of which a consulted division is part, in which case the division head will probably prepare a brief for his superiors at branch level, informing the originating division head that he is doing so. The proposal may thus escalate to branch level.

If not, as the divisional views begin to come back to the originating division head, he may be able to judge quickly whether the original proposal is a feasible one – in need of amendment in detail, perhaps, but 'definitely on', not a 'non-starter', 'worth pursuing', etc. (Hence the name for this part of the procedure; 'feasibility testing'.) If the alteration proposed is, on the other hand, clearly 'not on', even with amendment, it is 'back to the drawing board' for the originating section, unless they decide they can live with the present situation a little longer. The views expressed by other offices may nevertheless suggest either a refinement in the original perception of the difficulties, or a more appropriate 'desired state of affairs', or a more effective solution, perhaps to many other people's problems as well, in major change rather than minor.

Assuming, however, that the original proposal has passed the initial feasibility testing round, it is ready for developing. Using the criticisms received from other offices, perhaps exploring these criticisms and suggestions further with the divisions involved (in dyadic conversations, exchanges of papers, committees or working parties, as may be appropriate), and using further evidence of difficulties produced by the existing policies, further work on projections of the proposed changes, and so on, what was a proposal for change moves towards the specification of the alterations in working rules and practices that will actually take place if the change is authorised. The end of this phase is the preparation of another memorandum containing a clarified version of the problem (probably briefer than the original), a prescription of the action required and the specification of the new policies and procedures. It attempts to meet all of the objections raised by the previous memorandum and takes into account all the suggestions made for improvement – at least, all of them that were compatible with one another and with whatever decisions may have been reached at branch or higher levels. But the reformulations and revisions undertaken in the originating division as a result of the 'feasibility-test' round and later discussions may themselves have introduced new snags, side-effects and the like. So it is necessary for the new memorandum to be circulated all round again, but this time with more limited aims. The proposal is known to be feasible; it is not now open to objection 'in principle' or to 'escalation' – except, of course, upon admission of negligence in not speaking up earlier. What is wanted is assurance that the way is now clear for action to be taken in the manner proposed. Hence the name of this part of the procedure: 'clearance'. Minor objections to method or to timing, for example, must still be made if conflicts arise, and there is still opportunity for amendments to detail or improvements in presentation and the like.

Of course, mistakes will happen. Sometimes the developed proposal reveals unintended consequences that could perhaps have been picked up at feasibility stage but were not. A division or office omitted from the earlier circulation may come across a proposal only at a late stage. And there *are* problems of 'motivational' response that go under the names of 'defence of territory', *amour propre*, interpersonal rivalry, laziness and so on, which we are leaving out of this account – indeed, out of this book.

If the circulation of the 'feasibility-testing' memorandum had the secondary effect of notifying all concerned that a problem existed and change was in the wind, the circulation of the 'clearance' memorandum has the secondary effect of announcing that action is approaching and that agency instructions and practices may soon be revised. This can directly influence decisions – on planned changes in accommodation, on the size of a print order for forms that may become obsolete, on the degree of caution in replying to complaints about the present procedure and so on. In other words, the effect of a coming change can be felt in the agency before the change officially occurs.

The new memorandum is sent to all divisions to which the original was sent, plus any others whose interest has become apparent. The procedure on receipt is, in principle, the same as before: a downward progression to operating level (or its surrogate), followed by an upward progression of summarisation and collation. The originating division may have some more work to do on minor amendments or on removing newly discovered snags, and further consultation, or a repeat of the clearance stage in maybe one sector of the circulation list, may be required. But once clearance has been given, the proposal is ready to go for legal drafting (where necessary) and then to the stage of 'authorisation'.

'Authorisation' is the stage which, in other analyses of this kind, appears as 'the point of decision'. The latter name is apposite when what is presented to the appropriate body is a choice between two or more solutions to a problem, *each* of which has been tested for feasibility and cleared in some similar procedure to that described here. Eliding the choice or 'deciding' aspect of this stage into the choice between approving the proposal submitted or not approving it, and calling it the 'authorisation' stage, emphasises the view from below (an imbalance we shall perhaps redress in a later discussion). If the work has been impeccably done to this point, the 'decision' may be an easy one. 'Higher authority' (and it need not be 'highest authority': it will be the *lowest* level with responsibility for authorising such changes as are proposed) may be able to give formal approval without devoting serious attention to it. On the other hand, such review of the whole matter as is given at a higher level than has hitherto been involved may uncover faulty diagnosis of the problem clearly visible only from that height, or reveal engagement of other agencies not consulted, or suggest a dimension of outcome or side-effect that could render the whole proposal 'not on', for political or public relations reasons, for example. If so, the matter will return to whatever stage of its preparation has been found inadequate.

Even if the decision involved is only that to authorise or not, it marks a watershed. Authorisation ends the preparatory stages; it turns a proposal into an instruction or command (or the basis for one) with relevant sanctions. This may be registered by 'promulgation', requiring its own preparation, perhaps determining the dates on which the approved change or changes will come into effect, and often being published in a gazette or other formal publication. Then 'implementation' can begin.

In principle, this process or set of procedures is the way one sees an organisation like those we are concerned with go about all its decisions; routine processing of applications for service (at operating level), as well as the preparation of 'legislation' or its equivalent – even such matters as internal postings and promotions and other confidential matters, though of course in abbreviated circulation (sometimes called the 'need-to-know basis'). The initiative that sets the machinery going can take place anywhere in the system, and the machinery works in the same way ('in principle') for a problem that never rises above section head level as for one that involves the 'highest levels'. The machinery, as we shall perhaps see later, constitutes rather the ordinary functioning of a particular type of structure than anything added or imposed.

Adding complexity

We set out on this analytic account of the decision process in this type of agency, if you remember, because of the inadequacies of the simple 'linear' assumptions in predicting where a particular piece of work might be being dealt with at a particular moment. What we have been doing is trying to find what more complex assumptions might enable us to do that better. We need a 'better understanding' of the reality than the simple model gives us. What we have arrived at is not a number of empirical observations, even if the model is founded on several people's experience of reality. It is still a formal model, an 'in principle' abstraction, which will not adequately represent every actual example of the process that might be found. Some real processes will be simpler than the model portrays, their stages encapsulated so that the 'framework' disappears; other real processes will be so enormously more complicated that the 'framework' is swamped. How, then, can one ever tell that there *is* a 'framework' behind or beneath?

The answer, of course, is that one cannot. The 'framework' is essentially a construction of the observing theorist. It is only 'there' if other people, having had it pointed out, 'see' it too and find it useful to order their own thoughts about the matter, or perhaps to aid in 'prediction'. The argument is fundamentally circular, even tautologous: one looks for a better model, one that more nearly represents reality, so as to be able to understand (or predict) better: one knows it is a better model if one is able to understand (or predict) better. And neither understanding nor prediction is a yes-or-no affair; for general purposes, all one wants is *requisite* understanding, predictability within stated limits, knowledge to a given level of detail. Nor are models of this kind 'true' or 'false'. There may be several different ways of representing a single process, several different models, each of them 'true enough' in its own way.

With that interpolation on the logical status of what we are doing, let us see what the assumptions or axioms of this 'feasibility and clearance' model are, in comparison with earlier accounts of the decision process in a bureaucratic agency. It has several features in common with the Tullock/Downs account. It identifies the levels of consideration of a problem with the levels of rank in the agency, as they do – and as does the early Simon in the military illustration, for instance. It has a 'sine-curve' outline, though its dynamic is 'down-and-then-up-again' (like Litchfield's cycle) rather than up-and-then-down like that of Tullock. But it is more complex. First, it incorporates an 'out-and-then-in-again' component as well as a vertical component. The originating division (or section, or branch) consults relevant divisions (or sections, or branches), and they communicate their views to the originating division, which can thus be seen to take up a 'central' position in a lateral web. But only for that particular matter: any division can be 'central' for another matter, and at any one time virtually every division will be acting as 'centre' for some matter or other.

Second, in respect of any *one* such matter, the 'down-and-then-up-again' movement is seen as taking place more or less simultaneously at several points in the agency, from each node on the lateral web – on the originating 'plane' (divisional level, if the originator was a division head, etc.), down through the other 'planes' to operator or quasi-operator, and up again.

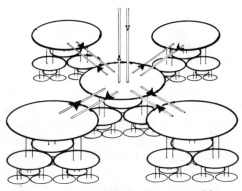

Fig. 10   The feasibility-clearance model

Third, the account postulates that this outward-and-downward pulse or probe, and its information-laden return, occurs more than once in the consideration of any particular matter: at least twice merely for 'feasibility testing' and 'clearance'. (We have not investigated what the 'promulgation' phase might look like, or what form 'implementation' takes in the same imagery.)

Consider, further, that if in the agency being studied there are several – perhaps scores or hundreds – such matters being considered at any one moment, or over a short period, it seems unavoidable that consideration of one matter will overlap with that of another, that proposals from different sources will be considered together, that what is analytically a separate matter to the external observer is not so seen by the internal participant. The participant, rather, takes it for granted that, in the network he inhabits, every node is a centre, every connection a two-way channel, every information-seeking probe also an information-carrier, every communication a conveyor of several messages. He is trained, also, to see the phases of the process together: preparation, decision and implementation must be in view simultaneously – that is, surely, what 'feasibility testing' means. Finally, it is part of his skill to relate one policy's preparation to another policy's implementation – that is, surely, what 'side-effects' are about.

Here is a complex model indeed: perhaps too complex. The more nearly a model comes to being a faithful representation of reality in all its richness, the less easy it is to grasp and use. Let us see what has gone wrong.

In the first place, we have slipped from considering the stages of a particular process of decision making into considering the nature of a dynamic structure embracing all such processes. The difference, to be sure, is only one of emphasis, or focus, but we have lost simplicity. If we return now to the idea of merely trying to predict where a particular set of papers will be found in the ministry (laying aside, that is, the 'dynamic structure' focus), then the outward-inward, downward-upward model is quite usable for this purpose. It gives probably adequate results – better, at least, than a simple linear or cyclical assumption. It would predict that (a) the papers will be in multi-copy form, or abstracted into several parts; (b) there will be a 'circulation list' of some kind naming the divisions (in this case) where papers will be found; (c) the 'cyclical' assumptions can be used, in conjunction with a local 'rate of progress' estimate for each division, to predict at what level in the local hierarchy relevant papers will be found.

In the second place, we have forgotten an earlier lesson, that it may be wise to separate time, logic and organisational sequences; hence odd conditions like the possibility of seeing preparation, decision and implementation together. Only the Deity is able to have past, present and future in view simultaneously. Let us repair this fault now and see what such statements ought to be.

Time, first. There can be no tampering with time, outside science fiction and our dreams. So any model which requires one to say that events have an effect before they occur, or the like, is just bad thinking, or consciously poetic treatment – 'casting shadows before'. If an effect can be demonstrated, then it is an effect of something which did occur earlier in time, not of something that has yet to happen. We may well *anticipate* the occurrence of an event: forecast it, and take the forecast into account in making a present decision, *as if* the event had already occurred. But it is the forecast that is the influence, not the event. Similarly, the preparation of one decision may influence the preparation of another decision, by an interaction of forecasts or conjectures.

Again, we may well, with hindsight, reassess the significance of an earlier event, perceive our recent history differently from how we perceived it at the time, because of something that happened later. We may, as it were, reformulate our assumptions about a 'chain of events', learn lessons and prepare a current decision in this new light. But it is nonsensical to speak in such circumstances of the later event 'having an effect on' the earlier event. The later event has not changed the earlier event, only our perception and description of it (which may be all there is to an 'event' anyway).

When Pressman and Wildavsky speak of programme implementation as a 'seamless web', the stages being related 'from back to front', they are referring not to time, but to logic:

> Considered as a whole, a program can be conceived of as a system in which each element is dependent on the other[s]. Unless money is supplied, no facilities can be built, no new jobs can flow from them, and no minority personnel can be hired to fill them. A breakdown at one stage must be repaired, therefore, before it is possible to move on to the next. The stages are related, however, from back to front as well as from front to back. Failure to agree on procedures for hiring minorities may lead the government to withhold funds, thus halting the construction. . . . (*Pressman and Wildavsky, 1973, xv*)

The failure to agree on procedures for hiring minorities clearly came, in terms of the calendar, before the decision on withholding (further?) funds. If a necessary condition for a next stage in the process was present on Monday, say, but by Tuesday was absent again, we do not sensibly say that we must return to Monday, but that on Wednesday we must try to repair the breakdown – to re-establish a necessary condition (and we might do it on Wednesday in a way different from Monday's attempt).

In a similar metaphor, Dorothy Johnstone, in a study of the introduction of value added tax in Britain (1975, 17 *and passim*), speaks of 'back-to-front planning'. Here she highlights the difficulties of planning to assorted timescales. For example, computers and buildings have long delivery schedules, so that if you want them to be ready to start operating in 1975 you have to order them in, say, 1972. But you cannot write a proper specification for a computer (or, within perhaps wider limits, a building) until you can say what work you want it to do. Yet you may not be able to determine exactly what you will require of it until after many consultations with all sorts of interests, including government, who will wish to retain as much flexibility as possible for as long as possible – and, but for the computer problem, many matters could well be left fairly open until, say, 1974 and still be ready for a starting date in 1975. So you have to make your 1972 decision concerning computers and buildings on a series of hedging bets and middle-of-scale points, trying not to be too far wrong whatever is eventually decided.

One could draw a kind of 'critical path' diagram backwards from the proposed starting date (the point when all time-paths must converge), showing the latest dates by which decisions on a number of issues would have to be taken. The 'calendar order' would then show that some 'early' decisions 'ought' not to be taken (i.e., 'rationally', or according to the desired logical sequence) until after some 'later' decisions – by which time, of course, it would be too late to take them. This may appear to put the poor civil servant in the position of being wrong whatever he or she does. But it is fact a very common phenomenon indeed: it would be more pleasant if one could always wait to make one's choice until the premises of choice were *certainties*, based upon known facts or unbrookable decisions; but many decisions (perhaps all decisions to some degree) have to be made on premises that are forecasts of probabilities and calculations of risk. If one prefers red apples to green apples, and one is presented with fully ripe apples to choose between, the 'choice' is easy. If one has to choose between apples on one tree and apples on another, long before the apples are ripe, the choice is one for an expert – but it is exactly the sort of thing experts are paid for. The expert might still choose wrongly, if there were not enough information available even for him; but his error is in a different league from the helpless coin-tossing of the non-expert.

So 'back-to-front planning' is really an exercise in skilled forecasting, and the 'seamless web' does not indicate that the order of events in time is somehow fluid or reversible.

Logic, next. What this means, whether in the 'developmental' or the 'aggregative' understanding of the implementation process, is that, wherever x is to become y via a number of partial transformations, there is only a certain selection of activities (out of all those available) that could *follow* any particular activity in the sequence and carry the process further; and at least one out of a certain selection of activities (from among all those available) must have *preceded* any particular activity in order for it to carry the process further. It may not be necessary, or sufficient, for a succeeding activity to follow immediately; there may be some choice, or 'slack'. It may not be necessary, or sufficient, for a particular preceding activity to have come immediately before. The logic of the process is the *pattern* of these necessary and/or sufficient conditions of the implementation happening at all. We might, of course, add specific adventitious conditions: the process to take the shortest possible time, or to use only available spare capacity, etc. But that would take us far beyond the mere logic of the process as such.

Like the time sequence in an implementation process, the logic sequence is not reversible. An implementation process cannot go backwards in logic, any more than the baby can become the egg again, or the motion produced by the burning of gasoline in a car engine reverse itself, so that rolling the car backwards might mysteriously fill the tank again. These impossibilities are based on the nature of chemical reactions; the impossibility of reversible implementation is based on the nature of *work* (activities, transformations, etc.).

Of course, *y* can become *x* again, in favourable circumstances: a disused railway branch line from which track, ballast and all has been removed, can become a busy railway again, conveying passengers in similar trains as before, if that is what is desired, by (in a sense) undoing everything that has been done, in reverse order. But that will require a fresh input of work; and undoing is also implementing. The uni-directionality of implementation, as such, is not a function of whatever substantive changes have been made: it is built into the naming of the process. As we have seen before, implementation simply *implies* one-way change. That is what the use of the word means. We merely confuse ourselves if we try to make it mean anything else.

In the aggregative model, activities that constitute some particular stage in some particular process of implementation may be indistinguishable from activities that constitute some stage in another process. They may, indeed, be 'going on all the time', and merely be 'switched into' the process in question. They are part of the logic of many different processes, but their own timing is independent of the logic of any particular process. One of the ways we 'went wrong' in over-developing the feasibility and clearance model was to mix up an analytic description of a generic logic sequence with an account of how several particular processes overlap in time.

Finally, the organisational sequence. It is this that gives the apparent 'up-and-down' or 'out-and-in' movement to the process. Failure to distinguish between logical sequence and organisational sequence leads to the assumption found in the earlier literature (including the early Simon, Tullock and Downs), that there is a progression in logic for every movement through the hierarchy; that different stages of the implementation process take place at different hierarchical levels; and that the process is either a steady climb up the ladder, rung by rung, or a steady descent down the ladder, step by step. If one leapt from top to bottom, or bottom to top, one would, on that assumption, be missing necessary stages in the logic of the process (Barnard, 1937, 177).

March and Simon, on the other hand, while not ignoring hierarchy, keep the logic of the process quite separate from it. The task of implementation in their understanding is the designing of a sequence of operations, of activities or packages of activities, such that each package can be linked to the next, its output acceptable as an input by the next, so that an initial state (what goes into the first 'work station') will be transformed into a desired outcome (what comes out of the final 'work station'). These activities clearly all take place *somewhere* in organisational space, and the dynamic path followed will, *de facto*, connect together units and officials related to each other either 'laterally' (across specialisms), 'vertically' (across ranks) or both; and in designing the divisions and 'commands' of an organisation, as March and Simon point out, there will be advantages in enclosing a number of frequently linked performance programmes into a single 'command'. But it is that way around, in March's and Simon's theory: the programming is basic, the authority structure (desirably) tailored to suit.

For Pressman and Wildavsky, their material presents the problem of multi-organisation programming. There is no given hierarchy; there is a congeries of separate hierarchies, each with its own authoritative rationale. The implementation process consists of the attempt to link appropriate units in different hierarchies in the appropriate order, so that (as in March and Simon) an unbroken transformation process can occur, from idea and intention to concrete fulfilment – in this case, minority personnel actually in newly created jobs. Each attempted linking is a decision point, a requirement for clearance or agreement, and the logic of the transformation process is not uni-linear but multi-linear, requiring divergences and convergences at strategic junctions, the 'co-ordination' of activities going on simultaneously in different organisations under separate control, with no machinery for effective programming in March and Simon's sense, simply because there is no authoritative overall hierarchy to enforce it.

'Organisational space', for Pressman and Wildavsky, is a population of organisations rather than of branches, divisions and sections; the organisational 'sequence' is not a 'command' pathway, or even a branching series of pathways, so much as a set of political relationships, the conditions of securing the co-operation of several separate organisations, and so of success in implementation. This set of relationships is seen either as not changing through the period or as changing relatively slowly as a result of the exercise itself. The communication channels and information exchange points connecting the organisations are not limited to those concerned with this particular implementation process, but in so far as there is, analytically, a subset of such channels and messages concerned only with this process, they are distinguished from other channels and messages neither by the 'necessary and sufficient' logic of the implementation process alone, nor by the time sequence of events, but by the interaction of both with the political relationships. These determine the actual time sequence and modify the logic sequence, selecting certain paths rather than their alternatives. The equivalent of the 'organisational sequence' is the dynamic path traced through these political constraints.

Thus in Pressman and Wildavsky we can see a clear separation of time sequences, logic sequences and organisational sequences in the implementation process. In our own partial model, concerned with feasibility and clearance, although there are points of similarity with the Pressman and Wildavsky model as presented here, separation has not yet been carried so far. We have assumed only one organisation, and although we have integrated the 'network' assumptions (lateral 'in-and-out') with 'pyramid' assumptions (many vertical hierarchies in the model, providing many simultaneous 'down-and-up' components of movement), the model (as yet) retains an identification of the stages in the logic of feasibility testing with the steps of a descent through the hierarchy of rank.

Not entirely, however. We do not assume the divisions and sections, their heads and staffs, to be there for the purpose of this implementation process alone, or indeed of any such implementation processes alone. They are there, specialised and arranged as they are, prior to the events that make up some process we are interested in, and they have other functions than implementation. Indeed, we perhaps ought to go further: we may recognise that it is our interest that delineates the process and not any self-consciousness of the actors or effect of the structure of the organisation itself.

The viewpoint of the observer

This is the principle behind March's and Simon's illustration of a customer's order 'passing through' a retail shop or a steel-making factory, for example. The order or job card may be all there is to identify the customer's interests at the outset but, given the acceptance of the order and the authorisation, it will gradually take on 'flesh and blood', or physical manifestations, as it passes from shelf to shelf or department to department, or as one specialist after another comes to add his contribution, until it emerges from the end of the process as 'just what the customer ordered'. But it is not the order that creates the stock divisions or departments or employs the specialists; it merely establishes the route. It represents the 'organising principle' of the execution of the order (or, as we should normally say, the 'filling' of the order): it is not the organising principle of the structure or procedures of the organisation.

Let us imagine a visit to the Ministry of Transport while the consent to the Wetherby closures was being considered. We want to trace the progress of the case. There are two analogies for what we are doing. The first assumes we are dealing with a complicated piece of machinery like a watch, and we want to find out what is making the hands take up the position they do. So we start from the centre spindle on which the hands are mounted, note the gearing and how the movement is transmitted from cogwheel to cogwheel, via the escapement and so on, back to the mainspring (assuming that the watch has such old-fashioned bits in it). We have traced the chain of transmission from output to input. (We could have done it the other way round.)

The second analogy assumes we are dealing with a complicated organism or perhaps a chemical 'plant', and we want to find out exactly what happens to a particular input. So we label it with an inert dye or the like and trace the presence of the dye at various intermediate points, or measure the amount of dye in various outputs: then we know where the dye has been and what has happened to the input we labelled. The dye, of course, has to be inert: the label must not influence the process.

The differences between the two analogies are these. The entire watch is there to make the hands turn and there is only one chain of transmission to trace. That is why it does not matter whether we start from the spindle end or the mainspring end. There is no distinction between the organising principle of what we want to do and the organising principle of the watch's structure. In the other case, there are by definition many possible paths or 'chains of transmission' through the organism or chemical plant and we want to demonstrate and display a particular one of them. The organism or plant, however, is indifferent to this interest of ours and simply goes on with its activities: its organising principles are independent of ours – and it is necessary (if we wish to gain the understanding we seek) that it be so.

A visit to the Ministry would speedily confirm that the second analogy is more appropriate than the first. The Ministry clearly does many things, and the case in which we are interested would be seen to be but one of thousands of matters under current consideration. At higher levels of the Ministry our interest would feel somewhat narrow and parochial, and the Wetherby closures would appear a mere incidental in a certain class of matters being dealt with as a class. At lower levels, we might see several persons each dealing with a single aspect of our case, along with the same aspect of other matters possibly remote from branch-line closure altogether, and perhaps no one would ever put the various aspects of our case together, in a single folder on a particular desk, to form the 'case' we would recognise. It would be forced in on us that the thread of our interest, a particular progression from a given application to a given 'consent' letter, is something we are imposing on the scene and not necessarily a conscious awareness on the part of all of the people whose work we are arbitrarily linking in this way. Their organising principle is different from ours. Perhaps only at one level, in respect of a small number of officials, will the two principles coincide sufficiently for us to be able, without strain, to discuss the Wetherby closures as such.

To generalise: the idea that individuals in the descending ranks of a hierarchy of authority are implementing a ministerial decision or carrying out a policy of his (or anyone else's) is *an abstract one*, one that derives from the interest of the observer or inquirer, and is not inherent in, or even manifest in, the internal structure of the Ministry. This is surely a not unimportant conclusion.

From their own point of view, the workers in the Ministry are just doing their job. It is the result of the way their jobs have been specified and of the procedures that have been laid down linking these jobs, that decisions of any particular kind can be implemented – whether as a 'one-off' or a regular routine.

Just occasionally, perhaps, an organisational unit will be set up to carry out one decision and one decision only. In that case, the organising principle of the implementation process (the logic sequence) and the organising principle of the structure (a unique organisational sequence) will coincide; and there will also be a simple, inseparable, linear time sequence. But that is surely a rare occurrence in organisational life and not one on which to base an account of the implementation process.

CHAPTER 5

Structures and Processes

We found that some of the isolable clusters of activities in the railway branch line closure study – the middle ones – seemed to be suitable for understanding by the 'developmental' hypothesis of the nature of implementation, and others – the later and earlier ones – by the 'aggregative' hypothesis. We can now perhaps postulate that this may have been because it was in the middle clusters that the time sequence, the logic sequence and the organisational sequence of the activities most nearly, or most frequently, coincided, whereas in the earlier and later clusters these sequences were separable – indeed, were brought together largely by the interest of the observer.

But this would not explain why we found five clusters and not merely three – anterior, central and posterior; it does not explain the difference between the second and third clusters, or between the fourth and fifth clusters, as set out on p. 130 above. There must be other scales for measuring these differences. This was the third of the five groups of assumptions which went towards the making of the various models of the implementation process we found in the literature: the character of each stage, how it differs from the others. (For the five sets of assumptions, see p. 118 above.)

'Order of comprehension'

The discussion has already thrown up several clues about this. It is in the nature of the activities in the 'demolition, disposal of scrap and sale of land' cluster that they might well be occasioned by some other kind of event than a branch line closure – a contingency shown most clearly, perhaps, in the activity of ballast lifting, where the people concerned are employed by an outside contractor. If your working life consists of the loading and transporting of rock and stone from one location to another, you do not need to know that a particular job is a 'branch line closure job' before you can perform it properly. You will see that it is a 'railway job' from the mere location; operationally, it is a 'ballast job'.

Traffic Facilities Section, whose activities were grouped in the 'running a railway, de-scheduling trains, etc.' cluster (the fourth), would have to know that it was a 'branch line closure' job they were dealing with, and they would know from their papers which branch line it was. But the arguments for and against closing this line would be irrelevant, for them, in the performance of their duties. A closure job is a closure job, however it comes about.

Railway B Division, and the Planning Officer (Reshaping) at BRB headquarters, who would appear in the third cluster ('mechanisms of reshaping, selection of lines for closure'), would clearly have as a central concern of their daily activity precisely this matter of the arguments for and against closing a particular branch line. But they would not need to know the reasons for fixing upon a certain number of route-miles to be eliminated, or to resolve the controversy over whether or not 'Inter-City' surpluses should subsidise branch-line and commuter-line deficits, before they could adequately discharge their responsibilities in this regard.

Similarly, those at ministerial level in the Ministry, and at Board level in the railway organisation, whose burden included just such considerations as the need for, and precise pattern of, reshaping, and the rights and wrongs (or advantages and disadvantages) of particular accounting conventions when drawing up corporate 'profit and loss' accounts (the second cluster), would thankfully conduct these activities on the basis of certain unargued decisions about whether or not the national railways were to be regarded as a commercial undertaking or a social service, and whether they should or should not have been taken into, or remain in, public ownership. These decisions, and any further discussion of them, they would say, are matters for Parliament, as led by Cabinet and guided by party doctrine. Their own activities must be carried on, and their problems resolved, within such decisions as 'givens'.

Here we have an ascending scale of some kind of the 'need to know'. What it is necessary to take into account, argue over and decide at one stage, it is not necessary to discuss or even know about at the next 'lower' stage in the scale. If one inspected the illustrations closely – loading ballast, de-scheduling trains, selecting lines for closure, fixing total route mileage to be eliminated, deciding that railways should be run commercially – one would probably conclude that one is seeing a widening of horizons. The distinction between cluster 5 and cluster 4, and so on, is that the people associated with the lower-numbered cluster must take a more general view of things, consider consequences over a broader field of action, expect to affect more people, possibly (though the material does not actually exemplify this) think on a longer time scale. Decisions in the fourth cluster comprehend a greater part of the railway closure universe than do those in the fifth cluster; and the 'comprehension', or scope, seems to increase by an order of magnitude at each transition from one cluster to the next.

This appreciation corresponds reasonably well with the literature, in which there is virtual consensus about a gradation in the implementation process from the more general to the more specific, occasionally said to be 'from the abstract to the concrete', or (as March and Simon imply) seen as a decrease in the 'range of purview' and in the complexity of matters dealt with. Barnard's 'pyramiding of the formulation of purpose' expresses a similar gradation. Urwick even specifies carefully that his six levels involve 'not gradations in the same kind of activity, but activities which differ in quality and character'. Urwick's six levels have names that would at some points fit the five 'orders of comprehension' we detected in the closures material; to abbreviate a little: (1) legislation, (2) governing authority, (3) managing direction, (4) general management, (5) operations supervision, (6) operations. Moreover, Urwick is clear that the labels attach to kinds of work and not to ranks in a hierarchy (Urwick, (1943) 1963, 63).

The images used in the literature sometimes imply, however, that the absence of the 'need to know' about the concerns of 'higher' levels in the graduated pyramid does not operate in the other direction. Do those carrying out the typical activities of the third cluster, say, need to know nothing of the concerns of those who operate in the fourth cluster? Is it not the case that, if it is your job is to arrange for the selection of branch lines to be closed, you *do* need to know something of how trains are de-scheduled and so on – about how railways are run?

The answer is not absolutely clear from the case material, but it seems safer to say 'yes' than 'no': it is desirable to know how railways are run, so that you know what sort of consequences one of your decisions may have for railway running, and may be able to avoid those you do not want. But you surely need not bother a great deal about what has to happen in the demolition and disposal area: decisions at your own level, selecting lines for closure, shall we say, cannot reasonably be expected to be governed by the effects they might have on disposal of ballast or the like.

Similar reasoning might apply as between other clusters. It would be foolish to take decisions on the extent and pattern of reshaping, with no consideration whatsoever of how the determined total of route miles for closure might be accumulated by the elimination of specific branch lines, or what problems that might give rise to in the way of hardship to users, strategic difficulties for other government departments and the like. But it would be going too far to include consideration of the on-the-spot problems of a regional official redeploying rolling stock, let alone demolition and disposal matters. Cabinet and Parliament, trying to make a decision on the 'commercial' nature of the railways stick, would be bound to take into account that this implied closure of many unremunerative branch lines, with consequent hardship to users. Procedures for just and equitable solution of these problems must, they would feel, be devised. But the difficulties of doing so could not be allowed to stand in the way of the *principle* of making the railways pay their way. As for regional railway management problems, 'Don't trouble us with such trivia' might be a not unreasonable Parliamentary response to a suggestion that there were consequences of that nature. No official or MP would even bring up the matter of the necessary demolition arrangements.

It appears, then, that the relationship between 'higher' and 'lower' clusters of activities is, indeed, not symmetrical: whereas you can do your job adequately in a 'lower' order of comprehension without taking into account considerations that belong in a higher order, the reverse is not true: you cannot do your job adequately in a higher order of comprehension without taking some account of considerations that belong in a lower order. This is surely only to be expected; the 'higher' order of comprehension *means* that more things are taken into account, and there is no reason to suppose that lower-order considerations are excluded from the necessary breadth of view.

But there appear to be limits. Those on a 'higher' level need not know about everything that takes place on all levels lower than theirs. If the illustrations are at all representative, a higher order of comprehension need take account of considerations relevant on the next lower order of comprehension only, and need not know about considerations of any lower order – indeed, will think these entirely 'beneath consideration'.

The exact number of 'orders of comprehension' there are, and what name should be given to each, it is, for present purposes, unnecessary to determine. We might want to climb even higher than the legislative level for some purposes; into 'ideological' considerations, perhaps, or those concerned with the nature of man and of knowledge. We might want to descend even lower than the ballast-loading level for some purposes: into time-and-motion study of the activity of shovelling, or into the mechanisms of muscle activation and control. If we did so, another dimension of the nature of the difference between such orders of comprehension might emerge more clearly than is likely while we keep our interest in railway closures as the focus. The orders can be of comprehension of the *same* activities ('comprehension' having its second meaning, of 'grasp' or 'understanding'). Let me make the point by analogy. Consider a man playing a piano.

From the point of view of a neurologist, each neuron in the motor units of each of the muscles in each of the man's fingers is responding to a series of impulses arriving at the several synapses or nerve ends by 'firing' when these messages arrive in a certain order and frequency, thus activating the muscle motors.

From the point of view of a physiologist, each of his hands is executing a series of previously learned programmed movements in response to complex signals from the cerebellum, which themselves are activated by volleys of message patterns from the memory area as modulated by information currently being received from the interpretation of signals from the sight, hearing and touch receptors.

From the point of view of a dog or a visitor from Mars, a human is seated before a box hitting it with his hands and producing a noise.

From the point of view of any civilised Western European adult, a man is playing the piano.

From the point of view of a moderately knowledgeable music-lover, a skilled pianist is performing Chopin's Nocturne in E Flat (let us say).

From the point of view of a music critic, he is playing a standard piece in a rather mechanical fashion, with the occasional slurred run and faulty intonation of *legato* passages (it may be).

Which account is the correct one? Who has most usefully observed what is going on? Who understands best? Clearly, none is more correct than another: what is observed depends upon the point of view, upon the universe of discourse, upon the interests of the observer and the ideas and terms he is accustomed to use, even when the 'objective' phenomenon (if we allow the possibility of such a thing) is common to all. None of the observers is making a mistake; all are accurate by their own criteria. Neither is there any dispute between the observers; one may doubt whether the neurologist and the music critic would share enough interests and a common language even to converse with one another, let alone to argue with one another about their respective perceptions; although the neurologist and the physiologist might, and the music-lover and the critic might.

Medawar makes a similar point when he says that biologists today tend to classify themselves by 'analytical plane' rather than by discipline, and he isolates molecular, cellular, whole-organism and population 'planes' of biology.

> Our instinct is to try to master what belongs to our chosen plane of analysis and to leave to others the research that belongs above that level or below. An ecologist in the modern style, a man working to understand the agencies that govern the structure of natural populations in space and time, needs much more than a knowledge of natural history and a map. He must have a good understanding of population genetics and population dynamics generally, and certainly of animal behaviour; more than that, he must grasp climate physiology and have a feeling for whatever may concern him among the other conventional disciplines in biology (I have already mentioned immunology and endocrinology). There is no compelling reason why he should be able to talk with relaxed fluency about messenger-RNA, and it is not essential that he should ever have heard of it. . . . (*Medawar, 1967, 101*)

The 'orders of comprehension' in the piano-playing illustration and (by implication) in Medawar's classification of 'planes of analysis' among biologists, as well as in the differences between 'clusters of activities' in the railway closure material, are, first, selections according to 'interest' of which phenomena to consider (out of all that is 'objectively' going on – no observer being ever able to observe everything at once) and which to leave to others; second, they are selections of concepts and ideas, language and theories, by which to order and understand these phenomena, by comparison with phenomena of similar kinds in other contexts. On any particular 'plane', therefore, one may expect to find a 'cognitive community' of people who 'talk the same language', understand the world in a mutually recognisable way, inhabit the same 'universe of discourse' and have heard of one another's concerns and interests. Conversely, if one moves to another 'plane', one may find communication somewhat difficult. An 'order of comprehension' is about how much is comprehended, in both senses of the word. We have discussed the first sense (of how much is included) at some length; now let us look at the second.

In-languages

The phrase 'universe of discourse' has been coined to denote each of several different 'worlds' an individual may inhabit and move between. Each 'world' has its own vocabulary, or characteristic selection of all the words that are possible in English, and also its characteristic modes of inquiry – the kind of question that gets asked, the sort of phenomenon to which attention is paid; its typical models and conceptual frameworks, or sets of assumptions about the nature of the world and the relationships of the things in it; its own epistemology, or way of knowing what is the case. The neurologist, the ordinary Western European adult and the music critic in the illustration (not to speak of the dog) gave radically differing accounts of the events perceived, because they were in different universes of discourse. A professional philosopher and a middle-aged bricklayer will tend to explain their own behaviour (even if it is 'objectively' the same behaviour) in vastly different terms. They seem to 'think differently'.

Speaking of languages within organisations, in these terms, is not very novel. Lilian Gilbreth (1914, 157), at a somewhat basic level, noted that it would be useful if the man who wrote job instruction cards and the man who used them were both masters of English; the substitute is 'standard wording', a formal language. Chester Barnard paid much attention to the difficulties of ensuring communication, noted that there is a language of behaviour that can supersede words and that men accustomed to working together evolve a 'special language' which cuts down the time of communication (Barnard, 1938, 108). Simon, Smithburg and Thompson give most of a chapter to a discussion of the 'barrier of language', of terms of reference and of 'status distance' in hindering effective communication in organisations (1950, 229–43). March and Simon develop the idea of an 'in-language' among those who work together. Organisational sub-units, given a separate task or subgoal, see their environment selectively, evaluating in terms of their subgoal; what they decide is validated by what they perceive as the effects of earlier decisions, and that too is filtered through this partial, restricted frame of reference. Any instruction or order received is understood via the same set of interpretations. In communication among themselves, and to some extent when communicating with others, members of the group come to 'hear' overtones and undertones not heard by others, and certain words (or other symbols) carry a penumbra of connotations that are not always consciously separated out by the members and never fully appreciated by outsiders. The use of technical jargon, and the tendency to develop 'in-jokes', reinforce the impenetrability of the 'in-language', though caused by other mechanisms.

We should try, as always, to distinguish the purely cognitive aspects of in-language formation from the social-psychological and motivational aspects. The mechanisms of the development of group consciousness and of group maintenance are well enough known (see Homans, 1950; Dalton, 1959; V. A. Thompson, 1961; J. D. Thompson, 1967; etc.). Thus, although we may assume that a new member of any such grouping will quickly learn and adopt the argot of the group so as to be accepted as a member, we also assume that he will continue to use the in-language because of a recognition that it really is necessary to express the nature of the problems faced in the daily work of the group and communicate about them. It is not just a badge or fashion or totem, like the schoolboy's secret and esoteric slang. To some extent, communication between individuals is always (as noted so carefully in the plays of Harold Pinter and others) subject to 'cognitive gaps': none of us can make effective use of information we do not fully understand; we cannot understand something we cannot recognise and classify; and our means of recognising and classifying derive from our personal stock of knowledge and experience, which, of course, is different from individual to individual. Where we have a strong interest in achieving communication, we devote effort to trying to 'understand the other person's language'; and this is true whether it refers to 'ethnic' tongue or 'universe of discourse'.

The normal method of acquiring an in-language is, like that of the child acquiring his 'native' language, by interaction with those who already speak it, though it can, like a second tongue, also be acquired by 'study', through books and the like – usually imperfectly.

The same mechanisms, we may assume, operate to form 'cognitive communities' of people in different organisations, or different parts of an organisation, who come to recognise that they 'speak the same language', perhaps because they deal with problems of the same order of comprehension, and come to discover that, although they have developed concepts and substantive vocabulary in isolation from one another in different organisations or divisions, these concepts and terms can be 'translated' into the interests of others. In the case of 'professional' people, of course, acknowledgement of the 'cognitive community' is quite overt: it develops during their professional training and persists to a large degree throughout their career, whatever sort of organisation employs them and whatever difference of subject matter or 'policy domain' may intervene. Other 'subject interest' communities have formed; the earlier in date, the nearer they are to the highly prestigious professionalised fields like medicine and architecture, law and accountancy. The number of associations of 'specialists' who are not quite professionalised (baths attendants, festival organisers, etc.) grows week by week.

'Cognitive communities' related to order of comprehension, as displayed in the railway closures material, can be easily identified – at least, at the 'higher' and the 'lower' ends of the scale which leads from 'generality' to 'specificity'. Politicians and statesmen are often conscious of 'living in a different world' from others; senior administrators and managers likewise; and at the operational end are communities linked by specific knowledge (tradesmen, etc.) and by common life-style and experience (trade unions). But, again, we should keep distinct placing on the generality/specificity scale and judgement of a different kind about 'level of comprehension'. That phrase can also mean the absolute capacity to grasp and understand, to take in and manipulate complexity, and assumptions are made that ability to grasp problems high on the generality/specificity scale is a function of 'intelligence', so that the cleverer you are the broader your concerns – with corresponding judgements about those who inhabit the 'lower' levels on the scale, who are said to have 'limited comprehension'. In another confluence of two ideas, the recognition that people who habitually deal with problems at a given level of generality develop a common mode of speaking about these problems becomes hopelessly confused with observation about social class and about variations in the use of the English language – accent, grammatical style, size of vocabulary and so on – which, however accurate in their own terms, are not at all what we are talking about here. That characteristic differences in 'intelligence' or length of formal education period, and in social class and manner of speech, *are* found to correlate in British organisations with the placing on a scale of generality/specificity of the work done we shall not try to deny; it just does not matter for the present analysis, and we are attempting (as explained in Chapter 1) to keep the discussions always on the plane of logical entailment rather than of empirical correlation. Social class distinctions and so on are not entailed in the logic of implementation and the execution process.

Translation

Given, then, that those who work within a particular 'order of comprehension' (for example, in one of the five clusters of activities we recognised in the railway closures material) should take into account, in their decision making, considerations appropriate at the next-lower realm in 'order of comprehension', and given that each 'order of comprehension' has its characteristic 'universe of discourse', set of ideas and terms, habitual outlooks and 'in-language', which is a necessary medium of communication within the cognitive community formed by working at that level (not a mere house slang), it follows that at least some of those in the 'higher' realm have to learn something of the 'language' of those in the 'lower' realm, in order to understand what kind of concerns the latter have, and at least some of those who work in the lower realm of 'order of comprehension' will come to know something of the language of those inhabiting the higher realm, through this interaction if in no other way.

Thus, even if the 'universes of discourse' are different, there will have to be people able to act as 'translators' from one language into the other. And, in the ordinary way, there will be such people. A number of those who work now in a higher realm will have at an earlier stage in their career worked in a lower realm and will know the language even if their factual knowledge is out-of-date. Other people who work now in a lower realm will have an expectation of coming to inhabit the higher and will have an interest in preparing themselves for it by 'learning the language'. (This is not a pejorative or slighting remark: 'language' here stands not only for the 'jargon', or the *appearance* of understanding, but for the ability to grasp and discuss the problems of a different order of consideration.)

But more important than either of these, as mechanisms for ensuring the availability of translators, is the nature of the organisational hierarchy. The idea of different 'orders of comprehension' is an abstract one: it belongs in the 'logic sequence', in our earlier terminology. There is no warrant for conceiving of a sharp boundary in *organisational* terms between 'orders of comprehension', or realms of consideration on the generality/specificity continuum, or whatever. Reifying the abstract idea, expressing it in terms of 'organisational space', may take different forms according to whether we talk about a single large organisation, or a group of large organisations, or a single small organisation, and so on. In the very small organisation interaction between all members may be so great that virtually everyone has at least a smattering of all the languages employed, and so direct communication between one member and almost any other member about almost any matter of business is possible. In the single large organisation with a fairly well defined hierarchy of rank the gradation of level of generality may be more like a spectrum of colour shades than bands of primary colours, the transition from one order of comprehension to the next being mediated through two or even three levels of rank. In such a case there will always be at least one organisational level which straddles the potential gap between 'universes of discourse' and is naturally 'bilingual'. In the group of large organisations linked (as in the railway closures case-study) by a series of common problems that recur regularly, it is quite customary to designate officers with special responsibilities for 'liaison' – on either side, as it were, of the boundary between one organisation and the next on any path of implementation. These officers do more than merely translate from one 'universe of discourse' to another, but they at least do that.

The case-study material suggested that while those in the realm of one 'order of comprehension' took into account, when making their decisions, the effects their choices might have at the next-lower level in 'order of comprehension', the kind of considerations appropriate to the level below that seemed somewhat too trivial to be brought seriously into the equation. There would be consequences at that level, it was recognised; but, constrained as those on the high level were by pressures from an even higher level, and taking relative importance into account, it couldn't be allowed to matter what these consequences were: they would just have to be sorted out by those who handled such questions at that level.

The reverse might be seen to be true also. To those who work on a low level of generality (which is the same as a high level of specificity), matters being discussed 'far above their heads' often seem unreal, even 'got up' to give them something to quarrel about – certainly nothing to do with their own difficulties. 'We have our own job to do, which is quite enough without worrying about theirs' may be a typical response from either group in respect of the other – those 'two up' in respect of those 'two down', and vice versa: from statesmen in respect of Traffic Facilities Section and vice versa, from Traffic Facilities Section in respect of ballast loaders and vice versa. More than one 'order of comprehension' apart, neither group feels that the other group's considerations are relevant to their own decisions.

It is just as well. For our later analysis has shown that the two groups would find it difficult to communicate with one another, to 'understand one another's language' – that is, appreciate the nuances of each other's technical terms, get into each other's way of thinking and so on. Interaction between persons on the margin between adjacent realms, in 'order of comprehension', is frequent enough for there to be a number of 'natural bilinguals'. In organisations such as the Ministry or the railways undertaking, which may span about three of the 'orders of comprehension' that we are dealing with, there may be about eight or ten levels of hierarchical authority or rank. So a bracket of three adjacent ranks may all still be within a single realm in 'order of comprehension'; superiors and subordinates all considering questions at more or less the same degree of generality (or specificity). But the lowest rank in the bracket of three is likely to be familiar with the language of the level below, while the highest is likely to be familiar with the language of the level above – not by a designed division of function, but by reason of the relative frequency of their respective interactions.

Interaction between realms in 'order of comprehension' that are not adjacent has no such mechanism to produce 'natural bilinguals'. It is not a matter of organisation that the universes of discourse are far apart; it is a matter of logic: ascription, not prescription. If interaction *were* frequent, then the two realms must be described as adjacent. If, nevertheless, direct communication clear across an intervening realm in 'order of comprehension' becomes necessary, the 'second language' must be studied, deliberately acquired, by means other than through daily interaction. The incentive to spend time and energy doing this would have to be extraordinarily great to overcome the natural tendency to rely on the succession of 'bilinguals' (a chain of translators) that the rank hierarchy provides.

Moreover, there is another complication. On any one level in 'order of comprehension', there is bound to be (inside the one organisation or outside it) more than one 'universe of discourse' and corresponding in-language to be learnt. Different sectors of the policy field, different specialisms in the 'horizontal plane', have their own special vocabularies and ways of looking at things. In the Ministry, perhaps, there would be a 'closures' jargon and 'terms of reference' that other railways divisions did not fully share, a 'railways' universe that was not inhabited by the 'highways' people in the Ministry, and so on. Broadly the same principles can be seen to apply to such differences in the lateral dimension as have been described for the 'vertical' dimension of 'order of comprehension'; indeed, they are much better understood, and conventionally treated. It is the notion of 'vertical' language barriers that is novel, not the idea that specialists (differentiated groups in the horizontal plane) have their own esoteric concepts and vocabularies which make it difficult to appreciate what they are trying to say. 'Natural bilingualism' operates in this plane also, between adjacent specialisms; language barriers between remote specialisms may be total. The interesting case is the 'cognitive community' that transcends both hierarchy and organisational boundary: for instance, one of the well established professions (law, medicine, accountancy). We shall return to these points later. For the moment, we need but note that the fact of many 'universes of discourse' on any one level in 'order of comprehension' reinforces the tendency to rely on a chain of 'bilinguals' in attempting to communicate outside one's own universe.

A visitor to the Ministry, the railways undertaking and (say) the demolition contractor could readily confirm the existence of different 'universes of discourse', should he ask to be taken along the 'dynamic path', or 'trace', of the Wetherby closures material through the several organisations. It is most unlikely that he would find one person able to conduct him from one end of the process to the other, explaining the several activities as they went. More likely, he would find himself accompanied along a stretch of the path by a particular guide, who would say that he 'knew broadly what went on in that area' although he was expert in only one section of it, and then he would be handed over at some boundary or other (which might or might not be visible to the visitor) to a second person, who, it would be said, could 'tell him more about that area' than could the first person (indeed, the first guide might well confess total ignorance of this new stretch). Before the end of the path, a third and perhaps a fourth guide would have appeared, each able to translate for the visitor and explain a limited, local area through which the dynamic path led. The visitor would end up knowing a very great deal more about the whole process than any one of the guides or any single person in any of the organisations and sections. This, I venture to suggest, is typical of all such 'traces' or 'dynamic paths', which, as we have seen, have their organising principle in the mind of the visitor in the first place.

Discretion

The visitor might also be able to confirm empirically what a 'descent' through the realms of lesser and lesser 'orders of comprehension' feels like: a sense of the narrowing of horizons or, perhaps, of growing concern with immediate practical effects. There was virtual unanimity among the writers we surveyed in Chapter 2 that real operative work – 'work on the world outside' (without which no policy maker would ever alter anything in reality) – took place only at the 'lowest' or 'final' stage, that of the front line, the business end, the operation. Now: if 'altering reality' includes changing the perceptions of people outside the organisation in such ways that the work *they* do on the world is then different, it has to be said that it is not true that operational effects on the world outside can be created only by the outputs of the 'final' stage or operating level. The declaration of an intention by a Minister, for example, can have immediate effects, leading people to behave in ways that leave the world quite definitely not the same as it was before the declaration. The raising of an imperial eyebrow in public may change the world. But no 'implementation process' is involved in such effects. If a statement of an intention to act to achieve a certain purpose results in the achieving of that purpose without the act, a form of self-fulfilling prophecy has occurred. If the statement of an intention to act to achieve a certain purpose results in the immediate achievement of some other purpose or effect, the act is still needed: an implementation process follows. Let us accept as axiomatic that we are interested only in effects that are the outcome of implementation processes, and that output from operating level is the only output we need concern ourselves with.

Precisely what signals the visitor might be reading, on his path from the intention to the fulfilment, as he experienced the narrowing of horizons or the growing concern with the immediate and the practical, can be left to the reader's imagination. There would, perhaps, be cues in the changing physical setting (the wider the horizons, the deeper the carpet), or in the speech and manners of the guide, which the visitor would interpret through his social knowledge, as we have noted earlier (and decided to discard as not logically entailed). But the main signs would be in the nature of the explanations given of what was going on at any point; what the purpose of the activity being observed was said to be.

According to some of the literature, the visitor tracing an actual dynamic path or process of implementation through a constellation of organisations, or parts of one organisation, should experience a sense of the diminution of 'discretion':

> The commands of the captain at the scene of a fire place much narrower limits on the discretion of the firemen than those placed on a fire chief by the city charter which states in general terms the function of the fire department . . . the discretion of a subordinate officer is limited only by the specification of the objective of his unit and its general schedule. He proceeds to narrow further the discretion of his own subordinates so far as is necessary to specify what part each subunit is to play in accomplishing the task of the whole. (*Simon, 1944, 18, 20*)

Again, in the March and Simon understanding of the process, the activities of persons at the lower levels of a hierarchy are more 'programmed' and specified than those of persons at higher levels, whose programmes, they say, are likely to specify desired outcome rather than to prescribe a particular activity; and the farther a programme goes in the latter direction (specifying outcome), the more discretion it allows for the person implementing it. Alternatively, the more *search* activity in a post (the more thinking, exploring, and conjecturing there is to be done), the more discretion; and search activity is more frequent at higher levels (March and Simon, 1958, 147).

On the other hand, we have to accommodate this apparently fairly straightforward equation of amount of discretion with hierarchical rank to two other concepts of the same writers: one, the notion of the 'province' of the subordinate; and two, the notion of 'absorption of uncertainty' at the points of contact between the organisation and the outside world. The early Simon article speaks of the US Army Field Service Regulations (1941), which state that an order of a superior should not 'trespass' on the province of the subordinate commander; and there is a hint that, although it is not spelt out in the Regulations, the nature of the system ensures that the private soldier, the lowest rank of all ('the man who actually does the army's "work" ', says Simon), also has, *de facto*, his 'province'. Barnard, even earlier, had been quite clear that the specifying of what work was to be done could only be made at the 'final stage, when and where the work is being done' – that is, by the men who do it, not by their superiors (Barnard, 1938, 232). What is the nature of this 'province', on which the superior should not – perhaps *cannot* (for lack of knowledge, Barnard suggests) – trespass?

March and Simon note that the perceptions of those actually in contact with 'reality', or their communication of those perceptions, are perforce taken as 'fact' by the rest of the organisation; 'uncertainty is absorbed', and 'a great deal of discretion and influence is exercised' by those who thus act as the sense organs of the organisation, because they also perform part of the 'brain function' in interpreting and screening sensory inputs. And since 'direct perception of production processes is limited largely to employees in a particular operation on the production floor', and direct perception of customer attitudes is limited to those who meet customers, and so on, then persons on these 'low' levels are endowed with discretions their superiors do not enjoy.

But here is a new thought: these are discretions of a different type, not just differences in 'amount of discretion'. It is, indeed, possible to clarify some of the problems in the use of the term 'discretion' in the literature by first substituting the scale of generality/specificity and seeing if anything is left. Thus, any observation that the discretion of a Minister, say, must be considered greater or wider than the discretion of a ballast loader, because the decision of the Minister would affect many more people, or have many more consequences or the like, would be analysed in two steps: first, to place the Minister and the ballast loader at their respective points on the generality/specificity scale and, second, to ask then whether the Minister's discretion at his level is or is not greater than the ballast loader's at *his* level. That would still require a scale to measure 'size' or 'amount' of discretion, level for level. And it would not tackle the matter of 'type' of discretion.

Let us look first at the concept of 'province', and go on after that to examine the nature of 'discretion' a little further.

'Province'

Consider again the model we developed earlier of the way in which a policy change in an organisation of the type represented by the Ministry or the Railways Board is initiated, scrutinised for the accuracy of its diagnosis of the problem, tested for the feasibility of its proposed solution, cleared for the disturbance it will occasion in other sectors of the organisation, and then authorised and promulgated. This may or may not be a good model: knowledgeable readers may have their reservations on several points. But I doubt that anyone will question the basic premise: that everyone at appropriate levels in the organisation who has an 'official interest' in a case or proposal has a right to be consulted about it before decisions are taken that would affect that interest or the responsibilities that legitimise it. Such a person does not, of course, have a right to win every battle; but, if the machinery works properly, he will know when a battle is impending and a defence will not go by default.

The nature of such 'rights' is interesting. There is an ancient sense of the word 'office' which implies a trust or duty, an obligation on the holder to discharge his function faithfully on appropriate occasions. Thus a newspaper can report that So-and-so 'discharged the office of "best man" with great aplomb', or the like. When the total of a Minister's responsibilities are parcelled out among a number of divisions and so on, something of this ancient sense is retained. In special circumstances, the direct placing of trust in or ascribing of duty to an officer is a matter of law – as in the function of a Public Health Inspector in condemning meat or the decision of a Chief Constable as to whether or not to prosecute in a particular case. In instances like that the officer's decision is not challengeable by his hierarchical superiors – or at least, the courts will uphold the subordinate if it should be so challenged.

The logic of bureaucratic structure, unsupported by the law in England, appears to produce a similar limitation on the sheer 'command' authority of a civil service superior. If a man has been appointed to occupy a particular post, and its job description includes phrases indicating that the post is concerned with a defined sector of the Minister's responsibilities (e.g. 'Section 56(8) Closures'), then the man acquires 'jurisdiction' over that sector; and although his superior clearly retains overall responsibility (for, say, 'reshaping' as a whole), it would be unthinkable for the superior to take decisions in respect of Section 56(8) closures – or to countenance anyone else taking such decisions – without the knowledge of the holder of the proper office. It would also be unusual for the advice of the holder of the office not to be accepted in a matter concerned *solely* with Section 56(8) closures. *Mutatis mutandis*, the same general principle seems to apply where a jurisdiction is acquired by other means – by prescriptive right or by delegation – even where there is no written job description or formal list of duties. Weber recognised the phenomenon in these words:

> When the principle of jurisdictional 'competency' is fully carried through, hierarchial subordination – at least in public office – does not mean that the 'higher' authority is simply authorised to take over the business of the 'lower'. Indeed, the opposite is the rule. (*Weber, in Gerth and Mills, 1948, 197*)

The Ministry, when it is considering a proposal for change in the way suggested earlier, is therefore to be seen as a congeries of jurisdictions – at different levels, jurisdictions within jurisdictions – some of which will 'have an official interest in' a particular matter, others not. The initial memorandum will be headed by a circulation list, designating recipients by name if above a certain rank, and by initials of the 'office' or section if below that rank. Most of these recipients are not to be regarded as 'experts' in the subject area of their jurisdiction, hardly even as 'specialists' in it, but rather as 'sovereigns', 'kings' or 'custodians'. The word 'competence' has two senses: the authority to do something and the ability to do it. One perhaps leads to the other in time: and in that way, what begins quasi-legally as mere 'jurisdictional competence' may become 'expertise'. But 'kingship' comes first.

An officer recognised as the custodian of a sector of responsibilities in this way is the person to whom it is expected everyone will turn for information and advice on that subject – even if he is known to have been in the post only a few weeks or days. He is 'the man to talk to about *X*', and he is supposed to know if anyone in the agency *is* talking about *X*. He is *entitled* to be consulted. He *ought* to be kept informed.

Why? It is clearly not a matter of absolute morals or ethics; it is entirely organisational. It is clearly not the same thing as professional or technical expertise (which would make it *prudential*, in his own interest, for someone to consult this man about *X*), for the obligation is present even when expertise is quite absent. It is not the same thing as possessing a monopoly of information on *X*, which would make it *unavoidable* for him to be consulted; for the predecessor of a man recently appointed to a post will know a great deal about the work of his former office and could be consulted about *X*: but such a predecessor will be among the most punctilious in upholding his successor's right to give a required piece of information to a third party, even if the new incumbent has to come to his predecessor for it first. At the least, he will try to ensure that the new man is kept fully informed about any exchange of information concerning *X*. This language – of rights, entitlements, obligations – is the language of jurisprudence and political philosophy, though entirely within the organisational boundaries. Weber simply observes it as a feature of bureaucratic internal structure. It is the way office-holders behave toward one another: perhaps a kind of 'do-as-you-would-be-done-by' – each saying to the other, 'I will help you to gain the wherewithal to discharge your responsibilities, if you will do likewise towards me.' Such equableness may not extend to all types of 'wherewithal'; but, as we may see later, there are strong inhibitions against putting a price on the use of information, running a market in it, and the consequence is that information is allocated by the main alternative mechanism – prescription of 'law'.

The right to information about *X*, then, is tied to an officer's duties in connection with or responsibilities for *X*. It is accepted that, having been judged fit to hold his office, and being held responsible by his superiors for the satisfactory discharge of its duties and 'trusts' (which include 'matters connected with X'), he has acquired official status that has to be recognised. This recognition is then transferred to the *advice* he gives, and to the decisions he makes that fall entirely within his jurisdictional competence. The advice may not be taken, the decisions may be adjudged erroneous or foolish, but his rights to give the advice and take the decisions will not be challenged; and indeed, there will be a presumption in the incumbent's favour that whatever the appearances from outside, the advice should be considered the best possible advice, the decisions the best possible in the circumstances, until evidence is adduced to the contrary.

There are problems arising, which we shall investigate at length in another place. But what we are describing in terms of a British government department is clearly a phenomenon of the same kind as described by the early Simon, quoting from the US Army Field Service Regulations: the 'province' of a subordinate officer. (See also Janowitz, 1959, 31–4; Thompson, 1961; Taub, 1969, 89–105; Haas and Drabek, 1973, 242–3.)

The 'province', let us note, is defined both horizontally and vertically. The organisation's total responsibilities are officially divided into sectors or subject areas, policy fields, or domains: but the responsibilities are also, we could say, divided into levels according to placing on the generality/specificity scale, or 'order of comprehension'. A 'province', that is to say, falls entirely within a particular realm in 'order of comprehension': this (as the Simon usage indicated clearly) distinguishes it from the notion of a 'command', which, as it were, goes all the way down. A 'province' may be vertically defined by the mere *rank*: a subordinate officer (upon whose 'province' the superior is enjoined not to trespass, in the field Service Regulations) also has subordinates, after all; perhaps each of them, too (if he has a recognised jurisdiction or competence) is entitled to have it treated as a 'province'. (But perhaps a subordinate, or subordinate unit, that could be effectively substituted by another without violating the principle of jurisdictional competence, simply does not qualify as a 'province'.) We will not, however, pursue the operational definition of 'province': it is a term of art, a fiction of jurisprudence, a theoretical concept, and if it does not seem applicable in some concrete instance, that will define its utility, not challenge it.

Simon's usage indicates that the concept of 'province' is one that gives a subordinate rights over his superior; it does not give to a superior any rights over his subordinate that he does not already enjoy.

The custodian of this 'province', let it be emphasised, is no tyrant. Everything he does is liable to be governed by rules or doctrines or pressures, and influenced by loyalties and fears and ambitions. He is incontrovertibly in a hierarchy of authority, of sanctions, which he wields over those below him and which are wielded over him by his own superiors. He cannot fly in the face of facts or of Nature. He must manoeuvre and choose allies and play politics in the internal power game emphasised by Bryson, Tullock, Downs and others. He can act only within the constraints imposed by the resources, material and other, allocated to him or which he can acquire in a legitimate manner. All that is claimed on his behalf is that, so long as he occupies the post he has been appointed to, he has a duty that is no one else's, a responsibility, a jurisdictional competence, a 'province' of which he is the custodian on behalf of the organisation as a whole: for no one else occupies quite the same 'niche' as he does, defined horizontally by division of specialisation of task, and vertically by placing on the scale of generality/specificity. This is the case whether he is the Permanent Secretary or a humble section head. Neither of them, nor anyone between, is there merely to give or receive orders: as we shall see, they are there to make choices and each is in a unique position to be able to do so.

It is clearly a very important concept. As between the two basic 'models' we elaborated earlier (the biological, developmental one and the mechanistic, aggregative one), the incorporation of the idea of the 'province', seeing an organisation as a complex of relatively autonomous jurisdictions or 'offices', at first sight powerfully reinforces the 'aggregative' assumptions about the nature of the implementation process. The mechanisms of 'switching-in' existing programmes of activities (hitherto considered as being of the quasi-routine or 'highly programmed' kind) can be extended to the linking of existing 'provinces', which are (almost by definition, but let us postpone the argument) non-programmed decision centres, loci of problem solving and 'search' activities.

But the idea of the 'province' is not incompatible with the 'developmental' hypothesis: that, too, assumes (in the strict biological analogy) that 'later' stages have their own rationale, their own connection, as it were, to the fount of original authority, the genetic blueprint in the chromosomes (or the policy decision). Activities in 'later' stages may be triggered off by the previous stage, and possibly influenced by it, but they are not determined or specified by it. The notion of 'province' rules out neither hypothesis.

The same is surely true of the idea of the 'order of comprehension', in its two aspects: a set of placings, or realm, on a scale of general (all-embracing) to specific (highly focused), on the one hand and, on the other, a 'universe of discourse', or set of outlooks, conceptual apparatus and terminology. This corresponds exactly with the March and Simon model of 'programmes-within-programmes' – indeed, was suggested largely by it – and it fits happily into the 'machine theory' analogue – a machine which gains its high variety by being composed of machines of somewhat lower variety, each of which is made up of machines of simpler specification still, and so on to the necessary number of levels, until fixed-relations machines are reached. Even the fixed-relations machines, however, are fitted (we saw earlier) with input-selecting devices which have two functions: they reject 'incompatible' inputs, or parts of inputs that they are not equipped to process, and they 'smooth out' inputs. The logic of this selection for compatibility is an analogue of the 'universe of discourse' or 'in-language' part of the 'order of comprehension' idea; you cannot accept what you cannot understand.

But the 'order of comprehension' schema is just as 'developmental', even in its own terms. It will accommodate comfortably the notion of an egg or policy 'containing' the blueprint of the specific final-stage result, actualised via stages of the shutting off of areas of potentiality differentially, from the 'general' to the 'specific' in many pathways of development. The 'triggers' of each stage, on each path, are an 'in-language' understood only by perceivers who are simultaneously at the same age of 'generations since ovum', and in the same location or site: there is no communication with any other perceivers, even if all receive the signal. (However, the 'trigger' chemical compound is not species-specific: the message can be 'understood' by cells of the same relative age and site in other species – which is an analogue of the 'cognitive community' that extends across organisational frontiers.)

Measuring discretion

Let us return to the consideration of 'discretion'. It appears that the ideas of 'province' and 'order of comprehension' will not support the view that the process of implementation entails a progressive 'narrowing of discretion'. To justify this view, one would have to find a single scale of 'amount of discretion' that could be applied to, say, the Minister and the ballast loader, and show the Minister always coming out with more. Now as suggested earlier, if we simply use the scale of generality/specificity for this purpose, the required result will follow. But that interpretation of the word 'discretion' is far from exhausting the meanings employed in common speech. There are perhaps two that it ignores. In the first the word connotes 'a judicious temper', an ability to discriminate wisely; thus a person may attain 'the age of discretion', in the sense that before that age he or she was *unable* to make necessary judgements, and one adult may be said to have 'more discretion' ('be more discreet') than another. In the second sense the word means the partial or total absence of external restriction or constraint upon choice, the ability to act at pleasure, or according to one's own judgement and not someone else's.

In neither of these two senses is it beyond argument that a Minister always has more of the quality than a ballast loader. Injudicious and indiscreet Ministers may be thought to be (at least in principle) just as common as injudicious and indiscreet ballast loaders. We can certainly conceive of circumstances in which a Minister or Permanent Secretary would be so hedged around by pressures and conflicts and constraints as to have very little 'room to manoeuvre', to act according to his own judgement – while another holder of the same office, or himself at another time, enjoyed considerably more 'freedom'. The same applies to a ballast loader: one might be almost completely free to load ballast as he saw fit, while another was time-and-motioned to distraction. We could not, therefore, say that a Minister as such enjoyed greater discretion than a ballast loader as such; although, given enough empirical information, it might well be feasible to arrive at the very broad judgement that, on the whole, and over most of their respective tasks, a particular Minister enjoyed greater discretion than a particular ballast loader (or the reverse). It might even be found that Ministers, as a class, enjoy more discretion in their job than do ballast loaders, as a class, in theirs. But that would be a finding, after research; there is no justification for an *a priori* assumption that that is the case.

Amount of discretion, then, is independent of rank as such, and independent of job as such; and also, it would seem, of 'order of comprehension' as such. People at different levels in an organisation, and people carrying out activities at different points in an implementation process, can be enjoying a lot of discretion or a little. Amount (and perhaps type) of discretion does vary, but when we take into account the effects of what we are calling the 'province' of a subordinate, and the change in 'order of comprehension' or placing on the scale of generality/specificity, 'amount of discretion' seems to be a way of speaking about the number and strengths of the various constraints that may act upon a decision maker. Some will be those imposed by a man's superiors and by the rules of the organisation. Others will be imposed by 'facts', or by the environment outside the organisation. It does not follow in logic, it is not entailed by the nature of the implementation process, that such constraints are invariably lighter at the beginning of such a process than at the end.

We shall be returning to the concept of 'discretion' many times.

The 'Babel House' model

Let us recapitulate the understandings we have so far reached in this chapter, before proceeding to the next stage of the argument.

Each agency through which the hypothetical visitor passes in his guided tour down the dynamic path of some particular multi-organisational implementation process should (if the argument so far is acceptable) be seen as a species of orderly Tower of Babel. It might be represented as a large office block, in which the rooms are occupied by administrative office-holders: that is, persons or groups each with an office to discharge – a task to do, a jurisdiction to maintain, a set of responsibilities – defined by, on the one hand, the sector of policy field or the professional specialism or type of work within their respective competences, and by, on the other hand, their placing in the vertical plane along a scale of generality/specificity. Each room is, naturally, on one or other floor of the building (the vertical dimension) and in one or other corner of the building (the horizontal dimension). Wider horizons are visible from the higher floors, but only on the ground floor can goods and services actually be taken into and out of the building. (However, it is possible to exchange signals with other buildings, from any floor.)

If the floors are conceived of as corresponding to grades of official rank (which is easiest), then there may be eight, nine or ten floors in the building. But we have to imagine that, by some quirk of landscape or of glazing, only three different views of the problem environment are obtainable from the many floors of the building: a characteristic 'top-floor' view, a middle-floor view and a ground-floor view.

The building is a Tower of Babel because a different tongue (concepts, vocabulary) is talked on each floor – amounting to a considerable linguistic disparity between top-floor speech and ground-floor speech – and different jargons and dialects are spoken on any one floor, in each of the corners and other areas. As between one floor and the next, or as between one office and its neighbour on the same floor, differences in language and habitual style of doing business can usually be noted, though it is quite easy for adjacent ranks, and denizens of adjacent offices, to understand one another. Messages from distant locations in any direction – from a far-away corner, or from a much higher or much lower floor – do not, by contrast, make much sense on first hearing or reading: the more distant, the less intelligible.

Only within the 'office', therefore, is communication uninhibited. Only there are there people whom one can rely on to speak one's own language as well as one does oneself and to pick up the nuances, the inflections, the conventional abbreviations and so on. All other messages require at least a modicum of translation.

This model of the organisation, or that kind of organisation with which we are dealing, as a polyglot government building (perhaps a 'Babel House', in the current Whitehall manner) is more complex and more explicit than the models assumed in the literature surveyed in Chapter 2, but it can accommodate most of the concepts we found there and even clarify them somewhat. Gulick (1937, 6) envisaged an administrative structure of subdivisions of work, co-ordinated by 'organisation' – which he defined as 'orders of superiors to subordinates, reaching from the top to the bottom of the entire enterprise'. Barnard discussed the 'scheme of organisation' – the definition of organisation positions and the communication between them – which turns given purpose, given objectives and direction at the top into specific jobs, named men and set times at the bottom. Barnard

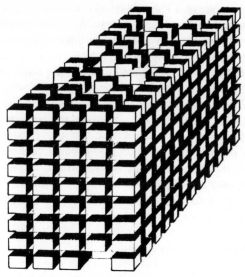

Fig. 11   Babel House

spelt out how this was done, too. Each chief at his own level speaks to his subordinates in this fashion: 'This means for us such and such operations now at these places, such others at those places, something today here, others tomorrow there' (Barnard (1938) 1971, 232). Simon, Smithburg, Thompson (1950, 229ff) noted that a chief must derive some of the knowledge required to speak like this from what he has learnt from his subordinates themselves; they, in fact, by selective communication, can influence the decisions the superior takes by determining what he knows. Tullock developed an arithmetical version of this, showing that 'distortion' of information passing upwards through the ranks of a hierarchy of authority to the decision maker at the top is cumulative, while the order that conveys the decision is subject to similar distortion on its way downwards to operating level (Tullock, 1965, 139). Downs (1967) incorporated much of March's and Simon's theory of non-motivational causes of selective perception and communication into his understanding of the same processes. Information, according to Downs, is 'screened' and condensed on its way up and knowledge of the degree of uncertainty it represents is suppressed, so that higher levels (or distant units, in the case of lateral communication) accept as working fact what is always to some extent an 'educated guess'. Orders, as they move from a higher to a lower level, must be expanded and made more specific, and at every level there is a 'discretionary gap' between the orders an official receives and those he issues (Downs, 1967, 134; see p. 63 above for full quotation).

These are the questions subsumed in the fourth set of assumptions underlying the two main models of the implementation process: the nature of the transition between stages of the process, how progress is actually made. The 'Babel House' model tends to emphasise the difficulties of communication, and the differences between realms in the 'order of comprehension' dimension. But organisations of this kind do continue to exist and to produce, and so these obstacles must be being overcome and these differences harnessed. Let us look first at what happens in this 'discretionary gap' to which Downs refers.

Pragmatisation and the 'P/Q relation'

Let us suppose that it has been decided on high that nationalised industries must become commercial enterprises. Where did the 'target surplus' formula for doing this come from? Suppose, again, that the 'target surplus' formula has been adopted: how did that become a confident figure of 'nil per cent' when applied to the railways? If it is desired to reduce cross-subsidisation between profitable Intercity rail traffic and unremunerative branch lines or commuter traffic, why were 'social grants' put up as the answer, rather than any of the other feasible ways of doing this? Once the principle of grants to socially necessary services is accepted, how does whoever-it-is know what should be written into the enabling legislation? And so on. Each of these examples can be called a 'policy decision', and answering these corresponding 'where?, how?, why?' questions a matter for a separate analysis of the historical circumstances and constraints. We are not going to pursue such answers here, for the present purpose is to illustrate the process and all of these examples are intended to be examples of the same phenomenon – the process of what was earlier called 'pragmatisation'. Given an intention, it is necessary to decide what is needed to 'put it into effect', or to 'make it work', or to 'implement it' – or any of a number of other ways of expressing this thought. To show that the phenomenon is not confined to the highest realms in 'order of comprehension', we could give as many illustrations from the 'demolition, etc.' cluster of activities in the railway closures case-study. A length of track is to be removed to another location by a certain day: somehow or other (how?) this becomes a whole series of entries on monthly and weekly work schedules associated with sending a particular gang and a particular mobile crane crew from one job to the next, this job being one of them. Ballast is then available for lifting, within certain restrictions as to time and points of access. This set of ideas turns into a letter to a contractor, and then into entries in his work schedules, and then into a job card handed to a foreman: three successive 'discretionary gaps', filled by different people.

This is the same phenomenon Barnard had in mind, clearly, when he had the chief executive talk to his department heads, who then spoke in similar terms to their division chiefs, saying, 'This means for us these things now', etc.; then the division chiefs added their interpretation of what 'these things' meant for them and their district chiefs – who did likewise for their own subordinates. It is what Simon meant in saying that the colonel assigned to each battalion its task; the lieutenant-colonel told each company what it then had to do; the captain each platoon. Tullock (and Downs likewise) spoke of decisions on policy being passed down through the pyramid, with each lower level making the 'administrative' decisions required 'to implement the policies set from on high'; and Tullock gave an account of the process in algebraic detail (it is to be found on p. 56 above, but is reproduced in part here for convenience):

> B is, presumably, only one of several direct subordinates to A. B will then have to decide what parts of the general policy direc-tives issued by A affect his particular division of the hierarchy. He will prepare orders and pass along to his inferiors, C_1, C_2, and C_3, only those parts of A's overall directive that he considers relevant. But to this directive he will add his own detailed administrative instructions. C_1 will do likewise. . . . (*Tullock, 1965, 139*)

Downs adds that the reason why A does not prepare directions for the C and lower levels as well as for B is that he lacks the time (Downs, 1967, 133).

There is in these accounts of the way in which an implementation process works an assumption that what A decides is a 'policy' for the whole organisation, a policy that somehow affects the work of everyone in it, albeit differentially, conveyed selectively as relevant, at each level, and distorted nearly beyond recognition, perhaps, by the time it reaches lower levels, and certainly 'interpreted' several times over; yet still assumed to give a unity to the performance, making an unbroken chain of causation, so that at least some proportion of what all the various people at H-level do is what A wanted and would have ordered if he'd had the time to spell it all out to each man directly.

The decision that British Railways must 'pay their way' in a quasi-commercial sense was, I suppose, a general policy of this kind, which perhaps ought to have had an effect on the work of everyone in the organisation. But in that case it is difficult to see how some *parts* only of such a decision would be relevant, and other parts irrelevant, at the level of B in Tullock's illustration; and it is difficult to see how *any* of that decision would be relevant at, say, the level of moving rail crossings from York to West Riding when District Engineers (York) was asked to supply manpower.

Are there not other kinds of top-level decision, and are they not much the more common kinds, where what is ordered is a particular result to be brought about by some part of the organisation only? Where A gives a directive to B only, and B in turn may instruct C_1 but not C_2 or C_3, and so on? And is it not the case that, at least sometimes, a directive by A only really applies to decisions by B and possibly by C, at which level the directive 'peters out' and is absorbed into routines which are quite unchanged by the decision of A? That, at any rate, is what we found in the branch lines closure material.

But, even laying aside such quibbles, these accounts of the implementation process do not take our present quest much farther forward. What we would like to know more about is how Barnard's department heads know what to say to their division chiefs; the nature of the work that the lieutenant-colonel does on whatever is said to him by the colonel, before he is in a position to tell the captain what his objective is; where Tullock's B derives his 'detailed administrative instructions' from that he adds for C's benefit to the relevant parts of A's directive. There is a 'discretionary gap' between the order a man receives and the order he gives. What does this mean?

We saw in Chapter 1 that what we are talking about is both a generalisation of, and a special case of, the familiar concept of the 'policy/administration dichotomy', or the relationship between 'policy' and 'implementation'. It is a generalisation because we can multiply examples at all levels of generality/specificity, not only at the 'higher' levels usually associated with policy making. It is a special case because we are asking questions about the relationship between one stage and the next, or one rank and its neighbours, whereas 'implementation' or 'administration' commonly describe *all* that has to happen between 'policy from on high' and the operative front line.

We decided in Chapter 1 to call this relationship between what goes before and what comes after, whether the former be 'policy' and the latter 'implementation', 'administration' or 'execution', or another pair of terms, the 'P/Q relation'. Let us consider one of these 'discretionary gaps', and see how (in principle) it has to be filled, from what we have found out about the nature of the process, the different possible sequences that one might be speaking about and how each stage of the process differs from the next.

The first observation to be made, even from the Barnard, Simon and Tullock/Downs accounts, is that such a 'discretionary gap' involves not two persons or ranks, but three. Each official (who is not at either the very top or the very bottom – neither of those has such a gap to fill) has a superior and a subordinate or, more likely, a number of subordinates of the next rank below. So let us adopt a Tullock-style hierarchy, and put ourselves temporarily in the shoes of someone around the middle of an *A*-to-*H* pyramid, say, those of *D*. The relationship looks like Fig. 12.

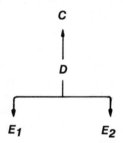

Fig. 12   The *C-D-E* triad

If we put ourselves, that is, in the shoes of (or at the desk of) *D*, then we place ourselves as the middle term of a *C-D-E* triad. *C*, *D*'s superior, is similarly the middle term in a different triad, *B-C-D*, and so on. The relationship we are speaking of is triadic, not dyadic.

Assume *D* to be District Engineer (York), for the sake of the argument, and the instruction from C to be Chief Civil Engineer's request to supply manpower for the recovery of points and crossings from the closed branch line for transfer to West Riding district. (We will not stop over the difference between 'instruction' and 'request'.) What does D do about this instruction, analytically speaking?

The first thing D does, actually as well as analytically in all probability, is to read it. But he reads it, perforce, with the eyes of D, not with the eyes of C who has issued it; already, an interpretation is taking place, even in the mere reading of what the instruction says. Reading is a brain activity and therefore tied in with a particular stock of knowledge and experience. It is extremely unlikely that any two people will make precisely the same sense out of any one written message.

Second: as he reads, D 'translates' it into his own 'language', the terms and concepts habitual to his 'office'. By 'translation' one understands the act of uttering in a second language the sense conveyed by a message in a first language, adding nothing and taking nothing away. One must know both languages well, even if one language is 'one's own' and the other 'foreign'. This can be a subtle and complex matter, but let us simplify. Suppose the wording of C's instruction to be 'Please arrange to supply manpower for transfer of crossings nos. so-and-so on such-and-such a date.' D might mentally turn those words, even as he reads them, into something like this: 'Work gang needed at the end of the month for an uplifting job.'

Analytically, D's next step is to decide what the *translated* order requires of him, what it *means* in terms of his jurisdiction. Now, that is not contained in the order, however many times translated: all that the order conveys is the result required. D himself has to supply the information which makes a problem out of the objective; that is, he has to list the means among which he is going to have to choose, survey the resources he has available to be allocated to this (and so not to some other) task and so on. D, in other words, perceives for himself whatever problem the instruction sets him; D specifies what his options are (within any general rules and constraints that may operate on any decision process). Even if the instruction contained words purporting to specify the problem, D would still have to decide whether he agrees, as District Engineer, with what C (Chief Civil Engineer) says his problem will be. He might consider that C has either underestimated or overestimated the problem, even if he has specified its nature correctly enough.

D's immediate vocalisation on receipt of the instruction might well indicate simultaneous perception of a problem. He might exclaim in some words that could be rendered as: 'Bless my soul, what are we going to do about this!' But the 'this' is the perceived problem, not the instruction as such. Let us assume that the problem *D* sees is how to fit together a work gang of the necessary skills and brawn out of what labour is left over after two previously committed gangs have been made up, and how to give them a foreman when there are only two foremen on the strength. Now *D*, if he were to take a second opinion on what the problem is (an alternative perception), might seek one from his subordinates; but let us skip that possible step, and move on. What *C*'s message has become is *D*'s perception of the problem he is presented with, and the next stage is to look for solutions.

Considerable philosophical and scientific attention has been devoted to conjecture about how humans perceive and solve problems. What a problem is can be described in some such terms as these: the perceived difference between an observed state of affairs and an intended or desired state of affairs is matched against a stock of known (experienced) possible transformations of the observed state, and a judgement made as to whether one or more such transformations (or possibly a programmed sequence of transformations) gives promise of removing or satisfactorily reducing the difference. If no such promise appears, a problem is perceived. (If *D* foresees no difficulties in his manning exercise, his immediate vocalisation might well be: 'That's all right: no problem.')

Two broad theories of how such a judgement is made exist. Those inclined to *Gestalt* psychology think in terms of a person seizing on a small number of key features of the presented situation, each of which recalls or 'stands for' a number of associated experiences – in the way that one can be virtually sure one has seen a friend in a crowd just from a glimpse at a distance of a shape of head, a colour of hair and the set of a neck. Recognition, then, is of 'bits' of actual situations one has met before and knows what to do about, and the problem is how to combine the 'bits' to fit this particular situation.

An alternative explanation relies on our experience of what usually follows what, of how one thing leads to another, so that it is chains of expectations, rather than key features, that are inspected for the necessary matching. The observed situation is (in principle) classified in several ways (as if one should say, 'It is personal/official/

social in certain proportions'; 'It is financial/legal/material in certain proportions'; 'It is supply/production/transport, etc. in certain proportions', and so on), according to one's own unique set of categorisations of life's rich tapestry, and each situation presents a 'profile' which (because of what we know usually happens) can be expected to change only in certain directions and within certain latitudes. The problem arises in trying to see how these latitudes can be used, remembering that a change in any one dimension is liable to alter the 'reading' on all the others.

Most authorities agree that one perceives the problems one can recognise or has categories for; aspects of a situation one has never met before do not throw up problems, but are consigned to a residual region of mystery, which one cannot be expected to cope with.

The literature on how humans *solve* problems once they have perceived them overlaps somewhat with 'decision theory', the study of how choice is made or ideally ought to be made. This in turn has various homes: in philosophy, in economics, in sociology, in politics; and also in social psychology, in individual psychology, in physiology, in biochemistry and in mathematics and logic. It has produced outputs as various as marketing and investment strategy, gambling systems, computer chess-playing programmes, international relations consultancy services and models of human brain functioning. This is far too large a literature to explore or even summarise here, and it is not wholly relevant. (On perception, etc., Dewey, 1933; Polya, 1945; Miller, Galanter and Pribram, 1960; Thompson, 1961; Vernon, 1962; Kuhn, 1962; Katz and Kahn, 1966; Wilson, 1970; etc. On decision theory, etc.: Grey Walter, 1953; Sluckin, 1954; Simon, 1957; Vickers, 1965, 1968; Beer, 1966, 1967, 1972; Edwards and Tversky, 1967; Audley *et al.*, 1967; Dror, 1968; Annett, 1969; Welsch and Cyert, 1970; Lindley, 1971; Self, 1972, 1975; etc.)

The first stage of problem solving after deciding what the problem is (perception) is generally called *search* – for a solution, or a number of possible solutions, or a way of approaching a solution. (For an extended discussion of 'search', see March and Simon, 1958, chap. 7; Downs, 1967, chaps. 14, 15.) There are (in principle) two ways of going about a search: algorithmically or heuristically. The algorithmic way would ensure that the entire set of possibilities was systematically explored by an exhaustive and foolproof method (an 'algorithm'), so that the 'right' solution would be bound to be considered. If a golf ball is somewhere in a pasture, an algorithm for finding it would ensure that every inch of the field was searched. This method can take a surprisingly long time, as instanced by Turing's calculation of the number of arrangements there are to be systematically inspected in the algorithmic search for the solution to a child's puzzle consisting of four-by-four sliding squares to be manipulated into some given pattern. The number is 20,922,789,888,000. At one arrangement per second, a man inspecting continuously day and night would take 663,457 years (Miller, Galanter and Pribram, 1960, 168).

A heuristic method makes use of whatever clues are available to narrow the area of search, more or less drastically. A heuristic for finding a golf ball in a pasture might involve reconstructing the trajectory from where the ball was hit and last seen. It is a much quicker method, but of course its chances of success depend upon the quality of the judgements of trajectory and point of origin. Relatively small errors can set one searching diligently in the wrong patch of field altogether. Searching one's memory for a similar problem that one has come across in the past, or searching one's files for precedents, is using a heuristic method for organisational problems, and is subject to the same sort of error. The assumption is that, once one has found a precedent, one can adopt or adapt the course of action taken then. ('Rule of precedent' means one *must* do so.)

An alternative is to review a number of easily available or frequently used solutions and to see whether any can be made to fit the presented problem. This is often the reason for classifying problems into one of a smallish number of categories – because there are that number of 'approved' solutions. As March and Simon put it, an organisation can operate in a relatively stable environment with:

(a) a repertory of standard responses,
(b) a classification of program-evoking situations,
(c) a set of rules to determine what is the appropriate response for each class of situation. (*March and Simon, 1958, 164*)

Students of behaviour in organisations are in fair agreement, also, that the process of searching for alternatives from which to select, in the kind of situation we are dealing with, is seldom continued after one or two acceptable solutions have been located. As Vickers says:

The difference between seeking the optimal and seeking the acceptable is important. . . . In examining possible solutions to a policy problem, we often review a series in order of familiarity and stop as soon as we find one that seems acceptable. If a familiar response seems good enough, why should we spend time trying out others? (*Vickers, 1965, 42n.*)

Simon calls this 'satisficing' (Simon, 1957, 204).

Our District Engineer *D*, we have said already, has not only to perceive his own problem, as it were, but also to search for his own options, his range of possible solutions. But he might well consider his problem 'solved' as soon as he has found *one* solution: he is not required to review all the possible solutions and choose the *best* – the first one that will actually 'work' will probably do for his purposes. If *D* were really stuck for even *one* solution, of course, he might seek help. He could extend his own problem-solving skills and equipment by turning the matter into an organisational sequence, asking other District Engineers for their advice, for instance, or going farther afield by seeking the help of professional specialists outside the organisation, or consulting his own subordinates. We have described earlier how, in the British civil service, if not quite so rigidly in the British Railways organisation, consultation of others is enjoined whenever a presented problem (or its proposed solution) contains references to the jurisdictional competences of other governors of 'provinces'. When the Assistant Secretary in the originating division received the hypothetical memorandum in the earlier illustration of 'feasibility and clearance' procedures, his 'search process' was collapsed into the mere scrutiny of the problem to determine which other Assistant Secretaries (or equivalents) had some 'official interest'. But, of course, in that narrative we paid no attention to how the originating division came by their proposal in the first place.

Let us, however (not to complicate matters unduly), assume that in *D*'s problem, of how to fit together a work gang (requiring a foreman) out of the men available, no 'outside' jurisdictions are involved: the problem is one for *D*'s province alone. Let us assume, further, that the solution which occurs to *D* is to reinforce one of the already committed gangs that is to be working about four miles from the uplifting site, and to ask the foreman of that gang to split his forces in two as he thinks best, designating one of the more senior workmen to take charge at each site during any periods when he himself will be away at the other. But whether or not he seeks and gets help from his subordinates in the problem-specifying or solution-seeking stages, *D* would be wise to consult them before settling finally on this particular solution. We already know why.

Factorisation

It is universally agreed in the literature we have surveyed that the reason for submitting a tentative solution (which will become an instruction) to subordinates is that they know more about the 'detail' than the superior: they are one step nearer operating level. That may be so; but it is simpler, surely, to say that the reason is that they are the people who will have to carry out the instruction if it becomes one. They have experience of which kinds of instruction *can* be carried out relatively easily and which not. (If *they* are uncertain about this, they can ask *their* subordinates, and so on; but whether any subordinate asks *his* subordinate is for him to decide.)

It is prudent, that is, for D to consult E_1 and E_2, his immediate subordinates, to receive their assurance that his tentative solution is a feasible one (that it *will* 'work'). From D's point of view, parenthetically, it would be only prudent for C to consult him (D) before C made whatever choice it is that needs an uplifting gang on that particular day. And of course, F_1, (E_1's subordinate) will hope that E_1 does not say anything rash to D without giving F_1 a chance to speak about it first. Every subordinate hopes that his superior will have enough sense to call on his relatively greater knowledge of his own province (of 'the practicalities', as he may see it), before committing himself to advice or instruction. Every subordinate feels conscious that if his superior does make a commitment without due consideration, it is the subordinate and his colleagues who will have to 'pick up the bits'. And the subordinates' problems in this regard naturally loom larger to the subordinates than they do to the superior – or to *his* superior, who might well think them not in the least pertinent.

So D, let us say, decides to pass his tentative solution to the manning problem down to his subordinates 'for checking'. Analytically, two operations are involved. First: we may assume that D's two assistants each cover one half of D's jurisdiction, but that D's jurisdiction covers many more activities than allocating work gangs. The decision to pass the tentative solution down for checking this involves either (a) the choice of which assistant to give the work to, or (b) the division of the elements of the solution into two lots, one to go to each assistant. In either case, of course, a statement of the perceived problem must accompany the statement of the proposed solution. (It does not, in principle, matter that both statements, in such a case as this, may be oral rather than written.)

Second: the communications must be in a 'language' the recipients understand. There will be no great difference between the office jargon of D and that of his assistant engineers. Nevertheless, if D were an introspective type, he would probably recognise that when speaking to C, he would find himself dropping into a *slightly* different vocabulary, simply because of the difference in the habitual concerns of Chief Civil Engineer, and he will do the same with his assistants – 'put things their way' – even if he never actually thinks about it. When it comes to speaking to the foremen, the differences will be more palpable and D may actually be conscious of the need to be sure he is 'getting across'.

The choice of which assistant to pass the work to, or its division into two pieces of work, is likely to be easy enough in practice. D's initial perception of the problem is inevitably in terms of the kinds of problem his office is accustomed to dealing with, and these problems will almost certainly be reflected in the division of labour in the office. D will think, when asked to supply manpower for a particular job, about what *can* be done, and what can be done will never vary greatly from what is being done already, since what is being done already will be reflected in the distribution of work in the office. It is still worth pausing, analytically, over the case where D has to ask one subordinate about some aspects of his tentative solution and the other about other aspects.

Let us say that one of the assistants is in charge of scheduling, of keeping records of what manpower resources were in use where and for how long and of planning their use for a month ahead, and the other assistant is in charge of personnel records – length of service, skills and personal qualities of the men employed, including foremen – and accustomed to dealing also with union matters, conditions of work and industrial relations. (Each, of course, will have other duties that need not come into this story.)

Because his assistants are specialised in this way, D tends to think about his own problems (at least, those about which he expects to seek advice from or give instructions to his subordinates) in these categories: on the one hand, the work scheduling and planning; on the other hand, the make-up and management of the gangs. Conversely (let us say), it is because most manning problems can be most conveniently factorised in this way that his assistants are thus specialised. All of D's fellow subordinates of C are specialised too, in complementary fashion to himself, in categories with which D is quite familiar, so that when he comes across a problem about which he is not confident of finding a solution he can apply within his own province, D will 'factorise' it into subproblems each of which corresponds to the specialism of one of his colleagues, so that a request for advice or assistance can be appropriately expressed and appropriately routed. To this extent, D is specifying the subproblems as he thinks his colleagues will see them, and is also using the 'language' he thinks they use about such things, so far as he is able. His colleagues may or may not agree with him completely, but unless D can 'make a stab at it', see the world as they see it at least a little, he will never be able to seek advice efficiently; he will be reduced to a generalised bleating. Nor will he be able to *give* advice efficiently. There is a marked difference between saying 'Here's what I would do', and saying 'Here's what I would do *in your place*'.

The same goes for D's approaches to his own subordinates. They are each more specialised than he himself is on their own aspects of manning exercises, though neither of them (by definition) is more specialised than he is on the manning problem *as a whole* – for if one of them were, D would not be handling the present case at all; he would simply have handed C's message down, as not being a D-level matter. This has to be emphasised. We have *assumed* that C's message produces a problem for D. It will not always be the case that a message from C presents a problem for D himself. If D does not habitually concern himself with manning problems, then although he may remain responsible to C for the work being done satisfactorily, the location of the perception and solution of the problem will move to where these matters are usually dealt with and D's role will be a merely supervisory one.

D, then, is seeking advice from his subordinates on the feasibility of the tentative solution he has come up with to the problem he faces. He has factorised both problem and solution into two subproblems, and is specifying for each of his subordinates how he thinks they will see the matter.

Since E_1 and E_2 are more specialised than their boss, they may well see it slightly differently. But that is only half of it. More significantly, the whole question may create problems for them, at their level, that D could not adequately foresee – and which in any case they will not expect D to solve, since they are not D's problems, but their own. Let us take this slowly, for it is important in appreciating the nature of the 'discretionary gap'.

On the assumption that manpower scheduling and supply is a D-level problem, it is not an E-level problem, although some aspects of it may be. D, in our illustration, is asking for advice on *his* problem: he is not trying to interfere (in this instance at least) in the way his subordinates handle *their* problems. When he comes to give his instructions on the matter, they will be instructions that deal with the problem he has been considering. They will not be instructions dealing with either (a) the problem C was dealing with when he committed District Engineer to supplying manpower as part of its solution, or (b) any problems that E_1 or E_2 usually handle. D's instructions may well *create* problems for E_1 and E_2, just as C's instruction has created a problem for D. The point of consulting E_1 and E_2 about the tentative solution before it is made into an instruction is, in part, so that any such E-level problems may be brought to light, and taken into consideration by D. If the consultation has been thorough, D ingenious and lucky, then the problems that E_1 and E_2 are left with will be simple ones, ones with known feasible solutions.

D's activity, therefore, is first to imagine how his subordinates will see D's problem, to put that version to them and then to listen to what they have to say not only about that, but about the problems it may create for them at their level (or *below* their level – but let us postpone that extension of the argument). Let us now assume that D has suggested his solution, of enlarging one of the already committed work gangs and then splitting it over two locations, to both E_1 and E_2, and that although E_1 has confirmed that as far as he can see the idea will work, E_2 has suggested that it would mean a rather complicated journey for the personnel transport, tying up a vehicle for about four hours each day, and he foresees problems in designating a workman as a temporary 'charge hand' at *both* sites – legal, union and insurance difficulties, let us say. Now this set of snags is either critical for the feasibility of D's solution or it is not: we need not pursue the course of the further consideration step by step. Let us move on to the point where D and E_2 (with, if necessary, the co-operation of D's colleagues) have found a solution that will work – probably by tinkering with D's original brainwave, but possibly by a completely fresh approach. In either case the solution will not now be the one that E_1 found to be workable, so the new one will have to be 'cleared' with him. Assuming it is all right (if it isn't, the cycle of feasibility testing has to be repeated; then there has to be a clearance with E_2, and so on), D is in a position to 'decide' what his manpower disposition on such-and-such a date will be, and to issue a set of orders accordingly. (In our earlier terms, he 'authorises' and 'promulgates' the solution decided upon.)

Analytically, E_1's reception of D's instruction sets off the same cycle in E_1's mind and office as did D's reception of C's instruction. Of course, in practice E_1 already 'knows all about' the instruction: he has had a hand in its making. He may not need to do much further 'thinking' about it: he has pre-solved the problems it creates. Nevertheless, there is still work to do – operations that he could not begin until it was an actual instruction (a commitment of authority) he was dealing with. He could not, for example, issue the necessary instructions to his own assistants, or to the foremen, until the solution to D's problem was reached and authorised, although he might well have been able to warn them that something of the sort was in the wind. Water having gone under the bridge since the question came up, new problems may have emerged. It is not at all the case that, D's problem having been solved, the rest is mere handing out of orders, any more than the instruction to D (which was a consequence of C having solved *his* problem) was the end of that matter. Each level has its own problems, influenced and even created by the solution to problems at higher levels – but not only by these, as we shall see.

We have here been expounding 'analytical' patterns. All the foregoing is part of what we earlier saw as a 'logic sequence', expressed in terms of an 'organisational sequence' involving three levels of rank hierarchy inside a single section, with an apparent 'time sequence' of a few days or weeks. But the pattern itself, I suggest, is analytically present, even where the logic sequence is collapsed into a single discussion, the organisational manifestation becomes a single meeting of those officially interested, and the time sequence a matter of minutes.

Operationalising

Let us review the 'pattern', remembering that the particular triad we

chose to focus on was but an illustration of all the possible triads there might be in the vertical plane of rank hierarchy. We were trying to extend the brief accounts given by Barnard, Tullock and others, to the effect that *D* (the focal figure) 'prepared his detailed administrative instructions'. We have, in fact, expanded and made more specific Downs's phrase, that 'orders from the top must be expanded and made more specific as they move downwards', and have considered how the 'discretionary gap between the orders an official receives from above and those he issues downwards' is actually filled (Downs, 1967, 134).

The ideas used to describe this activity by Barnard, Simon, Downs and others are usually those of 'translation' and 'interpretation'. But these terms are somewhat weak to stand for the operation we have just investigated. 'Translation' comes into it, certainly; we postulate that translation out of one 'in-language' into another occurs at virtually every transaction between offices and between levels in a hierarchy, and is a conscious activity where the offices or ranks are not near neighbours, organisationally speaking.

But the key activity is not mere translation (conveying in a second language the information contained in a message in a first language, adding nothing and subtracting nothing), nor even interpretation (which may be thought to be the conveying of the 'meanings' rather than the mere information contained in a message). The key activity is what we have called 'specifying', turning a message, instruction or request into a perceived problem. A superior 'specifies' for his subordinates to some extent, even in his allocation of work among them, but the more significant part is that done by the subordinate, whether after an instruction has been given or during the preliminaries of search, feasibility test and clearance. 'Specifying' an instruction, we may say, is turning someone else's prescription for your behaviour into what you know you will have to do before your behaviour can meet that prescription; spelling it out for yourself, specifying the problems it creates for you, in your position, with your responsibilities and resources. The activity begins with translation and interpretation of incoming information, but most of it consists of processing information available in the office and not available to the superior. Specifying the actions that an order requires for its implementation is something that can be done fully only at the level at which the order is received.

However, knowledge of what a 'specified' instruction would look like can be acquired by a superior through the mechanism we earlier called 'conjectural feedback' – information transmitted from lower levels about how the instruction will probably be specified if it is promulgated, on the basis of previous experience of 'real feedback'. And, of course, the conjecture need not stop at the specification necessary on the next-lower level; the mechanism can bring lower levels into consideration in the same way, so that it is possible to 'imagine' the likely consequent problems of an instruction at as many succeeding levels as appears necessary. Since the direction of this thinking is always towards the 'lowest' level in organisational terms, the level at which changes are made in the real world, what is called the 'operating' level, the word in use for this whole process of conjecture is 'operationalising'. This usage is akin to that of the word in the methodology of science, where if a variable is to be measured, the specifying of the scale on which it is to be measured is its 'operational definition', and turning a hunch about the relationship between two variables into an experimental setting in which the association can be tested is 'operationalising' the relationship. The word is used also in manufacturing, for instance; putting the design for a new product in a form in which it can be expressed as production specifications or 'blueprints' is 'operationalising' the design. It is an unlovely term, but it is the term in widespread use for this idea.

The following is a paragraph in the Annual Report of the Railways Board for 1966:

> . . . on the present method of preparing railway accounts an annual deficit of approximately £130m is being incurred. This sum includes large amounts for the provision of commuter services in conurbations and stopping passenger train services in rural and peripheral areas. . . . The deficit is not a reflection of the work of the Board and the sooner this is put right the better. . . .

A general statement of the problem, which then had to be 'specified' by someone in the Ministry, who wrote the terms of reference for the Joint Steering Group of the Ministry and the Board, into the following:

> (a) To establish an acceptable basis for costing and to identify those categories of services (both passenger and freight) which are not covering costs; to isolate those categories which are

potentially viable; to examine the remaining loss-makers and to isolate those with no prospects of becoming viable; and to cost in detail the annual loss on each passenger service which is unlikely ever to become viable so that the Government can decide whether it should be grant-aided on broad social and economic grounds; . . . (*Transport Policy, Cmnd 3057, July 1966, Annex, p. 35*)

Many other illustrations of the process of 'operationalising' could be drawn from the closures material: for example, the sequence at the 'recovery of track and assets' stage of the Wetherby closures, for which some quotations were given (see p. 113 above) from a letter of 15 June 1964 from Estates and Rating Surveyor to Chief Civil Engineer, listing such items as:

Penda's Way: total removal. Station access hand-gate to be removed . . .
Collingham Bridge: the following to be removed:
   Down side platform and waiting shed
   Footbridge No. 39
   Station coal house and lamp room. . . .

These are in the form of instructions, but they are not instructions. The letter was part of the process of seeking authorisation for the work, not of getting it carried out. These items (and the letter dealt with signal boxes, bridges and level crossings along the entire length of the two lines closed, as well as the stations) were of the nature of an operationalisation: specifying what in practice would have to be done if the decision to recover assets (and 'make good') were to be implemented.

Frequently a letter or memorandum of this kind gets transformed into a set of instructions at a later date, sometimes by a mere initial in the margin, or a rubber stamp across it — just as sometimes, on the film battlefield, say, a subordinate officer's lengthy report on the situation and what he thinks ought to be done is metamorphosed into a detailed, specified order by the superior officer's curt response, 'Right. Carry on'; or just as an estimates document, given approval, becomes the expenditure control document. Today's specification of the problem can become tomorrow's instruction. But analytically we should avoid telescoping the process.

The 'cognitive hierarchy'

What applies to 'translation' and 'interpretation', in the 'Babel House' model, may be seen to apply also – if anything, with more force – to 'specifying' and 'operationalising'. We noted that whereas it was relatively easy to use correctly the concepts and terminology of near organisational neighbours (in specialism or in rank), because one all but inhabited the same 'universe of discourse' and could appreciate their concerns, it was the more difficult to do so the farther distant the relationship. Similarly, 'specifying' for oneself the problems involved in an instruction received from one level higher in rank is relatively easy; operationalising a statement from a level higher than that, which has not had the benefit of one's immediate superior's attention and partial specification, is more difficult. One has in effect to do one's superior's work as well as one's own on the matter; adopting his perceptions, estimating the empirical knowledge available at that higher level, drawing one's own blueprints. It is not impossible, of course: it has actually to be done quite frequently, at holiday time and in case of sickness or other absence, and it is a poor subordinate indeed who cannot 'be his own boss' for a short time at least. But the cognitive and organisational problems of attempting the feat for a gap of more than two ranks (i.e. spanning two realms in 'order of comprehension', without the aid of 'marginal men') become very great.

This applies also in the downward direction. To envisage how a decision one might make oneself may be 'specified' at the next rank below is relatively easy, and no superior will last long who cannot do that with fair completeness most of the time. To do it for two ranks below is more tedious, but not out of the question. To try to spell out what it will become, in a dozen or more distinct versions, just one rank below that – even if within the same realm in 'order of comprehension' or just beyond – is not only very time-consuming (as Downs said), but also perilous. It is to run the risk of innumerable errors of sheer fact; it is to try to do the 'thinking' not only of one's immediate subordinates and their subordinates, but of *their* subordinates also; and it is to assume their familiarity with the raw empirical data of their offices, and their mental or even manual dexterities and skills. It may not be utterly impossible, but he would be an extraordinary superior who could do it.

This is a sufficient reason for having a hierarchy in an organisation: less a matter of 'authority' than of cognition. It is just as much a division of labour as is the 'horizontal' division into professional and jurisdictional specialisms.

Historically, there have been many social and 'political' reasons for a superior to wish to claim that he 'can do anything he might ask his subordinates to do'; and it may well be the case that an important part of his own authority may derive from the respect his people have for his ability to do their jobs as well as or better than they can. In the 'motivational' rather than the cognitive sphere, in an industrial setting, for example, an occasional demonstration by a managing director that he can 'get his jacket off', his hands dirty and so on, has had dramatic effects on morale (Gray and Abrams, 1954; Paterson, 1960; etc.). Field Marshal Montgomery, in military equivalents, is credited with inspiring an entire army to victory by such personal appearances. One has not heard of similar effects being generated by a Permanent Secretary's demonstration that he can issue a Giro payment order or the like, and the notion is clearly not felt to be appropriate in the civil service setting. But, in whatever setting, our analysis would indicate that such exercises are strictly for 'morale building', and are not operationally significant. 'Showing the flag' three, four or five hierarchical levels below one's own rank is one thing; giving commands or instructions (other than the trivial, such as 'Shut that door!') at such levels is something else and fraught with disaster where it is tried.

We will explore the need for and function of 'authority' in hierarchical formation in another place. It may well be that setting one person 'over' a number of others, in an arrangement of 'commands' and the like, is a social and 'political' need, a function of the nature of the society, rather than of the operational tasks. But we can perhaps see that getting rid of 'command' authority would not remove the need for a hierarchy altogether. A complex task, combining different skills and materials in some necessary sequence, requires an ordering of the kind we are analysing – a 'cognitive hierarchy'. A 'cognitive hierachy' is a function of the complexity of the task, not of the society.

The number of levels in the 'cognitive hierarchy', on this argument, is determined by the number of steps necessary to 'specify' problems successively, from the form in which they are (perceived as) problems for the organisation as a whole, to the form in which they are (perceived as) problems that can be dealt with by the operative skills and techniques that will finally dispose of them so far as the organisation is concerned, discharge the organisation's responsibility. These 'steps' are not necessarily of the same number for all problems; the size of the 'cognitive leaps' possible, and thus the length of the hierarchy, may depend upon the nature of the problem and the capacity of the individual doing the 'specifying'. But when the 'cognitive hierarchy' is reified as an organisational hierarchy, other considerations come into play in any case – workload, security of employment and so on; so that it is an academic exercise to speculate on what a 'cognitive hierarchy' would look like on its own, as it were.

Uncertainty absorption

It is a quirk of the subject's history that more attention has been devoted to 'vertical' relationships in organisational space than to 'horizontal' ones. Tullock, for example, does his 'distortion' calculations entirely in terms of the superior–subordinate relationship. On the other hand, the notion of conflict between jurisdictions inside an organisation in the struggle for resources, or for influence between 'arms' of the armed services, or for rewards and status between the 'professional' and the 'bureaucrat', is a staple of organisational dynamics writing (Dalton, 1959; Landsberger, 1961; Walton, 1966; Cyert and March, 1963; Crozier, 1964; Kahn and Boulding, 1964; Hall, 1972; Haas and Drabek, 1973; etc.); and the idea of communication barriers, of difficulties in understanding 'jargon' and technical talk even if the medium is nominally English in all cases, is commonplace. Indeed, it is because this is a commonplace for 'lateral' interactions that we have been able to make the point, not so often taken, that there are differences in 'universe of discourse' in the vertical dimension also. ('Communication in organisations' has as many literatures as has decision theory. It can mean how to write reports in good English, or installing electronic devices, or collecting information for management decision, or avoiding conflict. In relation to the present discussion, see relevant sections in Blau and Scott, 1962; Dorsey, 1958; Hall, 1972; Haas and Drabek, 1973; Kuhn, 1974.)

Downs, in a brief reference, says that Tullock's analysis of 'distortion' in upward-flowing messages is also relevant to horizontal flows: 'True, the average distortion per message is probably greater in vertical flows than horizontal ones. The former involve superior-subordinate relations, whereas the latter usually involve relations among equals' (Downs, 1967, 116). What Downs apparently means here is that the cognitive effects are probably quite similar in vertical and lateral flows, but that vertical effects, unlike lateral ones, are exacerbated by motivational considerations. However, given the 'conflict' literature, this seems doubtful; lateral effects are surely just as liable to be compounded by other than cognitive forces.

In any case, we are here concentrating on only cognitive effects. Let me revert to the 'Babel House' model, that aspect in which it is a congeries of 'offices' or jurisdictions. It can (we showed earlier) be used as a 'problem-solving machine', by first scanning the whole for offices with an 'official interest' in a matter and then linking these in a process of search, test and clearance. From the viewpoint of any one station in the complex, the denizens of that station will be in this kind of contact with some other stations not at all, with another set of stations infrequently, and with a third set frequently. Any particular officer, for a great proportion of his daily work, sits at the centre of a relatively small web or network of very frequent interaction, has rather less frequent interaction with a rather larger net and so on. The 'doctrine of levels' or of 'opposite numbers' in a British government department (by which one acquires a recognised contact at roughly one's own salary band in other Ministries and other branches of one's own Ministry), although possibly deriving from a concern for hierarchical propriety, has the property of reducing the variety of potential contacts and increasing the interaction rate with the selected ones. It also incidentally ensures equivalence in 'order of comprehension', or placing on the generality/specificity scale.

It is this frequency of interaction which defines who are 'organisational neighbours', rather than any physical propinquity. One can, in due course, learn a good deal about a close neighbour's subject material and way of thinking; and one will soon learn enough to appraise, and even criticise, the plausibility of any advice he may give on one's own problems. Similarly, when he makes a request for advice, one knows pretty well what he has in mind, what his words and his proposals means. The more infrequent the contact with another office, the more one is obliged to take what he says as gospel, because of inability to 'read between the lines' or do anything other than accept at face value what is said.

By a slightly different mechanism (the doctrine of jurisdictional competence, the notion of 'province'), the same treatment must be accorded to a properly authenticated 'divisional view' on a proposal. It has to be taken as a *given*, a statement behind which one does not go, an equivalent of 'fact'. Yet one knows from one's own experience how such 'divisional views' are prepared; one knows how much internal approximation and rough guessing goes into them, and how much difference of opinion on quite important issues, all of which disappears in the collation and summation and presentation of a single response.

This, of course, is the phenomenon March and Simon call 'uncertainty absorption'. All the range of variation, the boilings down and snap judgements, which if you knew about them would enable you to make your own estimate of the reliability of the information as 'evidence', are mopped up out of sight in the tidy 'official' presentation. The same thing occurs when a technical expert 'simplifies' something for the layman, in any form of averaging and when a mass of original survey data, for example, is presented in classified tables. A chartroomful of barometric and temperature readings from a score of weather stations is transformed by what is called 'inferential processing' into a four-sentence weather forecast. The replies of two thousand people to a specific (but not necessarily equally well understood) question is placarded as 'public opinion'.

But the absorption of uncertainty through inferential processing (the extraction of the inferences from the data) is not the same thing as the *distortion* of information. That label would apply to biased or skewed presentation, either in the deliberate attempt to mislead, or in the imposition of a pattern upon the data dictated by personal or organisational convenience (budgetary practice, for instance) rather than by regularities in the data themselves. It is also possible to withhold information or to release it selectively, to tell barefaced lies, and to make genuine errors. But all that is another story entirely, and separate from a cognitive treatment of uncertainty absorption.

Messages coming upwards in the hierarchy from levels of greater specificity, or inwards from 'distant' parts laterally, are necessarily subject to uncertainty absorption, often several times over. So every exercise of 'search, test and clear', the outward-and-downward probing operation by which proposals for change are considered in 'Babel House', takes place under these conditions. It could not be otherwise. An official who sent out and down a proposal of his for feasibility testing in, say, six other divisions simply could not handle (and often could not understand) all the scores of reports compiled at different levels in the different divisions that his initiative calls forth. He is (if he should think of it at all) no doubt merely thankful to rely on the inferential processing of the intermediate levels and of the division heads who eventually reply to him. There are checks: an office which may be 'distant' from his own is nevertheless surrounded by offices which are in close enough contact to evaluate its messages; one network is made up of offices each of which belongs to several other networks and messages are 'carboned' from one network to another, so that uncertainty is never wholly absorbed, the system does not get completely out of touch with reality – not altogether, not all of the time.

Tullock and Downs both made telling use of this phenomenon, particularly in the vertical dimension, though they both insisted on regarding it as 'distortion'. A distortion in a communication channel implies a theoretically possible undistorted communication along that channel. But a 'cognitive hierarchy' is not a 'channel' at all: information does not 'flow' upward, downward or in any other direction in 'Babel House'. It has to be transmitted from one person to another and received by the latter; if retransmitted, it is in a different form from that in which it was received; it is changed, not merely added to or subtracted from, at each step.

We have spent some time examining the operation in the 'downward' direction that we have called 'operationalisation'. There, stations are putting into a received message additional information, turning it into something they can use. 'Summation', or inferential processing, is the counterpart of this operation in the upward direction, as Downs noted. Here, stations are removing from messages 'crude' information which otherwise would overwhelm them and higher levels, using and sending onwards only what they infer from it. In 'operationalising', or 'specifying' (a kind of 'implication processing'), the injected information is generated from the station's internal resources, the knowledge of practicalities appropriate to that office or province, and that is precisely the kind of information which it removes from its upward transmissions. This balance of exchange of information is what keeps the 'cognitive hierarchy' stable. (The networks of the lateral dimension are in similar equilibrium.)

The stages of implementation

What we are saying about the nature of the transition between the stages of the implementation process, the way progress is made from one stage to the next (or the way one becomes the next), is, therefore, something like this.

Any particular specimen of implementation to which an observer or inquirer chooses to devote his attention may 'begin' in one realm of 'order of comprehension' and 'end' in another, with two, three or even four major shifts in 'order of comprehension' on the way – that is entirely dependent upon what the observer chooses as the beginning and end of his interest. If the specimen of the process on which he focuses involves an organisational sequence, or a series of them, in large organisations of the bureaucratic type, then the movement from 'beginning' to 'end' will be reified as a sequence of 'decisions' or 'instructions', each preceded by a preparatory phase or cycle of consultation between decision maker and advisers, between superior and subordinates and between one office and others of different jurisdiction. But the crucial activity in the preparation of any instruction, and in the carrying out of any instruction, is that which we have called operationalisation: an activity of spelling out the implication of an instruction in terms of the problems it poses for the receiving office, of making the instruction more specific than its actual words warrant. This is the operation which, repeated a large number of times, provides both the logic and the organisational sequence of the conversion of 'policy from on high' to 'action on the ground', turning words into deeds. Operationalisation is the engine of implementation.

Such an assertion, admittedly, assumes that the analysis of the operationalising activity which we carried out for one particular point in one organisational hierarchy is applicable at all points in any hierarchy, and at all points on the scale of generality/specificity. It assumes that operationalising is, as it were, the lever by which a matter is notched along a rack: the image is of an *?-A-B* triad becoming the *A-B-C* triad, that becoming the *B-C-D* triad, that becoming the *C-D-E* triad and so on. The limiting cases (apart from specimens of the process which do not include sequences in bureaucratic organisations) are at the very 'top' and very 'bottom' of the 'cognitive hierarchy'.

At the top the horizons are very wide indeed; operations of search, test and clear, though perhaps analytically detectable, may be in the realm of philosophical or religious discourse and may have no organisational manifestations at all, or only such as occur in party meetings and Parliament. At the bottom the horizons are very narrow; and if the activity consists of phases of perception, search, test, clearance, authorisation and promulgation, including operations of translation, inferential processing and implication specifying, then it may be necessary to assume that all of these phases and operations take place inside the head of one human being, and so also have no organisational manifestations. At this level the theory would become a theory of human thinking and choosing, and we could not illustrate it from the railway closures evidence.

But a theory of human thinking and choosing exists which would support this view of what would have to be happening inside one man's head as he 'operationalised' an order at the bottom of the 'cognitive hierarchy'. It has already been described in Chapter 1 (see p. 13), and it supposes that all human activity is governed by a cycle of neural processes that takes place at different cognitive levels *within* the human system. Miller, Galanter and Pribram (1960) called the cycle TOTE (Test Operate Test Exit); but even in their own account it might be better described as Perceive Search Test Operate (Test Exit) (the last two elements are in brackets because we are not yet in a position to appreciate their force in organisational terms).

We have rounded off other discussions by comparing the principles elicited with the principle implicit in the biological and machine theory analogues of the 'developmental' and 'aggregative' models. This chapter, however, is already lengthy, and the analogies to be discovered are very interesting. We shall give them a whole chapter to themselves.

CHAPTER 6

Analogy: Vertebrate Physiology

What, then, does happen after 'thinking and choosing' in the human being? How does any of us transform thought (or 'will' , if you like) into our own action? Let us look at the physiology of the motor nervous system in vertebrates. (I am no physiologist. The following account is put together from sources accessible to the layman: see Grey Walter, 1953; Sluckin, 1954; Koestler, 1965; Kennedy, 1967; Annett, 1969; Nathan, 1969; Merton, 1972; Evarts, 1973.)

Lifting a hand

If a layman asks questions about someone's movements, the kind of answer expected usually concerns him (or her) at 'whole organism' level. 'Why did you lift your hand?' can have many answers but, ordinarily, they will all be to do with the addressee's relationship with other persons or objects. 'How did you lift your hand?' is an odd question, but it could be asked in circumstances where the questioner is finding difficulty in copying the action, and the answer would not usually be in words but by demonstration.

But suppose the questioner means it in a different way, and persists: 'But how *do* you lift your hand?' Most people's response will be something like, 'Well . . . you just do it. You decide to do it, and it happens.' If you decided to do it and nothing happened, you would say you were 'paralysed'. We do not usually ask ourselves 'why' an arm lifts, in this sense: the answer lies below 'organism' level.

Physiologists know perfectly well, of course, how a man lifts his hand. You have to arrange for a number of flexor muscles to be activated (those that cause bending of the limb), and inhibit a number of extensor muscles (those that straighten it). You will also

need to arrange for some trunk muscles and muscles in the abdomi-
nal wall to be activated, so as to provide a firm anchor for the arm
movement; and if you are not sitting down, there might be a need to
move some leg muscles to take the strain of keeping your balance, as
your centre of gravity shifts a little. When you have taken care of the
arm movement, you may add a few more flexors for the wrist bend
that usually goes with it.

Such an account tells us too much and not enough. That may be
what goes on, but we are aware that we do not know how to do this
arranging: it is not something we have ever done, so far as we
remember, although we have seen it occur often enough. Actually,
we have 'done' it before: we once had to learn how to do it all from
scratch, but it was a long time ago. By adult standards, it was and is
well below consciousness.

But when we did it in the early days of life, we laid down patterns
or programmes ('software', in computer terms) that linked all
the relevant muscles in a network of well-trodden paths, to use
a familiar (if not quite accurate) analogy. Nowadays, we cannot
do anything about an arm lifting except 'switch-in' ready-made
programmes of that kind, and we have delegated even that to a lower
centre, a centre of lower order, than the 'consciousness' part of the
brain.

The switching centre for a 'lift arm' movement is in the spinal cord.
Seven major pairs of nerve trunks to and from the shoulders and
arms join the central nervous system near the top of the cord; from
the cord, they spread out into a number of more 'local' nerve centres,
each of which is associated with a set of muscles for a single joint or
the like. The 'switch' is not what you might think. The spinal cord
centre is not like a telephone exchange, with someone plugging in the
appropriate 'local' centres and then sending out messages along the
separate pathways leading to different joints and muscle complexes,
activating each of them in just the right way to ensure co-ordinated
movement. No: what the central nervous system sends out is of the
nature of a 'general call', or a 'to whom it may concern' message: a
single message goes out along the trunk nerve. Yet each local nerve
centre reacts differently, and of two centres connected by the same
pathway and hence receiving the same trunk message, one may react
and one not. Clearly, the local nerve centre has some means of
reading messages and discarding those not meant for it. What is
more, the trunk message is not received at all by any actual muscles:

even those local centres which react don't merely pass on the signal; they send out a different one.

The same, incidentally, is true for the communications between the highest nerve centre, the brain, and the spinal cord centres. All nervous activity connected with deliberate movement begins in certain small areas of the brain, the cerebellum and a particular sector of the cortex. (Reflex movements have a different 'headquarters'.) Messages from the brain to the spinal cord centres terminate there. What is sent out by the trunk nerve is a different message.

How is the 'reading' done? Always by the same mechanism at each centre, a kind of analogue computer measuring discrepancies. The entire nervous system is made up of different forms of a single kind of cell: the nerve cell or neuron. This consists of a cell body and several branching arms, one of which (the axon) is often several feet long, able to branch at the end. This is the cell's output channel. A 'nerve' is a bundle of neurons, their axons bound together in a sort of cable. A large nerve will contain thousands of such fibres. Each axon ends (in the network we are considering) either at another neuron cell body or at a muscle motor unit. One neuron can be connected to hundreds of other neurons, or to only one or two. A spinal-cord neuron cell body can have eight hundred or so nerve endings (input points) on its surface, and a muscle motor neuron about ten thousand. A cerebellum neuron (of which there are possibly ten million) will have more than a quarter of a million nerve endings terminating at that cell, able to deliver an input. The variety of the brain (see p. 126 above) is absolutely enormous: it has been estimated at two to the power ten thousand million. If you were set to write out the number this gives, at the rate of ten digits a second, it would take you a number of years. The number of years it would take you is itself a figure ending in three thousand million noughts (Beer, 1966, 365). The variety of the whole human nervous system is unimaginable.

Each nerve cell can thus be receiving a large number of input signals at any one time. They are all of the same kind. The axon of a neuron can transmit only one kind of signal: a pulse goes or it does not go; it is never a bigger bang one time than another. When it goes, it moves along the axon at a regular speed that may vary between neurons between half a metre and one hundred metres per second, but in any case is always of constant strength, for it consists of a 'travelling' chemical reaction – less like a pea in a pea-shooter than like a 'wave' travelling along a rope when you flick it sharply, but one which does not lose momentum. The neuron is never at rest: as soon as it has enough of a 'charge' (in electrical metaphor), which it accumulates from its inputs, it discharges or 'fires' – an impulse 'goes'. The difference in its activity is in the rate of firing: it can be at 'idling frequency', or at a frenetic maximum rate, or anything between, governed by the number of inputs from other neurons. If many pulses arrive simultaneously from many axons (strictly, from the nerve-end 'synapse' where the minute 'charge' is generated), the cell's charge rises quickly. Some inputs, however, are inhibitory rather than excitatory and so cancel out a certain number of other inputs; so the amount of total charge is a summation of positive and negative. Whenever this sum reaches a certain threshold (a figure 'built in' to each cell, invariable for that cell) – whether by low-frequency inputs from a great number of synapses or by high-frequency inputs from a smaller number (the cell has no way of distinguishing) – the cell 'fires'.

The way one local nerve centre may respond to a single trunk message while another does not may be explained thus. Postulate a mechanism like that in the ear, where each of a huge battery of acoustic analysers responds to one pitch of sound and one pitch only. A note from a flute excites only a few: a stroke on a gong sets several hundred resonating, but each is responding on its own, quite irrespective of what its fellows are doing. The trunk message from the central nervous system is like a gong stroke arriving by a large number of pathways, each neuron in the local nerve centre reacting quite individually and any bulk effect (responding or not responding) of the centre as a whole being the collective effect of these myriad individual summations of excitatory and inhibitory inputs. 'Bulk effects' are the result of learned programmes. A single neuron 'does' nothing, has no effect. All movements, however slight, are 'package deals' of incredible complexity if one tried to unravel them. Consider the movements of your body (eyes, hands, head) as you sit, relatively motionless, reading this. Consider a golf swing, or a man hitting a nail with a hammer. It is done by programming muscle movements, package deals within package deals within package deals. The metaphor of the onion's skins, the party game of 'pass the parcel' or the nest of Chinese boxes, box within box, perhaps eight or nine times, barely begins to portray the complexity.

In motor nervous activity, a 'higher-level' programme only selects among and activates a 'lower-level' programme – one level down. A 'local' nerve centre can activate a joint, but its impact is a package: the centre does not itself move the muscles independently. A spinal cord centre can move an arm: it has no way of moving a finger. There are higher centres which can trigger off the motions of walking or throwing a ball, but all they do is switch in these programmes; they cannot alter the position of an arm or leg independently – it needs a lower-order centre to manage that. So there is a real sense in which the brain can no more directly lift an arm than 'we' can: it, too, has to 'arrange' for it to happen, through several levels of lower-order centres. Thus the layman's somewhat baffled response to the question 'How *do* you lift your arm?' is a reasonable one: the nearest 'he' could get to knowing would be to understand what the 'brain' did, and the brain does not itself do much more than 'think about it'. (It is not quite true that then it 'just happens': the brain begins monitoring and altering what is happening, until the action required is completed. We shall consider this aspect elsewhere.)

Autonomy, spontaneity and discontinuity

Physiologists have suggested three principles which characterise the operation of the motor nervous system in vertebrates, which I shall call autonomy, spontaneity and discontinuity (the original terms can be found on p. 216 below).

Autonomy refers to a phenomenon we are all aware of at organism level ourselves, in that we know we do not have to remember to breathe or pump blood, though we can sense it happening. We can even 'make' the lungs and the heart work faster or slower, though (for most of us, at least) only in a roundabout way, such as by taking exercise. There are other major bodily organs, like the liver and kidneys, from which there is no sensory feedback, and so we cannot even know what is happening. We cannot, by taking thought, do anything at all about their functioning, nor 'arrange' for it to be done in even a roundabout way, unless we include drugs: there are no 'motors' to be activated, even by the autonomic nervous system which takes care of the lungs and heart.

There is, however, autonomy of two other kinds to be considered. Take a muscle. It is not necessary to go into how it 'works' or how it is triggered off by the nerve impulse arriving at the myo-neural junction or muscle motor. But if you removed a muscle from a leg (say, a frog's leg), and kept it in a jar for two years in a suitable solution, it will still contract to order when chemically stimulated. The muscle, as it were, is an entity on its own: its incorporation into a body is not a prerequisite of its functioning, although it may well be a prerequisite of its nourishment and hence 'survival', unless there is a scientist with a suitable jar around. The human body is made up of many parts like this.

Or take the neuron. It does not obey a 'command' from a higher centre, along a hot line. It sums up its situation and does what it is designed to do in the light of that calculation. It does not act on an instruction; it reacts to an environment. The human body is full of processes like that.

Autonomy means that a part (although indisputably a *part*) needs no stream of instructions, from outside or 'above', to tell it what to do. It functions the way it does because of what it is. A muscle will contract *in vitro*. A heart whose every sensory nerve has been severed will go on beating for as long as blood flows. A heart is for beating. It needs no commands from other parts of the body to set it doing so. The base of the spine is not told by the brain how to organise walking motion: the brain does not know how, and headless chickens can run about the farmyard for a gruesomely long time. Autonomy, or autonomous functioning, signifies the capacity to perform un-tutored.

'Spontaneity' refers, for example, to the finding that the millions of nerve networks in vertebrates are in ceaseless activity: the 'steady state' for a neuron (and hence for the entire nervous system) is not rest but 'idling frequency'. A message is sent not by producing impulses in a pathway or channel, but by modulating the frequency of pulses that are already being produced. Modulation is achieved by the influencing of two 'tendencies' that are built in to the chemistry of each cell: one which, if not inhibited, would cause the rate of firing to increase (to the physical limit); the other which, if not inhibited, would cause the rate of firing to decrease (to the chemical limit). The beat, or frequency, of the heart's action is 'fixed' in this way. Super-ficially it seems like a clock, and one might suppose its regularity to be maintained by some analogous mechanism, the correct rate for any particular conditions being set by some higher-order centre monitoring these conditions. But it is not so: the conditions act directly on the heart mechanisms by inhibiting one 'tendency' less than the other.

Lifting the arm is achieved in an oddly similar manner. Every muscle is acting all the time, pulling against sets or arrays of other muscles pulling in the opposite direction. 'Rest' is not inactivity, but balance. As one set or the other is inhibited in its activity, so the limb moves, as the contrary 'tendency' is permitted to work. The body is full of such mechanisms. Selective inhibition of contrary tendencies appears as the characteristic control mechanism in vertebrates. The water balance in the body, the sugar balance and many other balances in the body's functioning are also maintained by inhibiting one spontaneous reaction a little less than another.

The particular organ, or nervous subsystem, thus not only 'knows what to do without being told', it is 'doing it' all the time at a rate it fixes for itself unless influence is brought to bear; and no influence from outside can alter what it does or the method by which it is done, although it could stop it doing it quite so fast or quite so slow. This is what 'spontaneity' of function implies.

'Discontinuity' refers, for example, to the finding that 'messages' are relayed in steps or stages, and that what is transmitted further is always identifiably a separate transmission and may be identifiably a separate message. The surge of a neuron's discharge along its axon is not, as remarked earlier, like sending a pea along the tube of a pea-shooter. The axon consists of a large number of short segments: the cell body triggers a chemical reaction in the first and nearest segment; that reaction triggers a reaction in the next segment, which triggers one in the next and so on – a 'chain reaction' occurs along the axon in this way and hence the impulse does not lose strength as it travels. But it is equally fair to say that there is no direct communication between the cell body and the 'far end' of the axon, except via this chain of 'autonomous' reactions. Again, there is no direct communication between one neuron and another to which its axon (or dendrite) leads: there is a gap between the nerve end and the receptor organ of the second neuron, the synapse, and the mechanism for communication across the synapse is a different mechanism from that for passing an impulse along the axon.

Furthermore, as we have seen, there is no direct communication between high-order centres of the motor nervous system in vertebrates and low-order centres, or the ultimate 'muscle motors', save through a succession of intermediate-order centres. An impulse along a trunk nerve may or may not be 'felt' beyond one of these intermediate centres: if it is, it is because the intermediate centre has sent its own signal, not because of any kind of 'transmitted shock' or straight-through channel.

Another *kind* of discontinuity occurs, for example, at the muscle motor. Nerve activity has to be transformed into physical activity, deploying amounts of energy of an altogether different order. The muscle-motor endplate, or myo-neural junction, has a gap similar to that of a neuron synapse, but of enormously greater area (the surface is folded), and the trigger chemical, though of the same kind as the neuron trigger, works in a somewhat different way on the protein of the muscle fibres. One theory of how a muscle contracts is that each of its fibres is a complex of interlaced protein molecules, of myosin and actin; the thinner actin filaments are shifted between the thicker myosin filaments by a chemical 'ratchet' mechanism (a zigzag chain), one molecule of ATP (adenosine triphosphate, the maid-of-all-work energy-carrier of living cells) being used up for each 'notch'. This produces a relatively 'massive' effect, compared with events in the nervous system: it is as if an ant managed to move a boulder, or as if a man struck a match and a volcano erupted.

Similar shifts in order of magnitude occur between the nervous system and, say, the digestive system or the reproductive system. Across such gaps, as it were, we move into a different world. There is no direct communication across such boundaries; only a form of input or exchange at the boundary.

We can name these two different kinds of discontinuity 'transmission discontinuity' and 'system discontinuity'. 'Transmission discontinuity', let us say, refers to the lack of a straight-through channel in the motor nervous system, for instance, so that a high-order centre cannot communicate with a low-order centre save via the functioning of one or more intermediate centres. Lack of communication between the nervous system and the other systems of bodily functioning, or between any two such systems, save via specific exchange points, we shall call 'system discontinuity'.

System

The concept of 'system' requires a little elucidation. The term is used in many ways and the way it is being used here is but one of them; other usages have implications that are erroneous or superfluous in the present context. 'Systems analysis' in industrial usage refers to the description of what event has to follow what in a particular project and corresponds to what we earlier called the 'logic sequence' of an implementation process. Sometimes 'system' refers to the set of connections between an input and an output, that which effects the transformation of inputs into outputs, as in our machine theory analogy. So a 'closed system' is a set of elements related to one another but without connections between that set and any other set; an 'open system' has such connections and exchanges between the set and 'its environment' occur. Other usages of 'system' emphasise the interdependence of the elements in a set, so that what happens to one element affects the set as a whole or some other elements. Such an interdependent relationship is sometimes called an 'organic' one. In other usages, 'system' entails a 'functional' relationship between elements: a 'political system' (that aspect of a society we often call the 'state') has several requisite functions, such as the recruitment of politicians, the articulation of group interests, the harmonisation of these interests and media of communication among members, but the 'structures' or institutions that perform these functions may be very different from state to state. Finally, 'general systems theory' is a body of concepts of somewhat breathtaking universality, purporting to offer theorems that will apply to any pattern of relationships in which a whole is made up of interacting parts, whether the empirical context be that of physics, chemistry, biology, astronomy, demography or human society. The concept of 'ecology' is one now being employed in many contexts, in a particular application of general systems theory. But the use of 'system' in this book, although it does not exclude some other meanings of that kind, does not entail them. (For various usages of 'system', see Easton, 1953; Almond and Coleman, 1960; Beer, 1960; Kast, 1968; von Bertalanffy, 1969; Emery, 1969; Laszlo, 1972; Sutherland, 1973; Meyer, 1973; Kuhn, 1974; etc.)

Let me illustrate that present use, and also convey what is meant by 'system discontinuity', in a setting which is not that of vertebrate physiology but is quite familiar. A builder will see the 'structure' of a house as being its load-bearing framework, what keeps the roof up and the walls together. An electrical engineer might work with a different conception of the house: for him, the bricks and mortar are merely the carriers of his cables and appliances, and if one mentally excluded the walls and floors and could 'see' the wiring on its own, as it were, in a three-dimensional, full-scale wiring diagram, one would have an electrician's-eye view of the house. But the electrician's version of 'structure' does not stop at the boundaries of the house; the house is seen to be 'on the mains', and the mains are part of a wiring diagram which covers the whole town at a certain voltage; while the town, like other towns, is on the National Grid, which carries electricity at a higher voltage. (For accounting purposes, the 'house' begins at the 'mains switch' and meter.)

A plumber forms a different picture of a house. He sees water pipes instead of cables, and he thinks also of 'mains' – of two kinds, in most houses: cold water mains and 'main drainage' or sewers. Inside the house, he will 'see' a third interlacing structure: the hot water tank, pipes and boiler. Each structure – cold water, hot water and drainage – is separate, except at certain specific points: a sink, for instance, where hot and cold water can both be run off together and can both discharge into the waste pipes connecting with the drains. There may be *two* sets of cold water pipes, one running straight off the mains, one via a cold water tank or reservoir, and only the reservoir cold water enters the boiler to become hot water. The 'boiler' may, in fact, be an electric immersion heater: at such a point, the reservoir cold water, the hot water and the electrical diagrams will meet. If it should be a gas boiler, then a third kind of network can represent the house: the pattern of gas pipes, meters and appliances, again feeding off a 'main', interacting with the water diagram in the house at a boiler, but not outside the house, and only rarely with the electrical diagram, anywhere.

There may be other kinds of 'main' with structural manifestations in a house: telephone, 'cable' television or 'piped' radio, occasionally district heating or solid-waste disposal chutes. We usually call each of these structurings a *system* (the electrical system, the hot water system, the telephone system and so on), and it was difficult in the preceding paragraphs to remember not to use the word. Each system is not only separate from but of a different kind from the others, although they may, as it were, 'overlap' at certain points where special arrangements have been made. You do not mix water and electricity except where that is quite specifically part of your intention and where there is a device to allow the benefits of doing so without the dangers.

This, then, is 'system discontinuity'. The nervous system in the human body, the digestive system, the circulatory system, the respiratory system – all these correspond exactly (in terms of this meaning of 'system') to the various systems in a house. They are separate (visibly so, in most cases), of distinct kinds, as distinct as is a message from a meal, blood from air, yet interlinked, reacting with one another, exchanging energy by special mechanisms at certain points. (Each kind of system, too, has its own kind of exchange with the body's 'environment', but we need not make use of this property at the moment.)

'Discontinuity' in vertebrate physiology stands for the way that what the observer (or 'experiencer') sees or feels as a single coherent sequence of action or communication is, in fact, interrupted at several points, with boundaries to be crossed or translations to be made from one medium to another. We have discerned two types: one, of which 'programmes-within-programmes-within-programmes' is the paradigm, we have called 'transmission discontinuity'; the other, of which the change from a nervous-system event to a muscle-system event at the myo-neural junction is the paradigm, we have called 'system discontinuity'. Another way of writing 'programmes-within-programmes-within-programmes' is 'sub-subsystems within subsystems within systems'. This is confusing, but the terminology can be used so long as we can bear in mind that the relationship between system and subsystem is a hierarchical one, and not a difference between systems. The house is within the town is within the National Grid, but all these levels are to do with electricity; the 'mains switch' and meter, and the substation at which voltage reductions are made, are points of 'transmission discontinuity', not points (like the immersion heater) of 'system discontinuity'.

Analogy and homology

What have these principles of autonomy, spontaneity and discontinuity, as found in vertebrate physiology, to do with the implementation process in bureaucratic organisations? Well, we began the discussion because we had reached a point in the analysis where it became desirable to know whether or not the model of bureaucratic implementation was also a model of human-individual implementation. The model of human-individual implementation we have arrived at by starting afresh, as it were, apparently has these three principles. Are the same principles implicit in the bureaucratic implementation model?

Let us take 'autonomy'. This certainly fits well the conception of office-holder in his 'province' or jurisdiction, 'acting untutored' simply because he alone is in a position to know what is needed to be done within that province to meet any requirements that may be imposed upon it. The independence of a professional specialist is of the same nature. Fred E. Katz wrote a book (*Autonomy and Organization*) to support the proposition that 'autonomy' is 'part of the structure of social systems', incorporated into the very structure of social relationships:

> Each segment – each division, each department, each occupant of a position – has a sphere of action that is only minimally controlled by the whole organisation (in addition to a sphere that is very definitely controlled by the organisation's authority structure) . . . the accomplishment of functional contributions to a system requires a degree of autonomy from that system. . . .
> (*Katz, 1968, 4, 15, 23*)

We shall look elsewhere at this matter of control through authority, but Katz is certainly using terms in a way that suggests an identity of the organisational 'autonomy' principle with vertebrate physiology 'autonomy'. Another book, (*Autonomous Group Functioning*, by P. G. Herbst, 1962) is similarly dedicated to the study of the parameters and variables of the autonomy of social groups, including groups in organisations, although more from a 'motivational' than a 'cognitive' base.

'Spontaneous group functioning' is not yet a book title, but what the principle would have to mean in organisation terms (members doing what they are there to do continuously, all the time, rather than being 'at rest' until set in motion by a command from on high), is certainly not an unfamiliar concept, and might be considered the ideal that production engineering in manufacturing aims at – no 'idle time', whether of men or machines. It maps well on to the idea of an implementation process being a matter of 'switching-in' sets of activities or programmes that are already in operation, and which if not switched into one particular sequence (as defined by an observer's interest) will be switched into some other, not left doing nothing. The March and Simon concept for a work routine, a 'performance program', which can itself be linked with others into a programme of a higher order, is obviously immediately transferable to and from talk of 'package deals' in neuron activity.

'Transmission discontinuity' in vertebrate physiology is, also, clearly transferable to the implementation process in bureaucracies as we have come to see it: higher-order centres (decision centres high on the generality/specificity scale) unable to communicate directly with lower-order centres except through the functioning of inter-mediate centres, partly because of 'language' and 'universe of dis-course' difficulties, mainly because of the difficulty of *operationalis-ing* for more than one or two levels of rank above or below, let alone across larger distances in 'order of comprehension'. What 'system discontinuity' would have to mean in organisational terms is not something we have yet discussed explicitly, except in the context of differences in 'universe of discourse' on the horizontal plane. But it is not difficult to conceive of 'systems' in an organisation that are as distinct as are the digestive system and the respiratory system in the body: for example, a 'production system', a 'personnel management' system, a 'financial control' system and so on – each intertwining with the others, and requiring 'exchanges' at specific points (one having to 'take account of' another), but nevertheless separable in principle and working with quite different 'material' from one another.

It does seem, then, that the principles of autonomy, spontaneity and discontinuity apply to implementation in organisations as much as they do to implementation in the human individual. What would it mean to accept this? That organisations are 'really' organisms of some kind? No: we need not even contemplate that possibility. That, alternatively, the correct model for the organisational process must be an organic, developmental one? No: at some points the three principles suggest more obviously an aggregative, machine theory model and, perhaps more significantly, the description of the motor nervous system was itself in terms of 'mechanisms', inputs and outputs, variety and other concepts of machine theory. An organic model would apparently not portray this particular organism pro-cess. And as Grey Walter and others have demonstrated, an 'artificial animal' can be constructed, embodying principles like these, which will behave in an oddly 'human' (and not entirely predictable) way (Grey Walter, 1953). The distinction between 'an organism' and 'a machine' can hardly be sustained, on these terms, within these understandings.

Perhaps, since all descriptions are based on some theoretical model or other, I had these three principles of vertebrate physiology in mind from the start, consciously or unconsciously, and so was selecting what I chose to talk about, and the way to talk about it, in just such a manner as would indeed lead to correspondence between the description of the bureaucratic implementation process and the description of the process of lifting an arm? But it was not I who wrote books about autonomous group functioning, or performance programmes, or the pyramiding of the formulation of purpose. Nor was it I who suggested that these were the three principles which underlie the motor nervous system (though, admittedly, these three specific terms were my choice). Paul Weiss, in a contribution to a conference on cerebral mechanisms that has become known as the Hixon Symposium (Jeffress, 1951), said this:

> The working of the central nervous system is a hierarchic affair in which functions at the higher levels do not deal directly with the ultimate structural units, such as neurons or motor units, but operate by activating lower patterns that have their own relatively autonomous structural unity. . . . The structure of the input does not produce the structure of the output, but merely modifies intrinsic nervous activities that have a structural organisation of their own. . . . So we have experimental evidence that rhythmic automatism, autonomy of pattern, and hierarchical organisation are primary attributes of even the simplest nervous systems, and I think that this unifies our view of the nervous system. (*Weiss*, in *Jeffress, 1951, 140*: quoted in *Koestler, 1964, 435*)

For intrinsic nervous activities read spontaneous functioning; for autonomy read autonomy; for hierarchic organisation read discontinuity.

It is nevertheless true that in many of the books surveyed in Chapter 2, whether overtly, as in March and Simon, and in Downs, or implicitly, in parts of Barnard and Tullock, the parallelism between the organisational process and the organismic processes is already the basis of the authors' understanding. Already quoted (on p. 39 above) is March's and Simon's remark that organisations are the 'largest assemblages in our society that have anything resembling a central co-ordination system', although not as well developed as the central nervous systems in higher biological organisms (March and Simon, 1958, 4). Perhaps the coincidence of principles is built in that way: what people go looking for (central co-ordinating systems) they will find. It would be hardly surprising if, when earlier writers

based their accounts of organisation processes upon their understanding of the nature of central nervous system processes, later
writers, who base their accounts of organisation processes upon
those of the earlier writers, were to find that there is remarkable
similarity between these accounts and their own understanding of
central nervous system processes.

If this *is* the explanation, then the argument is circular and we have
merely produced a somewhat more sophisticated version of the old
attractive-but-fallacious sustained analogy between the human
organism and the human social organisation, where the head is the
commander and the hands are the organisational work force; money
circulation comes from blood circulation; national trade has parallels with digestion; the nervous system is the body's telegraph or vice
versa, and so on, every organ and function of the body having its
societal counterpart. The commoner metaphors of this old imagery
are now so familiar that they are 'dead'. No one now is aware of the
reference in a phrase like 'head porter', or 'member' of a group.
Perhaps we have done no more than freshen the metaphor a little, as
did Mason Haire (1959).

Haire began from D'Arcy Thompson's classic theorem in *On
Growth and Form* (Thompson, 1917) about the relationship in
organisms between size, shape and function: a deer cannot grow as
big as an elephant and still look like a deer; it has to look something
like an elephant. Jack in the fable was quite safe from the giant: if (as
he is usually portrayed) the giant was ten times as big as a man, but
still shaped like one, his weight would have increased in proportion
to his volume (10^3) while the cross-section (the area) of his leg bones
increased only in proportion also (10^2). But the material of which
bone is made will not stretch to supporting an increase in weight of
that order, unless the cross-section is also increased much more than
proportionately – which, of course, would have to mean that the
giant no longer had the shape of a man. A man-shaped giant ten
times as big in every way would break his legs if he stood up. (The
same principle, by the way, must apply to horror-film spiders and the
like: they cannot be as big as they are made to appear *and* still be
made of 'spider stuff'.)

Would this principle, Haire wondered, apply to the growth of
business firms? Using empirical data about numbers of employees in
four companies, the study found that, indeed, as the firms increased
in size, 'support' (mainly the proportion of administrative employees

to production employees) took up a progressively greater proportion of resources. More of the potential output had to be consumed in providing more complex management systems, and this was seen as an analogue of the disproportionately greater increase in skeletal structure as the overall weight of organisms increases.

Of course, the parallelism is faulty: ontogenesis and phylogenesis are being confused. An animal grows from an egg to an adult or from a lean adult to a fat adult; a species does not 'grow' from deer-like to elephant-like, which seems to be roughly what Haire is postulating. But that does not really matter so long as one is using an analogy merely as a generator of insights; imperfections of parallel are venial, because one is going to test new insights against empirical material, not come to conclusions, or make decisions, on the basis of the analogy. The specimen of reality will impose the necessary discipline on the argument.

If, on the other hand, one really is setting out to argue that two kinds of thing are alike in material respects, and that therefore whatever natural laws apply to the one can be held to apply to the other, then not only must the analogy be perfect; there must be *homology*. The relationship between the elements of one of the things must be shown to be *logically* identical to the relationship between the elements of the other thing: that is, it is the relationship that has known properties (expressed in mathematical terms, perhaps, or in formal logic or the like), and the relationships that are the same, however similar or different the appearances, and the laws that apply are, very strictly, only those governing the identity of relationship found.

Operational research, as developed from war-time juxtaposition-ing of scientists of different kinds working on the same problem, searches for homologies in order to suggest hypotheses for testing. An operational-research scientist who recognises in the mathematical expression of a road-traffic jam a similarity to an expression representing kinematic shock waves as found around an aircraft breaking the 'sound barrier', and also to that representing flood waters pouring through a gap, will be emboldened to make recommendations for the traffic problem based on knowledge of the super-sonic missile problem and the flood-control problem: but not because road traffic is 'like' Concorde or a river in spate, but because the relationship between flow and concentration is the relationship between flow and concentration. To him, the identity is complete, though formal. The layman's talk of the 'flow of traffic' is mere analogy, and would not by itself produce any scientific recommendation (Beer, 1966, 128).

One may argue, that is, from homology, but not from analogy. Plato likened a 'guardian' in his Republic to a watchdog, and straightway derived the proposition that guardians should be philosophers (lovers of knowledge) from the observation that watchdogs attack people or not according to whether they know them. It will not do. It is permissible to say that the managing director is the head of the firm or that he is the brains of his firm, but not that he ought to be the brains because he is the head.

Some may wish to say that what we have found is a homology: that a thought-to-action process is a thought-to-action process. Others may wish to believe that we have uncovered a property of systems as such (*cf.* Katz: 'accomplishment of functional contributions to a system requires a degree of autonomy from that system' – 1968, 23). For myself, I do not wish to argue either proposition. I can leave you, the reader, to make what you will of the curious affair of the autonomy, spontaneity and discontinuity principles. It does not matter for the argument of the book. At the very least, we have found a good analogy, for illustrative and heuristic purposes, to set us looking in the right area.

CHAPTER 7

The Nature of Implementation in a Bureaucracy

What can we say we have discovered about the nature of implementation in a bureaucracy by this method of taking thought about the terms already used in the literature, and applying these insights to the material of a single case-study?

First, the understandings we have arrived at about the nature of a bureaucracy. We have avoided definitions, preferring to quote usages, and 'bureaucracy' has been used in one of its looser colloquial senses to mean nothing more precise than 'a government department' or other organisation resembling one in its structure and working. However, nothing in this usage would conflict with the principal elements of Weber's ideal type, of an administrative structure in which tasks are distributed in functionally distinct offices, the distributions relatively enduring and endowing the office-holders with the requisite authority; where officials are trained to their jobs and arranged in levels of rank, with the rights of one rank over another specified by rules; where the office holder cannot appropriate his office for his own use, and the resources of the organisation are kept distinct from those of its members as individuals; where work consists of the application of general rules to particular cases, and all transactions are recorded in files. What we have done by exploring the implications of some of these elements in detail is to extend considerably the ideal type; in particular, to distinguish the notion of 'command' from the notion of 'office'.

Rank and scope

Each functionally distinct office in a bureaucracy is taken to be the 'province' of an administrative office-holder: a man, woman or small group with an office to discharge, a trust to uphold, whether legally constituted as such or merely in the logic of organisational structure; defined by the area of policy field or substantive task allotted to the office, or the area of professional competence or technical expertise practised (in the horizontal plane), and the placing of the office in the generality/specificity scale, or 'order of comprehension' (in the vertical plane). The identifying of this scale, and its conceptual distinction from the gradation of authority of rank (also in the vertical dimension), while in no sense a radical departure from common sense or the discussions in some of the previous literature, may be thought to be new, as an element in a bureaucratic model. High-generality/low-specificity connotes policy making, unprogrammed work, associated with Ministers and higher civil servants. Low-generality/high-specificity connotes 'operating' level, the practising of skills, trades or routines which directly produce the organisation's output (as distinct from arranging for its production). Although we made no serious attempt to *calibrate* the scale, both common usage and what evidence the case-study afforded suggested that it would be reasonable to see three or perhaps four distinct 'orders of comprehension' in a bureaucracy with a conventional hierarchy of eight or nine levels, although further levels were conceivable both 'upwards' and 'downwards'. The conventional names, 'top management', 'middle management', and 'operating level', seem to represent the same kind of understanding: they, too, distinguish between 'scope' and formal rank, and leave unclear just where (in terms of formal rank) the boundaries between 'orders of comprehension' are. To say (as someone accustomed to using these management terms might well do) that it is not a matter of rank but of the kind of work done, is to express the argument of this book exactly.

We distinguished, too, between placing on the generality/specificity scale and 'amount of discretion'. Although the discussion is not completed within this volume, we reached the position that there is no *a priori* case for supposing that a worker at a high-specificity level necessarily has a smaller amount of discretion (in any of its senses) than a worker at a high-generality level.

Information system

Since no other office can occupy quite the same niche (that is, be in the same 'order of comprehension' and deal with the same transactions), the office-holder acquires a kind of authority which is different from that conferred by rank: 'authority of confidence' (Parsons, 1949, 189; Simon, Smithburg, Thompson, 1950), or 'sapiential authority' (Paterson, 1960). Others will defer to him because of what he *knows*. In prudence, too, they will recognise the two important functions each such office fulfils in the internal communications of the organisation. First, it is a collecting point and storage centre for relevant information for that area of policy or technique at that level. Whether or not the office-holder personally absorbs this information, he is its bureaucratic custodian. He inhabits the niche where problems that can only be perceived by the possessor of that information are perceived (if they are going to be perceived at all), and where solutions that depend upon that information must originate (if they ever do). But even when others possess some of the information, and can alert the organisation to problems or suggest solutions, there is (at least in British central government) a strong ethos obliging others to consult the 'proper quarters' and listen to what the office-holder advises on matters within his jurisdiction.

The second communications function of each office-holder is the transmission of information. Conceptually, the office-holder can receive messages from all sides, from above and from below, and can send messages similarly. These messages arrive in several different 'languages'. For messages which come from organisational near neighbours in any direction, translation into the office's own 'language' is easy, partly because the office-holder 'speaks' their languages fairly well himself, partly because the messages have already been put into his own language to some extent. For messages from distant areas or levels of the bureaucracy, the office-holder may find translation difficult or may have to seek an interpreter, a middle-man who has enough of both languages.

If messages are not merely for the office's information but require retransmission (to superiors, to subordinates or to lateral colleagues in any direction), the office-holder has two kinds of operation to perform on them. One concerns their language: to ensure communication of their sense as he sees it, he should try to put them into the language of their recipients, to some extent at least. The other operation concerns the length or volume of the message. Messages destined for retransmission to superiors have to be summarised, abstracted, distilled, made more general, reduced in volume, while retaining their sense as it should be perceived higher up. Messages destined for retransmission to subordinates have to be expanded, spelt out, made more specific, operationalised into several distinct messages appropriate for the several subordinates in their respective niches or 'provinces'. Messages to be transmitted sideways may require either distilling or spelling out or neither, according to circumstances. These operations are necessary irrespective of whether the messages are called 'reports', 'instructions' or 'intelligence'.

There is thus a symmetry in the communications function of each office or 'work station': it extracts information (by 'inferential processing') from messages going upwards (or, in some instances, 'inwards'), and thus absorbs the uncertainty the full message displayed, and it injects information (by 'implication processing') into messages going downwards (and in some instances 'outwards'), thus absorbing the generality the original message displayed. Making messages more specific requires an input of information, and this is drawn from the office's stock of knowledge and experience. Making messages more general means that not all the information they contain is sent on: the 'surplus' is retained in the office. (It has to be admitted that this account conflates the semantic and the cybernetic senses of 'information'.)

This appreciation of a bureaucracy as a species of orderly Tower of Babel is the second main extension of the conventional model. A different 'language of discourse' (concepts, vocabulary, style) is talked in each of the three or four orders of comprehension – and let us leave social class out of it: we are not thinking of 'accent' or speech badges, but of the kind of problem being discussed. Those concerned with legislation, for example, seldom talk about the same things as those concerned with operations on the level of loading ballast or despatching Giro warrants. Again, different jargons are spoken on any one level in the generality/specificity gradation, as one moves from one policy field or task specialism to another. Even between one *rank* and the next, between one bureau and a neighbouring bureau, differences in habits of thought and conventions of speech may be noticed.

Of course, such differentiation of language can be overstressed.

Most internal communications 'barriers' of this kind are low ones, easily surmounted. But in studying implementation, it proved desirable not only to notice them, but to build them into the model, because of their importance in the elucidation of that phenomenon we have called 'the P/Q relation'.

Imagery

There is a problem in portraying these extensions to the Weberian model, that is to say, imagining (or drawing) the physical shape or configuration in space that such a structure might have. The conventional representation of a bureaucratic structure (the 'family tree' image) portrays well enough the official gradations in rank and distributions of task – who is whose superior and subordinate, and what 'commands' there are at each level (e.g., department, agencies or subdepartments, branches or groups, divisions, sections, etc.). This it can do on a flat sheet, in two dimensions. But the idea of 'comprehension', or increasing inclusiveness of scope as one ascends the rank hierarchy, is not well portrayed in a pyramid (even if one goes three-dimensional into the 'ziggurat' form). The point about the generality/specificity scale is that the higher levels *embrace* the lower and are not merely set over them. The concept of higher-level programmes containing lower-level programmes, and those in turn enveloping more specific programmes still (and so on, 'inwards' rather than simply 'downwards'), needs imagery corresponding to a set of 'Chinese boxes' – though each box would have to contain several smaller boxes, not only one (see Fig. 7 for a 'circles-within-circles' image portraying this idea – p. 86).

The second difficulty concerns the portrayal of the office or work station as a centre of communication, located at a point on a flat plane surrounded by other offices in all directions, some near neighbours, some more distant: and also sandwiched between a superior and one or more subordinates – each of those also constituting an office or 'province', for some purposes at least.

The centrality of an office at its own level, and its relations with near and distant offices on the same level, can easily be represented in a network image; and the idea that every office is a centre for its own bit of the task is easy to grasp, even if it would make for a complicated diagram if more than a handful of offices were to be shown.

Placing one such network in its 'vertical' setting – showing how the office-holder at the centre of the network is related to other office-holders above him and below him in rank – is also not inconceivable, especially if one draws in only *one* centre on the middle tier (each office-holder being treated as 'the centre of the world' in turn). But attempting to portray the bureaucracy as a whole in this convention is not so easy (see Fig. 10).

The image already used to convey the 'Babel House' model was that of the honeycomb, or mass of orderly cells related laterally in four directions and vertically in two. This can accommodate both the 'communication centre' idea and the idea of a 'command' fairly adequately, provided again one thinks of one office at a time – as if the environment, the enveloping 'Babel House', were built entirely for the convenience of that office. The difference between a 'command' and a 'province' is that the former 'goes all the way down', so that an office is at the peak of a hierarchical pyramid (small or great). Whereas the honeycomb can house a few such complexes of commands, the imagery begins to get sticky if one tries to 'see' all the hierarchical pyramids in the bureaucracy at the same time. One cannot easily portray the command pyramid and the office network for the whole of an organisation in the same 'physical' structure.

We are left with a group of three distinct images for different aspects of our model of a bureaucracy: the ziggurat, for gradations in formal authority and distributions of jurisdictional competence; the 'Chinese boxes', for the idea of 'order of comprehension' (or comprehensiveness) and of 'programmes-within-programmes-within-programmes'; and the network, or sandwich of networks (possibly envisaged as within a honeycomb of cells), for the idea of the office as information-storage, translation and transmission centre. A reader with a well developed imagination may be able to conceive of a single configuration which portrays all of these at once for an entire Ministry, but the writer's brain began to emit blue smoke when he tried.

Implementing

The present volume has been constructed on the framework of five sets of assumptions which, it was said at the end of Chapter 2, are implicit in the understandings of the implementation process shown by the authors whose writings were surveyed in that chapter. We have discussed four of them: (1) assumptions about whether implementation is a developmental or an aggregative process; (2) assumptions about the ordering or sequence of the elements of the process, distinguishing between time sequence, logic sequence, and organisational sequence (these discussions were in Chapter 4); (3) assumptions about how each element in the process differs from the others – we distinguished between 'discretion' as such and placing in the 'cognitive hierarchy', determining the degree of generality or specificity of function of any element in a particular progression, and expressible in the image of 'programmes-within-programmes', or minor routines enclosed in routines of wider scope; and (4) assumptions about the nature of the transition from one element of the process to the next, where we explored the concept of 'operationalisation', the injection of specificity (these discussions were in Chapter 5).

In the application of the developmental/aggregative assumptions to the case-study material, we suggested that some phases of the implementation process as shown there seemed to be adequately explained by a developmental hypothesis, while others required an aggregative hypothesis to make sense of them. In pursuing the phenomenon, we concluded that any account of a process of implementation in a real bureaucracy (or multi-bureaucratic setting) will be ordered by the interest of the observer and not by any necessary characteristic of the behaviours or matters observed. However, where there is *de facto* correspondence between the 'organising principle' of the interest of the observer, and the organising principle of the time, logic and organisational sequences of the operations observed, a developmental hypothesis will give good results; and where the interest of the observer is merely tracing a particular path through sets of behaviours and operations which have their time sequences, their logics and their organisational forms already fixed according to quite other principles, doing work that is not at all exclusively coincidental with the purposes that interest the observer, then only the aggregative hypothesis will give satisfactory results.

Thus the phases of the branch line closures process which were wholly about closing branch lines looked developmental, while those which were about Cabinet-level decisions, or concerned with effects on running a railway in general, or with selling property and so on, looked aggregative.

Since to another observer with a different interest even the branch line closure sequences might lose their identity and become merely a number of discrete examples of other principles at work, we ought to conclude (as we did in Chapter 4), rather surprisingly perhaps, that the idea that a number of individuals (or office-holders) in a bureaucracy are implementing a decision of the Minister or other supreme body, or carrying out a policy of his, is an abstract idea not inherent in, or even manifest in, the internal structure of a bureaucracy. Implementation is in the eye of the beholder.

At least, that would be the norm. Only where an organisational unit is specially created to carry out one decision, and that only, would implementation processes be explicit in organisational design. (But as to organisational design itself, we must leave that to another volume.)

For most purposes, therefore, the aggregative hypothesis will be the one that most often makes most sense. The office-holders (or workers) in a bureaucracy are all simply doing their jobs. It is the result of the way their jobs have been specified, and of the procedural and other rules that have been made governing the way these jobs are linked with (and *into*) one another, that any ministerial or other decision can be carried out. Implementation as a purposive activity, (as distinct from the description of a completed result of it), therefore, must consist in the identification of the requisite jobs, and the forging of the links between them, that will in practice, in a given bureaucracy, produce the output intended. It is still a matter of the interest of an observer: but the observer is now someone in the bureaucracy, someone with authority or power (or both) to obtain what he wants from it – or to try: Pressman and Wildavsky remind us that not all attempts at implementation succeed. 'The best laid schemes o' mice an' men/Gang aft a-gley.'

Programming

The notion of someone 'just doing his job' corresponds to the notion of 'office' used earlier. It is an organisational unit where personnel skilled or trained and experienced in a certain set of operations are endowed with a corresponding degree of jurisdiction, authorisation, equipment and materials to let them 'get on with it'. The name 'office' has been used for all kinds of such unit, at all hierarchical levels. Thus a Permanent Secretary's job is no more and no less an office than a counter clerk's job, the General Manager and the ballast loader both have an office to discharge. But common sense and common usage require two clarifications. First, the word 'office' is now more frequently applied to the place or room in which the job is done than to the work or responsibilities. So long as the sense of the argument is maintained, it will not matter whether the 'office' is the place or the work, provided it embraces an identifiable set of work operations requiring knowledge, skills or equipment not available elsewhere in the organisation. For simplicity, we have used the same term to cover operations of the unprogrammed, policy search and decision kind as well as of the programmed, more routine kind; and to cover operations of the administrative/clerical kind, concerned mainly with documents ('office work'), as well as of a manually dexterous, technical or machine-using kind, for which the term 'work station' is sometimes more evocative. For more refined treatments than are appropriate here such distinctions might need to be built into the model.

The second clarification bears on the 'individuality' of an office. Some kinds of job have to be thought of as being done by a number of persons who are substitutable for one another: for example, the typists in a typing pool, the shovellers in a ballast-loading gang. The 'office-holder', then, would be either a collective or an indeterminate individual from a given group. This complication can also be accommodated within our notion of 'office' or 'province' without making nonsense of it, and a 'command' (e.g., a division) still comprises a set of 'offices', arranged in a pyramid of several hierarchical levels, whether the holders are individuals or groups.

The model states that implementation in a bureaucracy is obtained (an order is fulfilled, a product or service produced, an application dealt with, a demand met, a stimulus responded to, a command carried out, etc.), by linking together a chain, train, combination or converging network of offices or work stations to assemble a sufficient number of appropriate work operations in a requisite sequence for the cumulated or final output desired.

Such linkings need not be fixed: in principle, each demand upon the bureaucracy might be met by a unique arrangement. In practice, an output that is frequently required will result in a particular combination being frequently assembled. A bureaucracy that is created or designed ('organised') for the express purpose of meeting a given set of demands repeated regularly may be seen as comprising a number of such trains or chains in more or less permanent connection. There are advantages to be gained from enclosing such permanent linkages within separate commands.

Each linking of a number of offices to produce a cumulated output can be called a 'programme'. In the usage of March and Simon, the word is reserved for well established and frequently used linkings (resulting in 'programmed behaviour'). We have used it that way too, though we have also used the word 'routine' for that idea. 'Programme' is in common use, however, for a single one-off linking, as in the concert programme, establishing the sequence of and (at least in a well-thought-out one) the cumulation or even development of the impressions made by the several independent items, as in 'a programme of early Beethoven'.

One may in this way speak of 'programming' an organisation to produce a particular output, or of 'engineering' a certain effect. But the understanding of this depends as much upon *control* as upon implementation.

The concept of control

Indeed, there is much yet to be discussed before our understanding of the implementation process in a bureaucracy can be said to be complete. For the fifth set of assumptions which we elicited from the literature were assumptions about the relationship of the process to 'authority', and we have not yet begun to consider this in any detail. To leave things at the point we have reached would leave us with several puzzles.

If an office-holder is essentially autonomous, the custodian of specialised knowledge, entitled to be consulted and to be listened to, entitled even to the right of decision within his sphere of competence and so on, what is left of his subordinate status? How can he be autonomous and subject to authority?

If an officer with a specialised function (or 'mystery', in the medieval term) is to be considered more expert than his superior in that function, regarded as knowing what to do spontaneously without being told, if the work operations unique to an office are merely triggered off, or 'switched-in', by a command signal, and are not conveyed or specified by it and so on, what becomes of the notion of a superior's 'instructions'? How is spontaneous functioning made or kept relevant?

If the preparation of reports and instructions and intelligence of all kinds is subject to interpretation, inferential and implication processing, summation or amplification, selection and uncertainty absorption and so on at every junction in the communication system, if a superior of senior rank is (practically speaking) incompetent to supervise what is being done by those in his own command three or four grades or rank below his own, what is left of his 'responsibility' for their actions? If transmission and comprehension are discontinuous, but accountability is not, how is compliance assured?

Again: it is one thing to programme a command, or the bureaucracy as a whole to produce a desired output; it is another to ensure that the output is produced. What happens if something goes wrong? How, for that matter, would one know whether something has gone wrong or not? If there is a delay or other unforeseen circumstance that interrupts the operation of the programme, how does a bureaucracy cope?

In the treatment of the implementation process in this volume we have worked on the assumption that when a decision has been taken at its appropriate level, operationalised into instructions at succeeding levels until operating level is reached, and so has become an output to the environment, whatever it was appropriate should happen at any point in the process *has* happened. We have assumed 'perfect implementation': that the Minister, having given his consent to closure, could take closure for granted; that the General Manager having by a Works Order ordered works, works thereupon (by the processes described) took place. Since we were studying the idea of implementation as such, this was not unreasonable, and even analytically unavoidable.

But there are at least two huge gulfs in such an account, ways in which it is so unrealistic as to be useless as a descriptive model of what has to happen in a bureaucracy when implementation of such a 'consent' or 'order' is in progress. The first has to do with the coping with inevitable 'imperfections' in implementation: overcoming gaps in information, monitoring the exercise of discretion, ensuring compliance, adapting to unforeseen circumstance. Even if (as we are doing) we leave out of account variations in the commitment of the actors, the effects of self-interested behaviour and other matters of 'affect' in interpersonal relations (the staple of so much of the 'pathology' literature), there are still many contingencies of timing or routing or precise configuration of material constraints for which unprogrammed, on-the-spot choices, or 'feedback' to higher decision levels, are indispensable. One such decision may then have unintended consequences for other parts of the bureaucracy: other superiors may have to cope with the outcomes of coping with an unplanned event. The counterpart to programming activity, in facilitating desired outputs, is *co-ordinatory* activity.

The second gulf that would be left by an assumption that the implementation process is primarily a matter of programming is particularly relevant to bureaucracies, in our loose definition of that term; that is, as 'public bodies'. Briefly put, Ministers and heads of other public bodies, much more than the heads of other organisations, are accountable for the actions of their subordinates not only in respect of the results achieved, the outcome or the impact, but also in respect of the processes by which the outputs were produced. Indeed, it is sometimes said that public bodies have to pay more attention to the manner of their doing something than to the matter of it: more attention to procedural correctness than to substantive success.

Any implementation process in a bureaucracy, therefore, has to take place within a set of constraints imposed by the simultaneous seeking of a large number of organisational goals, or satisfying of a large numbers of concurrent criteria. Some are substantive (to do with aims in the policy domain concerned); some are procedural (to do with generalised government objectives, such as efficiency and probity); and some can be called structural (to do with the 'survival' or growth of the organisation as such). Conflict between such multiple goals is endemic and, as it were, a mere condition of production; but implementation in any instance requires either the establishment of priorities by explicit processes or the containment of conflict in equilibrium by implicit processes.

The concept which unifies all these ideas (authority, accountability, compliance, monitoring, feedback, correction, coordination, equilibrium, etc.) is the concept of *control*. This is the subject of the companion volume, *Control in a Bureaucracy*.

Let us summarise the understanding of implementation that we have reached in the form of a number of propositions.

1. An office pre-exists a programme, and may in principle be included in many different programmes.

This is the basic aggregative assumption and follows from the appreciation that the number of distinguishable professional or trade skills, the number of divisions of knowledge and the number of types of equipment are all much smaller than the number of organisational jurisdictions which can be put together employing them; and that in its turn is infinitely smaller than the number of orders that can be executed, or policies implemented, in and through such organisations.

2. Each office has a specialised function, an operation combining knowledge and skill and equipment, and applies a particular technique to some raw or partly processed material so as to produce a characteristic office output or range of outputs.

This is an expansion of the definition of 'office'. A corollary is that one office is not, as such, substitutable for another office, unless a duplicate has been created to cope with work-flow demand (as in a three-shift system, for example). In that case offices with the same function might be found in different commands; it does not greatly matter whether the two or more duplicates are considered as one office split or as separate offices. It is quite feasible, however, that a programme may be substitutable by another programme; that is, a quite distinct combination of offices may be able to produce an identical cumulated output. More than one sequence may be available to implement a given policy.

3. To produce an office's output, several kinds of input are required: materials, which may be the partly processed outputs of other offices, and may include stored materials or stocks; energy, used in the work operations or conversion of inputs into output, and including labour and the stored energy or capital represented by accommodation, furniture, machines, etc.; information, the input which triggers off the operation, but including stored knowledge represented by standing instructions, training and rules governing the operation, and other knowledge and experience applied to it.

These, too, are corollaries of the definition. It is to be noted, however, that whereas an operation may be wholly or selectively triggered by a command signal (an instruction or 'word of command'), it may also be triggered by the mere appearance of work at the input end; alternatively, the *non*-appearance of work may trigger a part of the work operation. In any event, the operations are not *specified* by the signal. The operations of the office are governed by the physical, mechanical or logical necessities of the work (technical requisites), and by the organisational rules (structural, procedural and substantive) laid down for it.

4. An office can only operate on materials in a specific state or in one of a small range of states.

The more 'routinised' the office, the narrower the range of problems it will be able to do anything at all with, but the same applies in principle to the range of inputs processible by units at higher-generality or policy-making levels. There is (conceptually) in all offices a 'doorkeeping' or recognition function, in which presenting inputs are scanned for 'fit' or processibility and (if they fall within the acceptable categories and limits) prepared for operations (e.g., 'clients' are turned into 'cases'). A programme, accordingly, is governed by the logic of a domino game, each office's input pattern having to be matched with compatible output patterns of the requisite other offices (and vice versa). Depending upon the ranges of such compatibilities, there may be several alternative sequences in a programme: one office's operations may be suitable to come before or after another's. A complex, 'branching' programme may be constrained by the time or logic sequences of its points of convergence (as in critical path analysis).

5. Between the input and output of an office, there may occur not simply one operation or single set of operations in a fixed pattern, but a sequence of operations, each itself a programme linking subordinate offices, and incorporating selection among such subordinate programmes in order either (a) to produce constant output from a variety of inputs or (b) to produce a variety of outputs from constant inputs or (c) some combination of the two.

Here we encounter again the problem of accommodating hierarchy in network. Just as the notion of 'programmability' of offices to produce a variety of outputs means that the bureaucracy cannot be seen as a 'fixed-relations machine' of the stamp-vending kind, so the fact of specialisation at subordinate levels within a command gives the office-holder the resources of a 'mini-bureaucracy' to draw on, so that his *command* is programmable. If he has no command, this proposition is of course inoperable. Where a subordinate office-holder himself has subordinates, he, too, has a programmable command, and the operations of an office several ranks up in the bureaucracy have to be seen as potentially including 'programmes-within-programmes-within-programmes', to the requisite number of inclusions. (This is the case whether or not the programmes are routinised ones.)

By analogy: the operator of the sophisticated domestic washing-machine can programme it for temperature of water, length of wash, number of rinses, length of spin and so on. The controls having been set, the machine goes through its operations. But each spin, for example, is a programme of its own, involving timing triggers, a rotation-speed governor, a braking sequence and so on. And, seen separately, the braking sequence (for example) is itself a programme, a complicated enough piece of engineering, incorporating pawls and springs and levers arranged to cope with a variety of conditions. The action of any one lever in this set is a programme. The regress of programmes-within-programmes, if not infinite, is quite lengthy.

On much the same principles, the wrist action of a clerk shaping a letter or figure in a document is a programme. The entry he is making is part of a programmed work operation, that itself fits into a scheme designed to produce reports or records for use in a wider programme, and so on (upwards or outwards), until organisational-level work operations (the purpose for which the bureaucracy as a whole is programmed) are in view.

6. Such programmes, and programmes-within-programmes, form the bureaucracy's repertory of responses to presenting problems; and the degree of appropriateness of final output to presented problem is limited (at maximum) to the combinatorial possibilities of the repertory.

This proposition is derivable from the others, but it also sums up, in our terms, a set of well-known 'truths' about bureaucracies: their limited flexibility and adaptiveness. Of course, one bureaucracy may be more flexible than another, according to the proportion of its activities that are heavily routinised or relatively unprogrammed. And the sixth proposition does not apply only to government organisations, by any means. Here, however, we begin to move into another definitional field, one where bureaucracy *means* 'an organisation that cannot correct its behaviour by learning from its errors' (Crozier, 1964, 187).

Documents in the Case Study (Chapter 3)

1. Relevant subsections of Section 56, Transport Act 1962
2. Formal Notice of Closure
3. The Minister's Consent Letter

1. TRANSPORT ACT 1962, Section 56

56—(1) There shall be established in accordance with this Section –
  (a) a Central Transport Consultative Committee for Great Britain (hereinafter referred to as the 'Central Committee'), and
  (b) Area Transport Users Consultative Committees (hereinafter referred to as 'Area Committees') for such areas of Great Britain as the Minister may from time to time direct, but so that there is no part of Great Britain which is not within the area of an Area Committee and so that there is at all times an Area Committee for Scotland and an Area Committee for Wales and Monmouthshire.

(2) [Constitution of the Committees]

(3) [Term of office of members]

(4) Subject to the following provisions of this section, it shall be the duty of the Central Committee and of each Area Committee to consider and, where it appears to them to be desirable, make recommendations with respect to any matter affecting the services and facilities provided by any of the Boards –
  (a) which has been the subject of representations (other than representations appearing to the committee to be frivolous) made to the committee by or on behalf of users of those services or facilities, or
  (b) which has been referred to the committee by the Minister or by a Board, or
  (c) which appears to the committee to be a matter to which consideration ought to be given;

and copies of the minutes, conclusions and recommendations of each committee shall be sent to the Board concerned and –

(i) in the case of any Area Committee, to the Central Committee; and

(ii) in the case of the Central Committee and the Area Committees for Scotland and for Wales and Monmouthshire, to the Minister.

(5) Nothing in the last foregoing subsection shall entitle any committee to consider the charges made for any service or facility, or to consider any question relating to the discontinuance or reduction of railway services except as provided in the following provisions of this section; and the Central Committee shall not be obliged to consider any representation which appears to them to be more suitable for consideration by an Area Committee or which has been previously considered by an Area Committee.

(6) Where the Minister receives a recommendation under subsection (4) of this section he may give to the Board concerned such directions as he thinks fit with respect to the matters dealt with in the recommendation.

(7) Where the Railways Board or London Board propose to discontinue all railway passenger services from any station or on any line (hereinafter referred to as a closure), they shall, not less than six weeks before carrying their proposal into effect, publish in two successive weeks in two local newspapers circulating in the area affected, and in such other manner as appears to them appropriate, a notice –

(a) giving the date and particulars of the proposed closure, and particulars of any alternative services which it appears to the Board will be available and of any proposals of the Board for providing or augmenting such services; and

(b) stating that objections to the proposed closure may be lodged in accordance with this section within six weeks of a date specified in the notice (being the date on which the notice is last published in a local newspaper as required by this section);

and copies of the notice shall be sent to the appropriate Area Committee.

For the purposes of this and the next following subsection the appropriate Area Committee is the committee for the area in which the station or the line, or any part of the line, affected by the proposed closure is situated.

(8) Where a notice has been published under the last foregoing subsection any user of any service affected and any body representing such users may within the period specified in the notice lodge with the appropriate Area Committee an objection in writing, and where such an objection is lodged the committee shall forthwith inform the Minister and the Board concerned and the closure shall not be proceeded with until the committee has reported to the Minister and the Minister has given his consent.

(9) A committee with whom an objection has been lodged under the last

foregoing subsection shall consider the objection and any representations made by the Board concerned and report to the Minister as soon as possible on the hardship, if any, which they consider will be caused by the proposed closure and the report may contain proposals for alleviating that hardship.

Where objections with respect to any proposed closure have been lodged with more than one Area Committee, the committees in question –

(a) may report to the Minister jointly, or

(b) may agree that the consideration of objections and representations relating to the closure and the making of a report to the Minister shall be delegated to any of those committees appearing to them to be principally concerned;

and copies of every report under this and the next following subsection shall be sent to the Central Committee and to the Board concerned.

(10) The Minister may require an Area Committee to make a further report; and if in any case the Minister considers that a report or further report has been unreasonably delayed he may, after consulting the committee and making such enquiries as he thinks fit, consent to the proposed closure without awaiting the report or further report.

(11) In any case in which a closure requires the consent of the Minister under this section, the Minister may give his consent subject to such conditions as he thinks fit and may from time to time vary those conditions; and the Minister may in connection with the closure from time to time give such directions to the Board concerned, as he thinks fit.

Where a condition attached to a consent or direction requires the Board to provide or assist in the provision of alternative services, the Minister may refer to an Area Committee any matter relating to those services, and the committee shall consider and report to the Minister on that matter.

(12) [Frequency of meetings of committees]

(13) Where for the purposes of subsection (9) of this section a committee decide to hear an objector orally, or to hear oral representations made on behalf of a Board, they shall hear the objector and the representations in public.

(14) [Quorum at meetings]

(15) [Annual reports]

(16) [Staffing and accommodation, allowances etc.]

(17) [Transition provisions]

(18) [Shipping services]

(19) [References before vesting date]

2. Formal Notice of Closure

BRITISH RAILWAYS
NORTH EASTERN REGION

PUBLIC NOTICE

TRANSPORT ACT 1962

Withdrawal of Railway Passenger Services

The North Eastern Railway Board hereby give notice in accordance with Section 56(7) of the Transport Act, 1962, that on and from Monday, 9th September, 1963, they propose to discontinue all railway passenger services between Harrogate and Cross Gates (via Wetherby) and between Church Fenton and Wetherby and from the following stations:-

SPOFFORTH	SCHOLES
WETHERBY	PENDA'S WAY
COLLINGHAM BRIDGE	TADCASTER
BARDSEY	NEWTON KYME
THORNER	THORP ARCH

It appears to the Board that the following alternative services will be available:-

LEEDS CORPORATION TRANSPORT Service No 40.
Between Leeds and Penda's Way station. Hourly service with 15, 20 or 30 minute service at peak times.

WEST YORKSHIRE ROAD CAR CO.
Services 38 and 39 between Leeds and Knaresborough and Leeds and Wetherby via Bardsey, Collingham and Wetherby, at half-hourly intervals except at morning and evening peaks when there is a 15 minute interval.
Services 41 and 42 between Leeds, Scholes, Thorner, Tadcaster, Thorp Arch and Wetherby at hourly intervals with additional buses at peak times.
Services 43, 44, 45, 46 and 91 between Leeds, Scholes, Tadcaster and York at half-hourly intervals.
Services 47 and 48 between Leeds, Penda's Way and Scholes at half-hourly intervals with additional buses at peak periods.
Service 76 between Harrogate, Spofforth, Wetherby, Thorp Arch and Tadcaster at hourly intervals.

WEST RIDING AUTOMOBILE CO. LTD.
Services 186 and 187 between Castleford, Church Fenton and Tadcaster – five buses daily each way.

It is proposed to introduce additional stops at Cross Gates in the following trains:

    8.20 am York to Leeds   (8.44 am at Cross Gates)
    5.30 pm Leeds to Scarborough   (5.37 pm at Cross Gates)
and to re-time the 7.40 am York–Leeds to call at Cross Gates at 8.17 am to replace the Service leaving there at 8.13 am.

Any user of the railway services it is proposed to withdraw, and any body representing such users desirous of objecting to the proposal may lodge objections within six weeks of Friday, 21st June, 1963, i.e. not later than 3rd August, 1963, addressing any objection to the Secretary of the Yorkshire Area Transport Users' Consultative Committee at address:

                    Toft Green Chambers
                    Toft Green
                    YORK.

Note: If any objections are lodged within the period specified above, the closure cannot be proceeded with until the Transport Users' Consultative Committee has reported to the Minister, and the Minister has given his consent (Section 56(8) of the Transport Act, 1962).

3. *The Minister's Consent Letter*

MINISTRY OF TRANSPORT

St Christopher House, Southwark Street, London SE1
Telegrams: Transminry London Telex
Telephone: WATerloo 7999, *ext.*

Our reference: RB.3/6/034
Your reference:

The Secretary,
British Railways Board,
222 Marylebone Road,
LONDON NW1   18 October, 1963

Sir,

    I am directed by the Minister of Transport to inform you that he has received the report of the Transport Users Consultative Committee for the Yorkshire Area upon objections and representations relating to the proposal to discontinue all railway passenger services between Harrogate and Cross Gates (via Wetherby) and between Church Fenton and Wetherby in the County of York, West Riding, involving the discontinuance of all railway passenger services from the stations at Spofforth, Wetherby, Collingham Bridge, Bardsey, Thorner, Scholes, Penda's Way, Tadcaster, Newton Kyme and Thorp Arch. This proposed discontinuance is referred to in this letter as 'the closure'.

2. The Minister has considered the report of the Consultative Committee and all other relevant factors. He accepts the view of the Committee that having regard to the bus services at present being provided and to the willingness of the West Yorkshire Car Co. Ltd. to duplicate, at peak times as the need arises, their service between Scholes and Leeds, hardship from the closure would arise only in isolated cases. He has therefore decided that the measure of hardship likely to be caused by the closure would be insufficient to justify the continuance of the services to which the closure relates.

3. Accordingly the Minister, in exercise of his powers under Section 56 of the Transport Act 1962, hereby gives his consent to the closure subject to the following conditions:

  (a) Whenever the Board become aware –

    (i) of any proposal for an alteration of any of the bus services at present being provided which are set out in the Annex hereto by withdrawing or substantially reducing the frequency of any such service, whether it is then being provided by the person named in the Annex or by any other person; or

    (ii) of any such alteration having been made,

  the Board shall forthwith notify the Minister of any such proposal or alterations as the case may be and give him all such information as he may reasonably require.

  (b) The Board shall take reasonable steps to keep themselves informed of any such proposal or alteration as is mentioned in the last foregoing condition.

  (c) The foregoing conditions shall have effect until the Minister notifies the Board that they are no longer to apply or until they are varied Section 56(11) of the Transport Act 1962.

4. I am directed by the Minister to make it clear that in imposing the conditions contained in paragraph 3 of this letter the Minister has been concerned only to discharge his functions under section 56 of the Transport Act 1962, and that these conditions have been framed in the light of the information before him for that purpose. In particular it should be clearly appreciated that the existing bus services can only be maintained in so far as their maintenance is authorised by road service licences issued by the Traffic Commissioners under the Road Traffic Acts and that nothing in this letter affects the powers and duties of the Traffic Commissioners under those Acts in relation to the maintenance of any of these services. Furthermore in the event of any appeal to the Minister from any decision of the Traffic Commissioners the Minister will deal with that appeal in accordance with the

provisions of the Road Traffic Acts and in the light of the information properly before him on the appeal.

I am, Sir,

Your obedient Servant,

J. H. H. BAXTER

Assistant Secretary

RB 3/6/034

ANNEX

EXISTING BUS SERVICES PROVIDED UNDER ROAD SERVICE LICENCES GRANTED UNDER THE ROAD TRAFFIC ACTS 1960 TO 1962

Services operated by the West Yorkshire Road Car Company Limited

Service No. 38.   Leeds–Wetherby–Knaresborough
          39.   Leeds–East Keswick–Wetherby
          41.   Leeds–Boston Spa–Wetherby
          42.   Leeds–Boston Spa–Tadcaster
          43.
          44.
          45.   Leeds–Tadcaster–York
          46.
          47.   Leeds–Barwick–Aberford
          48.   Leeds–Scholes–Barwick–Aberford
          76.   Skipton–Harrogate–Wetherby–Tadcaster
          91.   Leeds–Tadcaster–York

Services operated by the Leeds City Transport

Service No. 9.   Leeds Ring Road, Selby Road–Bradford Road
          38.   Moortown–Whitkirk
          40.   Leeds Central Bus Station–Stanks (Kelmscott Green)

Service operated by the West Riding Automobile Company Limited

Service No. 187.   Castleford–Brotherton–Sherburn–Tadcaster.

Books and Articles Referred to in the Text

ALBROW, Martin (1970), *Bureaucracy*. London: Pall Mall Press, 1970; Macmillan Papermac, 1970; New York: Praeger, 1971.

ALLEN, G. Freeman (1966), *British Rail After Beeching*. London: Ian Allan, 1966.

ALLISON, G. T. (1971), *Essence of Decision: Explaining the Cuban Missile Crisis*. Boston: Little, Brown, 1971.

ALMOND, Gabriel and COLEMAN, James eds (1960), *The Politics of Developing Areas*. Princeton, NJ: Princeton University Press, 1960.

ANNETT, John (1969), *Feedback and Human Behaviour*. Harmondsworth, Middlesex: Penguin Books, 1969.

APPLEBY, Paul H. (1949), *Policy and Administration*. Alabama: University of Alabama Press, 1949.

ARGYRIS, Chris (1960), *Understanding Organizational Behavior*. Homewood, Ill: Dorsey Press, 1960; London: Tavistock Publications, 1960.

AUDLEY, R. J. et al. (1967), *Decision Making*. London: British Broadcasting Corporation, 1967.

BACKOFF, R. (1974), 'Operationalising Administrative Reform for Improved Governmental Performance', *Administration and Society* 6(1): 73–106, May 1974.

BAILEY, Thomas (1966), *Presidential Greatness*. New York: Appleton-Century–Crofts, 1966.

BAKKE, E. Wight (1950), *Bonds of Organization*. New York: Harper Bros., 1950.

BARDACH, E. (1977). *The Implementation Game*. Cambridge, Mass.: M.I.T. Press, 1977.

BARNARD, Chester I. (1938), *The Functions of the Executive*. Cambridge, Mass.: Harvard University Press, 1938; *new edn*, 1968.

BAUER, R. A. and GERGEN, K. H. eds (1968), *The Study of Policy Formation*. New York: Free Press, 1968.

BEECHING, Richard (later Lord) (1963), Chairman, British Railways Board, *The Reshaping of British Railways* (The Beeching Report). London: HMSO, 1963.

BEER, Stafford (1960), 'Below the Twilight Arch', *in General Systems*, Yearbook of the Society for General Systems 5:9–20. Ann Arbor, Mich.: Society for General Systems Research, 1960.

BEER, Stafford (1966), *Decision and Control*. London: John Wiley and Sons, 1966.

BEER, Stafford (1967), *Management Science, The Business Use of Operations Research*. London: Aldus Books, 1967.

BEER, Stafford (1972), *Brain of the Firm: The Managerial Cybernetics of Organization*. London: Allen Lane The Penguin Press, 1972.

243

BENDIX, Reinhard (1960), *Max Weber – An Intellectual Portrait*. London: Heinemann, 1960.

BENTHAM, Jeremy (1843), *Constitutional Code*, Vol. IX *in* BOWRING (1843).

BERGER, Robert and SEABORNE, A. E. M. (1966), *The Psychology of Learning*. Harmondsworth, Middlesex: Penguin Books, 1966.

BLAU, Peter M. (1955), *The Dynamics of Bureaucracy*. Chicago: University of Chicago Press, 1955.

BLAU, Peter M. and SCOTT, W. Richard (1962), *Formal Organizations*. San Francisco: Chandler Publishing Company, 1962; London: Routledge and Kegan Paul, 1963.

BONAVIA, Michael R. (1971), *The Organisation of British Railways*. London: Ian Allan, 1971.

BOSANQUET, Bernard (1899), *The Philosophical Theory of the State*. London: Macmillan and Co Ltd, 1899; 4th edn, 1923; reprinted 1951.

BOURN, J. B. (1968), 'The Main Reports on the British Civil Service since the Northcote–Trevelyan Report'; Memorandum No. 10 submitted to the Committee on the Civil Service, *Report* of the Committee, 3(2): 423–65. London: HMSO, Cmnd 3638, 1968.

BOWRING, John ed (1843), *The Works of Jeremy Bentham*; 10 vols. Edinburgh: William Tait, 1843.

BRITTAN, Samuel (1964), *The Treasury under the Tories 1951–64*. Harmondsworth, Middlesex: Penguin Books, 1964.

BROCK, J. R. (1958), *The Railways of Harrogate* (typescript; in Leeds Public Library), 1958.

BRODIE, M. B. (1962), 'Henri Fayol: "Administration industrielle et générale" – a reinterpretation', *Public Administration* 40:311–17, 1962.

BRODIE, M. B. (1967), *Fayol on Administration*, (an Administrative Staff College Monograph). London: Lyon, Grant and Green, 1967.

BROWN, R. G. S. (1970), *The Administrative Process in Britain*. London: Methuen, 1970; University Paperback, 1971.

BRYSON, Lyman (1951), 'Notes on a Theory of Advice', *Political Science Quarterly* 66:321–339, 1951.

CAIDEN, Gerald (1970), *Administrative Reform*. Chicago: Aldine Publishing Company, 1969; London: Allen Lane, The Penguin Press, 1970.

CHAPMAN, Richard A (1969), *Decision Making: A Case Study of the Decision to Raise the Bank Rate in September, 1957*. London: Routledge and Kegan Paul, 1969.

COMFORT, Alex, *et al.* (1964), *The Science of Man 3: Egg to Adult* (booklet to accompany a series of television programmes). London: British Broadcasting Corporation, 1964.

COOMBES, D. (1966), *The Member of Parliament and the Administration*. London: George Allen and Unwin, 1966.

CREEL, H. G. (1964), 'The Beginnings of Bureaucracy in China: the Origin of the Hsien', *Journal of Asian Studies* 23(2):155–83, February 1964.

CRENSON, M. (1971), *The Unpolitics of Air Pollution*. Baltimore, Md: Johns Hopkins Press, 1971.

CROZIER, Michel (1964), *The Bureaucratic Phenomenon*. Paris: Edition du Seuil, 1963; London: Tavistock Publications, 1964; Chicago: University of Chicago Press, 1964.

CUTHBERT, Norman (1970), 'Fayol and the Principles of Organization', *in* TILLETT *et al.*, 1970:108–23.

CYERT, Richard M. and MARCH, James G. (1963), *The Behavioral Theory of the Firm*. Englewood Cliffs, NJ: Prentice-Hall Inc., 1963.

DALTON, Melville (1959), *Men Who Manage*. New York: John Wiley and Sons, 1959.

DERTHICK, Martha (1972), *New Towns In-Town*. Washington, DC: Urban Institute, 1972.

DEWEY, John (1933), *How We Think*. New York: Heath and Company, 1933.

DOLBEARE, Kenneth M. ed (1975), *Public Policy Evaluation*. Beverley Hills, Calif: Sage Publications, 1975; London: Sage Publications Ltd, 1975.

DOLBEARE, K. M. and HAMMOND, P. E. (1971), *The School Prayer Decisions: From Court Policy to Local Practice*. Chicago: University of Chicago Press, 1971.

DORSEY, John T. Jr (1958), 'A Communication Model for Administration', *Administrative Science Quarterly* 2(3):307–24, 1958.

DOWNS, Anthony (1967), *Inside Bureaucracy*. Boston: Little, Brown and Co., 1967.

DROR, Yehezkel (1968), *Public Policymaking Reexamined*. Scranton, Penn: Chandler Publishing Company, 1968.

DUNSIRE, Andrew (1973), *Administration: The Word and the Science*. London: Martin Robertson, 1973; New York: Halsted Press, John Wiley and Sons, 1973.

DYE, Thomas R. (1972), *Understanding Public Policy*. Englewood Cliffs, NJ: Prentice-Hall Inc., 1972.

DYE, Thomas R. (1976), *Policy Analysis, What Governments Do, Why They Do it, and What Difference it Makes*. University, Ala: University of Alabama Press, 1976.

EASTON, David (1953), *The Political System*. New York: Alfred A. Knopf, 1953.

EDWARDS, Ward and TVERSKY, Amos eds (1967), *Decision Making: Selected Readings*. Harmondsworth, Middlesex: Penguin Books, 1967.

ELLIS, C. H. (1959), *British Railway History 1877–1947*. London: George Allen and Unwin, 1959.

EMERY, F. E. ed. (1969), *Systems Thinking: Selected Readings*. Harmondsworth, Middlesex: Penguin Books, 1969.

EVARTS, Edward V. (1973), 'Brain Mechanisms in Movement', *Scientific American* 229(1):96–103, July 1973.

FARRAR, M. F. (1931), *How To Make The British Railways Pay*. London: Pitman, 1931.

FAYOL, Henri (1916), 'Administration Industrielle et Générale', *Bulletin de la Société de l'Industrie Minérale*, No. 3, 1916; Paris: Dunod, 1925; *new edn* 1962; transl. Coubrough, *Industrial and General Administration*. Geneva: International Management Institute, 1929; transl. Storrs, *General and Industrial Management*. London: Pitman, 1949.

FLETCHER, Ronald (1971), *The Making of Sociology: A Study of Sociological Theory*; Vol. I, *Beginnings and Foundations*; Vol. II, *Developments*. London: Michael Joseph, 1971.

FRIEDRICH, Carl J. (1937), *Constitutional Government and Politics*. New York: Harper Bros., 1937.

FRY, Geoffrey (1969), *Statesmen in Disguise: The Changing Role of the Administrative Class of the British Home Civil Service 1853–1966*. London: Macmillan, 1969.

GARRETT, John (1972), *The Management of Government*. Harmondsworth, Middlesex: Penguin Books, 1972.

GEORGE, Claude S. Jr (1968), *The History of Management Thought*. Englewood Cliffs NJ: Prentice-Hall Inc., 1968.

GERGEN, K. (1968), 'Assessing the leverage points in the process of policy formation', *in* BAUER AND GERGEN *eds* (1968), chap. 5.

GILBRETH, Lilian (1914), *The Psychology of Management*. New York: Sturgis and Walton Company, 1914; London: Pitman, n.d.

GOLEMBIEWSKI, Robert T. and MUNZENRIDER, Robert (1977), 'Some Managerially

Relevant Covariates of Hierarchical Status', *Administration and Society* 9(1): 3–12, May 1977.

GOODENOUGH, W. H. (1963), *Cooperation in Change*. New York: Russell Sage Foundation, 1963.

GOODNOW, Frank J. (1900), *Politics and Administration*. New York: The Macmillan Company, 1900.

GRAY, A. P. and ABRAMS, Mark (1954), *Construction of Esso Refinery, Fawley*. London: British Institute of Management, Occasional Paper 6, 1954.

GREY Walter, W. (1953), *The Living Brain*. London: Duckworth, 1953; Harmondsworth, Middlesex: Penguin Books, 1961.

GROSS, Bertram (1966), 'Activating national plans', *in* LAWRENCE ed. (1966), 449–82.

GROSS, Bertram (1967), *Action Under Planning, The Guidance of Economic Development*. New York: McGraw–Hill, 1967.

GROSS, N., GIACQUINTA, J. V., and BERNSTEIN, M. (1971), *Implementing Organizational Innovations*. New York: Basic Books, 1971.

GULICK, Luther (1937), 'Notes on the Theory of Organization, with special reference to Government in the United States'. A Memorandum prepared as a member of the President's Committee on Administrative Management, December 1936; revised June 1937. Paper I *in* GULICK AND URWICK eds (1937), 1–45.

GULICK, Luther and URWICK, Lyndall F. eds (1937), *Papers on the Science of Administration*. New York: Institute of Public Administration, Columbia University, 1937.

HAAS, J. Eugene and DRABEK, Thomas E. (1973), *Complex Organizations, A Sociological Perspective*. New York: Macmillan, 1973.

HAIRE, Mason ed. (1959), *Modern Organization Theory*. New York: John Wiley and Sons, 1959; London: Chapman and Hall, 1959.

HALL, Richard H. (1972), *Organizations: Structure and Process*. Englewood Cliffs, NJ: Prentice-Hall Inc., 1972; London: Prentice-Hall International Inc., 1974.

HANSON, A. H. (1961), *Parliament and Public Ownership*. London: Cassell, 1961.

HECLO, H. (1974), *Modern Social Policies in Britain and Sweden*. New Haven: Yale University Press, 1974.

HECLO, H. and WILDAVSKY, A. (1974), *The Private Government of Public Money*. London: Macmillan, 1974.

HERBST, P. G. (1962), *Autonomous Group Functioning, An Exploration in Behaviour Theory and Measurement*. London: Tavistock Publications, 1962.

HERRING, E. Pendleton (1936), *Public Administration and the Public Interest*. New York: McGraw-Hill, 1936.

HILL, Michael J. (1972), *The Sociology of Public Administration*. London: Weidenfeld and Nicolson, 1972.

HININGS, C. R., PUGH, D. S., HICKSON, D. J., and TURNER, C. (1967), 'An Approach to the Study of Bureaucracy', *Sociology* 1:62–72, January 1967.

HOMANS, George C. (1950), *The Human Group*. New York: Harcourt Brace, 1950; London: Routledge and Kegan Paul, 1951.

HOOD, Christopher C. (1976), *The Limits of Administration*. London: John Wiley and Sons, 1976.

HOWE, M. (1964), 'The Transport Act, 1962, and the Consumers' Consultative Committees', *Public Administration* 42: 45–56, Spring 1964.

HOWE, M. and ELSE, P. K. (1968), 'Railway Closures: Recent Changes in Machinery and Policy', *Public Administration* 46: 127–42, Summer 1968.

HOWE, M. and MILLS, G. (1960), 'The Withdrawal of Railway Services', *Economic Journal* 70: 348–56, 1960.

JANOWITZ, Morris (1959), *Sociology and the Military Establishment*. New York: Russell Sage Foundation, 1959.

JEFFRESS, L. A. *ed*. (1951), *Cerebral Mechanisms in Behavior – The Hixon Symposium*. New York: John Wiley and Sons, 1951.

JOHNSON, R. M. (1967), *The Dynamics of Compliance*. Evanston, Ill: Northwestern University Press, 1967.

JOHNSTONE, Dorothy (1975), *A Tax Shall Be Charged: Some Aspects of the Introductin of the British Value Added Tax*. London: HMSO, Civil Service Studies 1, 1975.

JONES, C. O. (1970), *An Introduction to the Study of Public Policy*. Belmont, Calif: Wadsworth, 1970.

KAHN, Robert L. and BOULDING, Elise *eds* (1964), *Power and Conflict in Organizations*. New York: Basic Books Inc., 1964.

KAST, Fremont (1968), 'Systems Concepts and Organization Theory', *in* LE BRETON (1968), 147–54.

KATZ, D. and KAHN, R. (1966), *The Social Psychology of Organizations*. New York: John Wiley and Sons, 1966.

KATZ, D., GUTEK, B., KAHN, R. L. and BARTON, E. (1975), *Bureaucratic Encounters: A pilot study in the evaluation of government services*. Ann Arbor, Mich: University of Michigan Institute for Social Research, 1975.

KATZ, Fred E. (1968), *Autonomy and Organization, the Limits of Social Control*. New York: Random House, 1968.

KAUFMAN, Herbert and COUZENS, Michael (1973), *Administrative Feedback*. Washington, DC: The Brookings Institution, 1973.

KENNEDY, Donald *ed*. (1965), *The Living Cell: Readings from* Scientific American. San Francisco and London: W. H. Freeman and Company, 1965.

KENNEDY, Donald *ed*. (1967), *From Cell to Organism: Readings from* Scientific American. San Francisco and London: W. H. Freeman and Company, 1967.

KERLINGER, F. (1964), *Foundations of Behavioral Research*. New York: Holt, Rinehart and Winston, 1964.

KOESTLER, Arthur (1964), *The Act of Creation*. London: Hutchinson, 1964.

KOESTLER, Arthur (1967), *The Ghost in the Machine*. London: Hutchinson, 1967.

KUHN, Alfred (1974), *The Logic of Social Systems*. San Francisco and London: Jossey-Bass Publishers, 1974

KUHN, Thomas S. (1962), *The Structure of Scientific Revolutions*. International Encyclopaedia of Unified Science, 2(2). Chicago: University of Chicago Press, 1962. 2nd *edn*, enlarged, 1970.

LANDSBERGER, H. (1958), *Hawthorne Revisited*. Ithaca, NY: Cornell University Press, 1958.

LANDSBERGER, H. A. (1961), 'The Horizontal Dimension in a Bureaucracy', *Administrative Science Quarterly* 6: 298–332, 1961.

LASSWELL, H. D. (1963), *The Future of Political Science*. New York: Atherton Press, 1963.

LASZLO, Ervin *ed*. (1972), *The Relevance of General System Theory*. Papers presented to Ludwig von Bertalanffy on his seventieth birthday. New York: George Braziller, 1972.

LAWRENCE, J. R. *ed*. (1966), *Operational Research and the Social Sciences*. London: Tavistock Publications, 1966.

LE BRETON, Preston P. *ed*. (1968), *Comparative Administrative Theory*. London: University of Washington Press, 1968.

LEPAWSKY, Albert *ed*. (1949), *Administration: the Art and Science of Organization and Management*. New York: Alfred A. Knopf, 1949.

LIKERT, Rensis (1961), *New Patterns in Management*. New York: McGraw-Hill, 1961.

LINDLEY, Dennis V. (1971), *Making Decisions*. London: Wiley-Interscience, John Wiley and Sons Ltd, 1971.

LITCHFIELD, Edward H. (1956), 'Notes on a General Theory of Administration', *Administrative Science Quarterly* 1(1): 3–29, 1956.

McGREGOR, Douglas (1960), *The Human Side of Enterprise*. New York: McGraw-Hill, 1960.

MACKENZIE, W. J. M. and GROVE, J. W. (1957), *Central Administration in Britain*. London: Longmans, Green and Co, 1957.

MARCH, James G. and SIMON, Herbert A. (1958), *Organizations*. New York: John Wiley and Sons, 1958.

MAUD, Sir John (later Lord Maud) (1967), Chairman, *Report* of the Committee on the Management of Local Government. Ministry of Housing and Local Government. London: HMSO, 1967.

MAYO, Elton (1933), *The Human Problems of an Industrial Civilisation*. New York: Macmillan, 1933.

MECHANIC, D. (1962), 'Sources of Power of Lower Participants in Complex Organizations', *Administrative Science Quarterly* 7: 349–64, December 1962.

MEDAWAR, P. B. (1967), *The Art of the Soluble*. London: Methuen, 1967.

MERTON, P. A. (1972), 'How We Control the Contraction of our Muscles', *Scientific American* 226(5): 30–7, May 1972.

MERTON, Robert K., GRAY, Ailsa P., HOCKEY, Barbara and SELVIN, Hanan C. *eds* (1952), *Reader in Bureaucracy*. New York: The Free Press, 1952; London: Collier-Macmillan Ltd, 1952. 3rd printing, 1968.

MEYER, Poul (1973), *Systemic Aspects of Public Administration*. Copenhagen: GEC Gad Publishers, 1973.

MILLER, George A., GALANTER, Eugene and PRIBRAM, Karl H. (1960), *Plans and the Structure of Behavior*. New York: Henry Holt and Company, 1960.

MILLS, G. and HOWE, M. (1960), 'Consumer Representation and the Withdrawal of Railway Services', *Public Administration* 38: 253–62, Autumn 1960.

MONTESQUIEU, Charles Louis de Secondat, Baron de (1748), *De l'Esprit des Loix*. Genève: Barrillot, 1748; *transl.* Nugent, *ed.* Neumann, *The Spirit of the Laws*. New York: Hafner Publishing Company Inc., 1949.

MOONEY, James D. and REILEY, A. C. (1931), *Onward Industry!* New York: Harper Bros, 1931; *2nd edn* as *The Principles of Organization*, New York: Harper Bros, 1939; *rev. edn* by Mooney, 1947.

NATHAN, Peter (1969), *The Nervous System*. Harmondsworth, Middlesex: Penguin Books, 1969.

NOVOGROD, R. Joseph, DIMOCK, Gladys O. and DIMOCK, Marshall E. (1969), *Casebook in Public Administration*. New York: Holt, Rinehart and Winston, 1969.

PARRIS, Henry (1965), *Government and the Railways in Nineteenth-Century Britain*. London: Routledge and Kegan Paul, 1965.

PARSONS, Talcott (1949), *Essays in Sociological Theory Pure and Applied*. Glencoe, Ill: The Free Press, 1949.

PARSONS, Talcott and SMELSER, N. J. (1956), *Economy and Society*. London: Routledge and Kegan Paul, 1956.

PATERSON, Thomas T. (1960), *Glasgow Limited*. London: Cambridge University Press, 1960.

PERROW, Charles (1961), 'The Analysis of Goals in Complex Organizations', *American Sociological Review* 26: 854–66, December 1961.

PERROW, Charles (1968), 'Organizational Goals', in SILLS *ed.* (1968), 305–11.

PERROW, Charles (1970), *Organizational Analysis, A Sociological View*. Belmont, Calif: Brooks/Cole Publishing Company, Wadsworth; London: Tavistock Publications Ltd, 1970; Social Science Paperback, 1971; 3rd impression 1974.

PERROW, Charles (1972), *Complex Organizations, A Critical Essay*. New York: Scott, Foresman and Company, 1972.

PFIFFNER, John M. (1935), *Public Administration*. New York: The Ronald Press, 1935.

PLAMENATZ, John (1963), *Man and Society*. 2 vols. London: Longmans, 1963.

POLYA, G. (1945), *How To Solve It*. Princeton, NJ: Princeton University Press, 1945.

PRESSMAN, Jeffrey L. and WILDAVSKY, Aaron B. (1973), *Implementation, How Great Expectations in Washington are Dashed in Oakland, etc.* Berkeley and Los Angeles: University of California Press; London: University of California Press Ltd, 1973.

RAPOPORT, Anatol and HORVATH, W. J. (1960), 'Thoughts on Organization Theory and a Review of Two Conferences', *General Systems Yearbook* 4(2). Ann Arbor, Mich: Society for General Systems Research, 1960.

REID, Graham L. and ALLEN, Kevin (1970), *Nationalised Industries*. Harmondsworth, Middlesex: Penguin Books, 1970.

RHODES, Gerald (1965), *Administrators in Action*, Vol II. London: George Allen and Unwin, 1965.

ROETHLISBERGER, Fritz J. and DICKSON, William J. (1939), *Management and the Worker*. Cambridge, Mass: Harvard University Press, 1939.

ROSE, Richard *ed.* (1947), *The Management of Urban Change in Britain and Germany*. London: Sage Publications, 1974.

ROSE, Richard *ed.* (1976), *The Dynamics of Public Policy*. London: Sage Publications, 1976.

ROUSSEAU, Jean-Jacques (1762), *Le Contrat Social*. Geneva: 1762; *ed.* Vaughan, C. E., *The Political Writings of Jean-Jacques Rousseau*, Oxford: Basil Blackwell, 1962; *transl.* M. Cranston, *The Social Contract*, Harmondsworth, Middlesex: Penguin Books, 1968.

RYLE, Gilbert (1949), *The Concept of Mind*. London: Hutchinson, 1949.

SAPOLSKY, Harvey M. (1972), *The Polaris System Development, Bureaucratic and Programmatic Success in Government*. Cambridge, Mass: Harvard University Press, 1972.

SAYRE, Wallace S. (1958), 'Trends in the Study and Teaching of Public Administrations', *in* SWEENEY (1958), 37–43.

SCHULTZE, C. L. (1969), 'The Role of Incentives, Penalties, and Rewards in Attaining Effective Policy', *in Analysis and Evaluation of Public Expenditures: The PPB System*. Papers submitted to the Subcommittee on Economy in Government of the Joint Economic Committee, Ninety-First Congress, First Session: 201–25.

SELF, Peter (1972), *Administrative Theories and Politics*. London: George Allen and Unwin, 1972.

SELF, Peter (1975), *The Econocrats and the Policy Process*. London: Macmillan, 1975.

SELZNICK, Philip (1949), *TVA and the Grass Roots*. Berkeley: University of California Press, 1949.

SHARKANSKY, Ira (1970), *Public Administration, Policy-Making in Government Agencies*. Chicago: Markham Publishing Company, 1970; *2nd edn*, 1972.

SILLS, David L. *ed.* (1968), *International Encyclopaedia of the Social Sciences II.* New York: The Macmillan Company and The Free Press, 1968.

SILVERMAN, David (1970), *The Theory of Organizations, A Sociological Framework.* London: Heinemann, 1970.

SIMON, Herbert A. (1944), 'Decision-making and Administrative Organization', *Public Administration Review* 4: 16–25, 1944.

SIMON, Herbert A. (1957), *Models of Man, Social and Rational.* New York: John Wiley and Sons, 1957.

SIMON, Herbert A. (1964), 'On the Concept of Organizational Goal', *Administrative Science Quarterly* 9: 1–22, June 1964.

SIMON, Herbert A., SMITHBURG, Donald A. and THOMPSON, Victor A. (1950), *Public Administration.* New York: Alfred A. Knopf, 1950.

SLUCKIN, W. (1954), *Minds and Machines.* Harmondsworth, Middlesex: Penguin Books, 1954; *rev. edn,* 1960.

STOUT, G. F. (1896), *Analytic Psychology.* 2 vols. *In* Muirhead Library of Philosophy. London: Sonnenschein and Co., 1896.

SUTHERLAND, John W. (1973), *A General Systems Philosophy for the Social and Behavioral Sciences.* New York: George Braziller, 1973.

SWEENEY, Stephen B. *ed.* (1958), *Education for Administrative Careers in Government Service.* Philadelphia: University of Pennsylvania Press; London: Oxford University Press, 1958.

TANNENBAUM, Arnold S., KAVČIČ, Bogdan, ROSNER, Menachem, VIANELLO, Mino and WIESER, Georg (1974), *Hierarchy in Organizations, An International Comparison.* San Francisco: Jossey-Bass Inc., 1974.

TAUB, Richard P. (1969), *Bureaucrats Under Stress.* Berkeley and Los Angeles: University of California Press, 1969.

TAYLOR, Frederick Winslow (1910), 'Shop Management', paper to the American Society of Mechanical Engineers, 1903; *Shop Management*; New York: Harper Bros, 1910.

TAYLOR, Sir Henry (1836), *The Statesman.* London: 1836; reprinted in *Collected Works,* 1878; with *intro.* By H. J. Laski, Cambridge: Heffer, 1927; with *intro.* by C. N. Parkinson, New York: Mentor Books, The New American Library, 1958.

THOMPSON, Sir D'Arcy (1917), *On Growth and Form.* Cambridge University Press, 1917; *new edn,* 1942; abridged *edn, ed.* J. T. Bonner, 1966.

THOMPSON, James D. (1967), *Organizations in Action.* New York: McGraw-Hill, 1967.

THOMPSON, Victor A. (1961), *Modern Organization.* New York: Alfred A. Knopf, 1961.

TILLETT, Anthony, KEMPNER, Thomas, and WILLS, Gordon (1970), *Management Thinkers.* Harmondsworth, Middlesex: Penguin Books, 1970.

TÖNNIES, Ferdinand (1887), *Gemeinschaft und Gesellschaft.* Leipzig: 1887; *transl.* C. S. Loomis, *Community and Association,* New York: American Book Company, 1940; London: Routledge and Kegan Paul, 1955.

TULLOCK, Gordon (1965), *The Politics of Bureaucracy.* Washington, DC: Public Affairs Press, 1965.

URWICK, Lyndall F. (1937), 'Organization as a Technical Problem', *in* GULICK AND URWICK *eds* (1937), 47–88.

URWICK, Lyndall F. (1943), *The Elements of Administration.* London: Pitman, 1943; *2nd edn,* 1947; ninth impression, 1963.

VAN METER, D. S. and VAN HORN, C. E. (1975), 'The Policy Implementation Process:

A Conceptual Framework', *Administration and Society* 6(4): 445–88, February 1975.

VERNON, M. D. (1962), *The Psychology of Perception*. Harmondsworth, Middlesex: Penguin Books, 1962.

VICKERS, Sir Geoffrey (1965), *The Art of Judgement: A Study of Policy Making*. London: Chapman and Hall, 1965; New York: Basic Books, 1965.

VICKERS, Sir Geoffrey (1968), *Value Systems and Social Process*. London: Tavistock Publications, 1968; Harmondsworth, Middlesex: Penguin Books, 1970.

VILE, M. J. C. (1967), *Constitutionalism and the Separation of Powers*. Oxford: Clarendon Press, 1967.

VON BERTALANFFY, Ludwig (1968), *General System Theory, Foundations, Development, Applications*. New York: George Braziller Inc., 1968; London: Allen Lane The Penguin Press, 1971.

WALDO, Dwight (1948), *The Administrative State, A Study of the Political Theory of American Public Administration*. New York: The Ronald Press, 1948.

WALTER, GREY – see GREY WALTER.

WALTON, Richard E. (1966), 'Theory of Conflict in Lateral Organizational Relationships', *in* LAWRENCE ed., (1966), 409–26.

WELSCH, Lawrence A. and CYERT, Richard M. *eds* (1970), *Management Decision Making: Selected Readings*. Harmondsworth, Middlesex: Penguin Books, 1970.

WHITE, Leonard D. (1926), *Introduction to the Study of Public Administration*. New York: Macmillan, 1926; 4th edn, 1955.

WIENER, Norbert (1950), *The Human Use of Human Beings: Cybernetics and Society*. New York: Houghton, Mifflin, 1950.

WILLIAMS, W. (1971), *Social Policy Research and Analysis: The Experience in the Federal Social Agencies*. New York: American Elsevier, 1971.

WILLOUGHBY, W. F. (1919), *The Government of Modern States*. New York: D. Appleton-Century Company, 1919; 2nd edn, 1936.

WILSON, Bryan R. *ed.* (1970), *Rationality*. Key Concepts in the Social Sciences. Oxford: Basil Blackwell, 1970.

WILSON, Woodrow (1887), 'The Study of Administration', *Political Science Quarterly* 2: 197–222, 1887; reprinted 56: 481–506, 1941.

YATES, Douglas T., and NELSON, Richard R., *eds* (1967), *Innovation and Implementation in Public Organizations*. Farnborough: Lexington Books, 1967.

Index

253